LONG
TRAIL
GUIDE

Green Mountain Club

LONG TRAIL GUIDE

Hiking Vermont's High Ridge

VERMONT HIKING TRAIL SERIES
VOLUME 1

TWENTY-FIFTH EDITION

Green Mountain Club
Waterbury Center, Vermont 05677

Editions

First Edition 1917	Fourteenth Edition 1951
Second Edition 1920	Fifteenth Edition 1956
Third Edition 1921	Sixteenth Edition 1960
Fourth Edition 1922	Seventeenth Edition 1963
Fifth Edition 1924	Eighteenth Edition 1966
Sixth Edition 1924	Nineteenth Edition 1968
Seventh Edition 1928	Twentieth Edition 1971
Eighth Edition 1930	Twenty-first Edition 1977
Ninth Edition 1932	Twenty-second Edition 1983
Tenth Edition 1935	Twenty-third Edition 1985
Eleventh Edition 1937	Twenty-fourth Edition 1996
Twelfth Edition 1940	Twenty-fifth Edition 2003
Thirteenth Edition 1947	

The Green Mountain Club, Inc.
4711 Waterbury-Stowe Road
Waterbury Center, Vermont 05677
(802) 244-7037
gmc@greenmountainclub.org
www.greenmountainclub.org

The information in this guide is the result of the best effort of the
publisher, using information available at the time of printing. Changes
resulting from maintenance and relocations are constantly occurring,
and, therefore, no published route can be regarded as precisely
accurate at the time you read this notice.

Cover and book design by The Laughing Bear Associates,
Montpelier, Vermont
Format by Electric Dragon Productions, Montpelier, Vermont
Cartography by Map Adventures, Portland, Maine
Watercolor paintings by Dave Blumenthal
Illustrations by Ed Epstein, Clyde H. Smith, Duncan Wilkie

Twenty-fifth Edition

ISBN 1-888021-08-X

Printed in Canada

To all those who have worked
as volunteers to maintain
the Long Trail, Vermont's
"footpath in the wilderness," and,
in particular, to Bob Northrop.
In August 2001, at the age of
eighty, he completed his seventh
end-to-end hike of the Long Trail
as a fundraiser for the
Long Trail Protection Fund.

Editors-in-Chief
Dave Hardy
Steve Larose
Ben Rose

Editors
Scott Christiansen
Bill Clark
Smith Edwards
Katy Klutznick
Mary Lou Recor

Initial Transcription
Doris Washburn
Karen Zbikowski

It is impossible to list every person who assisted in the production of this edition of the guidebook, but many deserve special recognition. Thank you for your creativity, patience, and enthusiasm for the *Long Trail Guide*.

Contributors

Pete Antos-Ketcham
Brian Aust
Paul Austin
Deb Brown
John Buddington
Ann Burcroff
Cosmo Catalano
Jane Coffey
Russ Eastwood
Marge Fish
Don Foote
Keri Foster
Cathy Frank
Pam and Robert Gillis
Steve Gladstone
Richard Goldsmith
David Goodman
Julia Grand-Doucet
Deane Helms
Dick Krompegal
Mike LaRoss
Bob Lincoln

Peter Mackey
Cheryl McQueen
Matt Moore
Ed Myers
Jeff Nugent
Herb Ogden
Bill Osgood
Tom Paquette
Bill Perry
Sylvia Plumb
Fred Putnam
Doug Reeves
Weiland Ross
Gary Salmon
Gary Sawyer
Roy Schweiker
Cheryl Shanks
Susan Shea
Andy Squires
Val Stori
Greg Western
Paul and Joanne Woodward

Contents

CONTENTS

Foreword

Welcome to the twenty-fifth edition of the *Long Trail Guide*. This book, like the trail it describes, is bigger than any one writer, hiker, reader, or maintainer. In fact, it's the culmination of the backcountry labors and joys of nearly a century of Green Mountain hikers. Don't let that scare you away; every hike begins with that first step, and the planning of each Long Trail trip can begin with the turn of a page.

Why yet another edition of this book? The Long Trail is a continuous work in progress. New shelters are built, sections of trails are relocated, and sometimes the weather causes an unplanned trail revision: in the past five years Vermont has seen a major ice storm, two shelters closed by heavy spring snows, the tail end of a hurricane, flooding, and droughts.

Thank you for picking up this guide. We hope it leads to many Long Trail adventures. This edition features trail updates throughout the state, yet the format of the guide still retains the look of the previous edition developed by Sylvia Plumb. We've added improved maps by Map Adventures of Portland, Maine. Care was taken to retain the look of the maps that were painstakingly updated for previous editions by Don Hill. Thanks to improved printing technology we were able to return the maps to the start of each trail division, and for the first time we've added elevation profiles so folks can preview a trip's vertical relief, which may or may not be a good thing.

Remember a hiking guide is just that, a guide. Each visit to the mountains reveals something previously unseen. Dozens of people have worked to make this edition as accurate as possible as of the beginning of 2003. But just as a simple typographical error can change a trail into a trial, you may see things we didn't. Please contact GMC at gmc@greenmountainclub.org to point out errors or suggest changes for future editions.

We thank Dave Hardy for burning the midnight oil writing text, editing maps, and guiding this project to a successful conclusion, as well as the folks of the GMC Publications Committee for their support. We especially wish to thank artist Dave Blumenthal for his beautiful watercolors; Karen Zbikowski and Doris Washburn for typing; Mary Lou Recor and the Old Ridgerunner, Smith Edwards, for their valuable initial reviews of the first draft; and Bill Clark, Steve Larose, and Scott Christiansen for striving to make the text readable and accurate.

Happy Trails,

Marty Lawthers

Marty Lawthers,
GMC President

Ben Rose

Ben Rose,
GMC Executive Director

Using This Guide

The *Long Trail Guide* is the official guide to the Long Trail and its network of side trails. It is produced and updated by Green Mountain Club volunteers and staff who maintain and manage the trail. This guidebook and the club's companion publication the *Day Hiker's Guide to Vermont*, which includes trails outside the Long Trail System, together cover the majority of hiking trails in Vermont.

This guide divides the Long Trail into twelve divisions, numbered from south to north. Each division has four components: map, elevation profile, division summary, and trail description.

Maps

The scale of the maps is about three miles to the inch. The contour interval is 100 feet. The Long Trail is shown as a heavy red line. Double-dashed lines depict roads that may not be passable; solid lines represent roads that probably are.

Division Summaries

Tables of mileage and elevation information are provided for each division. The northbound hiker will read the tables from the bottom up. They are useful for quickly determining the distance and net elevation gain or loss between one point on the trail and the next. The listed features in bold type correspond to features mentioned in the Long Trail descriptions. Mileages are cumulative. Long Trail elevations are given in both feet and meters.

Trail Descriptions

The Long Trail and Appalachian Trail descriptions read from south to north. Distances are cumulative within each division. Distances between shelters are given in both miles and kilometers and include northbound hiking times. Southbound times are in parentheses. Cumulative distances to Massachusetts and Canada from the beginning (i.e., the southernmost point) of the division are given at the top of the first page of each division. Many trail features, such as shelters, summits, side trails, and road crossings that appear in bold type in the descriptions are also listed in bold type in the summary tables. Side trails are noted in the Long Trail description where they intersect the trail. Side trails are described after the Long Trail descriptions.

Mileages used in the division summaries and trail descriptions are actual hiking distances, including twists and turns, based on surveyor's wheel measurements. Bear in mind that road distances are from odometer readings and everyone's odometers are different! Hiking times are based on the age-old formula of one half hour for each mile plus one half hour for each 1,000 feet of ascent. These figures are for actual walking time; allowances should be made for breaks, ruggedness of terrain, hiking experience, and also for trips to summits and other viewpoints reached via side trails. Of course, everyone has their own pace, and actual times are likely to differ from "book time."

Elevation Profiles

This new feature provides a sense of the ups and downs of the Long Trail for each division. We are still tinkering with this but hope readers will find it useful. Observant readers with keen eyes will notice that a miniature version of each division's elevation profile is at the start of the division trail descriptions.

Abbreviations

AT. . . . . Appalachian Trail

ATC. . . . Appalachian Trail Conference

CCC . . . Civilian Conservation Corps

DOC . . . Dartmouth Outing Club

ft. . . . . . feet

GMC . . . Green Mountain Club

GMNF . . Green Mountain National Forest

hr. . . . . hour(s)

km. . . . . kilometer(s)

LT . . . . Long Trail

m. . . . . meter(s)

mi. . . . . mile(s)

Mt. . . . Mount

Mtn. . . . Mountain

Rev. . . . . Reverse time for side trails

SB . . . . . southbound

USFS . . . U.S. Forest Service

DFPR . . Vermont Department of Forests, Parks, and Recreation

Welcome to the Long Trail

Vermont's Long Trail System, with its 272-mile footpath, 175 miles of side trails, and seventy backcountry campsites, many featuring shelters, offers endless hiking opportunities for the day hiker, weekend overnighter, and extended backpacker. The Long Trail follows the main ridge of the Green Mountains from the Massachusetts–Vermont state line to the Canadian border, crossing Vermont's highest peaks.

Although the Long Trail is known as Vermont's "footpath in the wilderness," its character may more accurately be described as *backcountry* since *wilderness* now represents a specific management regimen on federal lands. On its way to Canada, the trail climbs rugged peaks and passes pristine ponds, alpine sedge, hardwood forests, and swift streams. It is steep in places, muddy in others, and rugged in most. Novice and expert alike will enjoy the varied terrain of the trail as it passes through the heart of Vermont's backwoods.

Built by the Green Mountain Club between 1910 and 1930, the Long Trail is the oldest long-distance hiking trail in the country. It was the inspiration for the Appalachian Trail, which coincides with the Long Trail for over one hundred miles. As Long Trail manager, the Green Mountain Club works to ensure that the trail — one of Vermont's most significant recreational features — is protected and maintained for everyone's enjoyment.

Guidelines for the Use of the Long Trail

With proper care, a hiker of almost any ability and experience can enjoy an excursion on the Long Trail. Hikers are encouraged to plan their hikes with both their ability and weather conditions in mind. For the latest information on trail and shelter conditions, contact GMC or visit www.greenmountainclub.org.

Please treat all trail lands with respect. Portions of the Long Trail in northern Vermont cross private land. It only takes one inconsiderate hiker to cause a landowner to close the trail. Park so as not to block access to roads or driveways. Practice Leave No Trace. Carry out all trash. Landowners may be farming, grazing, maple sugaring, or logging on lands adjacent to the trail, activities that are an integral part of Vermont's economy and way of life.

Trail Marking

The Long Trail is marked by two-by-six-inch white blazes. Intersections are usually marked with signs. Double blazes may mark important turns. In open areas or on rocky summits, blazes are often painted on rocks; cairns and scree walls may also define the trail. Property lines, snowmobile routes, and cross-country ski trails marked in various colors occasionally cross the route, but the well-worn footpath and standard white blazes distinguish the Long Trail from these. Nearly all side trails are blazed in blue and signed. Hikers should always pay special attention at trail intersections as signs may be missing and blazes faded.

Taft Lodge
1998
DEV

Camping and Fires

Because the Long Trail System passes through private, state, and federal lands, regulations vary from one part of the trail to the next. Guidelines for each type of land ownership are described below. Unless you know you are on federal or state land and in areas where primitive camping is permitted, camp only at designated sites. The trail description provides information about where dispersed camping is allowed in each division. For more information, contact the appropriate state or federal agencies.

PRIVATE LANDS. Camping on private lands is limited to designated sites. Fires, when permitted, are only allowed in the permanent fireplace at each site. Use of these areas is permitted through the generosity of the landowners. Abuse of our long-standing arrangement could result in closure of the Long Trail on private lands. If you are unsure whether or not you are on private land, camp only at designated sites.

STATE LANDS. Primitive camping is permitted below 2,500 feet, 100 feet from water, and 200 feet from any trail if Leave No Trace practices are followed. Any other exceptions are noted in each division. Fires are permitted but discouraged below 2,500 feet unless otherwise noted in trail descriptions. Camping is limited to no more than three consecutive nights in the same area. See page 17 for information regarding group use permits.

FEDERAL LANDS. Camping between shelters is permitted along much of the trail in the Green Mountain National Forest between the Massachusetts border and Vt. 140 and between Sherburne Pass and Mount Ellen if Leave No Trace principles are followed. Exceptions are noted in each division. Small wood fires are allowed unless noted in trail descriptions. See page 17 for information regarding outfitter-guide special-use permits.

Overnight Sites

There are nearly six dozen Long Trail overnight sites spaced no more than a moderate day's hike apart. These range from fully enclosed lodges to three-sided lean-tos and tenting areas. All sites, although primitive, have a water source (purity and reliability cannot be guaranteed) and privy. Visitors must carry their own food, backpacking stove, and overnight gear.

The overnight structures along the trail are designated as shelters, camps, and lodges. Shelters usually have open fronts in the Adirondack style. Some camps are enclosed and have doors and glazed windows. Larger enclosed structures are lodges. Any exceptions to these classifications are noted.

These facilities are used on a first-come, first-served basis until filled to their stated capacity. Please make room for other hikers. Use of any overnight facility is limited to three consecutive nights. Shelters are intended for individual or small group use. Larger groups of more than six should not plan to use shelters and should carry tents or tarps. Organized groups should follow group hiking guidelines on pages 11 to 17. Anticipated shelter changes are noted in each division.

To improve outhouse efficiency and reduce odors, whenever possible urinate in the woods well away from water sources. As part of its waste management efforts, GMC composts sewage at some overnight sites. Please follow any special instructions posted on the outhouse door.

Site and Summit Caretakers

Throughout the hiking season, hikers may find GMC caretakers at sensitive, high-use overnight sites along the trail (identified in the trail description). Through informal conversation and example, these caretakers educate hikers about Leave No Trace principles and perform trail and shelter maintenance. Caretakers compost sewage at all fee sites on the Long Trail.

Green Mountain Club caretakers are experienced hikers. They are happy to provide backpacking suggestions and tips as well as basic information about the trail and the club. Caretakers and their field supervisors also work up and down the trail with volunteers taking care of backcountry privies and addressing other maintenance and management problems that crop up each season. This important program is partially funded by a modest overnight use fee charged at caretaker sites. Site fees cover less than half of the program's cost to GMC. This is a use fee and applies to tent as well as shelter users.

To protect Vermont's alpine areas and fragile summits, GMC sponsors summit caretakers on Mount Mansfield, Camel's Hump, Mount Abraham, and Stratton Mountain, as well as ridgerunners on the Coolidge Range (Killington and Pico Peaks) and Glastenbury Mountain when funding is available. These caretakers talk with hikers about the fragile summit ecosystems, local camping and fire regulations, and provide first aid and fire assistance.

Water

Although the Green Mountain Club makes every effort to locate shelters and campsites near water sources, the quality and quantity of water cannot be guaranteed. During dry weather, water sources may fail. Areas that are particularly prone to water shortages are noted in the trail description.

Contamination of water supplies is a problem, even in remote areas. Water may look and taste clean but still be unsafe to drink. Giardiasis, caused by the intestinal parasite *Giardia lamblia*, is just one of many illnesses caused by drinking contaminated water. Other bacteria and viruses may also be present in water sources. If giardiasis symptoms such as severe cramping and diarrhea occur, consult your physician.

Hikers and dogs are probably the main carriers of *Giardia*. Often, they carry the parasite and unknowingly contaminate water supplies through the careless disposal of waste. People can pass it on to others by failing to wash their hands after making a pit stop.

The best way to prevent illness is to treat all drinking water. To kill *Giardia*, water must be boiled for one minute, filtered with a water purifier guaranteed to remove the *Giardia* parasite (filters may not remove all contaminants, such as viruses), or treated with a chemical purifier (follow the directions on the bottle). To kill all viruses and bacteria, water must be chemically treated or boiled for ten minutes.

Spring and Fall Mud Seasons

The Green Mountain Club strongly encourages hikers to avoid higher elevation trails during the spring mud season (usually late March through the end of May). Snowmelt creates extremely muddy trails and makes them vulnerable to damage from foot traffic, which is often compounded when hikers walk beside the trail to avoid the mud.

Late fall presents similar muddy conditions. From late October until snowpack, early snows produce moisture but don't cover the ground enough to protect it from damage. Freeze and thaw cycles during this period can wreak havoc on heavily used trails. Severe winter thaws create similar conditions. During these times, hikers should find other recreational activities and allow mountain trails to freeze or dry, which will protect them from further damage.

Guidelines

• If a trail is so muddy that you need to walk on the vegetation beside it, turn back and seek another place to hike.

- Plan spring hikes in hardwood forest at lower elevations.
- Avoid spruce-fir (conifer) forests at higher elevations before Memorial Day and after the end of October.
- The State of Vermont closes trails in the Camel's Hump and Mount Mansfield areas from mid-April until Memorial Day weekend. Please do not hike here. Also avoid Stratton Mountain, the Coolidge Range (Killington and Pico Peaks), Lincoln Ridge (Lincoln Gap to Appalachian Gap), and Jay Peak during this time of year.

Special Natural Areas and Wildlife

Alpine Areas

Vermont is fortunate to be home to three arctic-alpine areas. These fragile ecosystems, found on the summits of Mount Mansfield, Camel's Hump, and Mount Abraham, contain plants normally growing 1,500 miles to the north. Although these plants are hardy enough to survive the harsh climate of mountain summits, they are vulnerable to trampling. Please protect these special natural areas by staying on the marked trail, walking only on bare rock, and leashing your dog to ensure that it does not wander off the trail. Camping is prohibited above timberline.

Wilderness Areas

In parts of the Green Mountain National Forest, the Long Trail crosses federally designated wilderness. These generally remote areas were established by the United States Congress as places where human impact is minimal. Appropriate recreation and scientific research are encouraged. Hunting and fishing are allowed, but logging, roads, and mechanical equipment (including mountain bikes) are not. In time, the forest will regenerate from past clearing, and the wilderness will approximate the primeval lands early European explorers first encountered. The Long Trail crosses four wilderness areas: Lye Brook (Division 3), Big Branch and Peru Peak (Division 4), and Breadloaf (Divisions 7 and 8).

Limiting day and overnight group sizes to fewer than ten people is particularly important in wilderness areas. Campers should practice Leave No Trace. Trail blazing and brush cutting are limited. Signs are less frequent and they often omit mileage figures. There may be more downed trees across the trail, reflecting a reduced intensity of trail maintenance. Bridges are often more primitive, and there are occasional stream fords.

Peregrine Falcons

After almost a thirty-year absence, peregrine falcons have returned to nest in Vermont. They are still rare with twenty-three nesting pairs reported in 2001. Peregrines prefer high cliffs and outcrops. With many of these locations on or near the Long Trail, such as Smugglers Notch and Mount Horrid, they are easily disturbed, especially by hikers above their cliffside nests.

During the nesting season, from mid-March to mid-August, hikers may encounter portions of the Long Trail or side trails that have been closed or relocated. Please stay away from such areas until young falcons have fledged. For information call the Green Mountain Club or the Vermont Department of Fish and Wildlife at (802) 241-3700.

Animals

Mice, raccoons, and squirrels are particularly adept at gnawing through packs in search of food. Take food, trash, and items resembling food (toothpaste, peppermint soap) out of your pack and hang them in separate bags.

Porcupines enjoy gnawing on shelters and outhouses. Close and latch privy doors and lodge doors to keep them from chomping on the interior. They love salt; never leave your boots where porcupines can reach them. Hang boots to keep porcupines away and also to help them dry out. Hang packs because the animals will chew sweaty pack straps and belts, too.

Although black bears exist in Vermont, they are generally not a problem, being shy and seldom seen. Don't feed them and please follow Leave No Trace practices so bears do not become a problem.

Dogs

Many Long Trail hikers bring their dogs along. The Green Mountain Club and public land managing partners strongly recommend keeping dogs under control at all times. If you bring your dog along with you on the trail, you should bring a pair of pliers in case you both meet a porcupine. Sad experience has shown that dogs don't learn from their first porky encounter.

Leash your dog when hiking in alpine zones, near roads, and at overnight campsites and their water sources. Please don't allow your pet to muck up a small water source! Please also leash dogs at other hikers' request; not everyone is comfortable around your lovable pet.

Hunting

All the land crossed by the Long Trail is open to hunting. Hikers should be aware of the various hunting seasons that are underway from September 1 through mid-December. Deer rifle season, from mid- to late November is a time of particular concern. Wild turkey season takes place during the month of May. Hunting is a time-honored Vermont tradition, and hunters and hikers have coexisted happily for generations.

Late fall offers some of the best, bug-free hiking of the year, with leafless trees affording greater long-range visibility; but hunting season necessitates that hikers take certain precautions during this time of year. Wear bright, visible colors, preferably fluorescent orange. Avoid wearing brown, tan, black, or patches of white that might be mistaken for the white tail of a deer. For information on hunting seasons, write or call the Vermont Department of Fish and Wildlife at 103 South Main Street, Waterbury, Vermont, 05671; (802) 241-3700.

Leave No Trace

Learn about Leave No Trace principles. This nationwide effort educates backcountry travelers about the importance of practicing low-impact camping and travel techniques to reduce potential negative impacts on the land, wildlife, and other visitors. Practice of the seven Leave No Trace principles promotes sustainable use of the backcountry. The Green Mountain Club offers a variety of Leave No Trace workshops. Participants will leave each course with an understanding of wildland ethics and sound backcountry practices. We encourage you to contact the Green Mountain Club to find out more or visit the Leave No Trace Web site at www.lnt.org. The seven Leave No Trace principles are:

PLAN AHEAD AND PREPARE. Familiarize yourself with local regulations. Visit in small groups; split larger parties into groups of four to eight. Groups should plan to not occupy shelters; use the table on pages 14 and 15 to plan your itinerary. Repackage food to minimize waste. Prepare adequately for extreme weather, hazards, and emergencies. Trails can be difficult and travel slower than it appears on a map, especially in northern Vermont. Be prepared to purify all drinking water. Carry and know how to use a map and compass. Bring enough tents for everyone.

TRAVEL AND CAMP ON DURABLE SURFACES. Stay on the trail; avoid shortcuts that erode soil and damage vegetation. Camp at designated sites. Use tent platforms if available to avoid compacting soil. Groups should use recommended group-use campsites. Concentrate activities on existing trails and campsites. Avoid camping where impact is just beginning. Walk single file in the middle of the trail, even when wet or muddy, to avoid widening the treadway. Walk on rocks whenever possible, especially in fragile areas such as shorelines and alpine zones.

DISPOSE OF WASTE PROPERLY. If you pack it in, pack it out! Shelters and campsites are equipped with privies. Otherwise, bury human and pet waste in six-inch deep cat holes at least 200 feet away from water sources. Pack out all trash including hygiene products (opaque bags are helpful). To wash yourself or your dishes, carry water seventy steps away from streams or ponds and use little or no soap. Strain food particles from dishwater and pack out. Keep pets away from water sources to protect water quality.

LEAVE WHAT YOU FIND. Take only pictures, leave only footprints. Flowers and other natural wonders are best enjoyed in their natural states. Removal of these items is illegal on public lands. Let others enjoy nature and cultural artifacts as you originally found them. Remember that removal of these items is illegal on state and federal lands. Please don't carve into trees or shelters along the trail. After breaking down camp, leave your site cleaner than you found it.

MINIMIZE CAMPFIRE IMPACT. Know local regulations — wood fires may be prohibited. Campfires cause lasting impacts to the backcountry and are discouraged along the Long Trail. Use a portable stove for cooking instead of a fire. Where permitted, if you choose to build a fire, use only preexisting fire rings. Keep fires small using only dead, downed wood. To minimize impacts to the campsite, collect wood on the way in. Burn all wood and coals to ash, extinguish completely, then scatter cool ashes. Pack out all foil and plastic packaging — these don't burn!

RESPECT WILDLIFE. Observe wildlife from a distance. Feeding animals damages their health, alters natural behaviors, and exposes them to predators. Protect wildlife and your food by storing food securely. If you must bring a dog, keep it leashed and dispose of its waste in a privy or a cat hole, especially in fragile areas and at campsites. Consider leaving your pet at home.

BE CONSIDERATE OF OTHER VISITORS. Respect other trail users and the quality of their experience. Limit group size to no more than ten on overnight outings or trips to fragile areas (alpine summits, pond sites and shorelines, and designated wilderness areas) and no more than twenty on day trips. Be courteous and yield to others on the trail. Take breaks away from the trail and other visitors on durable surfaces. Travel and camp quietly.

For further information about Leave No Trace, visit www.lnt.org, or join a GMC workshop.

Group Use

Group use of hiking trails in the Northeast is on the rise; more than 370 groups hiked on the Long Trail in 2002. It is estimated that more than 200,000 people take a hike on the Long Trail annually, with 40,000 visiting Mount Mansfield alone.

Groups exert a disproportionate impact on water quality, alpine vegetation, wildlife habitat, trail treadway, backcountry campsites, and the experiences of other hikers. Groups can minimize their impacts by following these guidelines.

Leadership

Experienced group leaders are vital to an enjoyable and safe backcountry experience. Not only do they keep the group together and accounted for, but they also help the group act responsibly and safely. All groups need a sufficient number of leaders. The recommended leader-to-participant ratio is one to four. Experienced group members can be designated as assistant leaders if necessary.

GMC's *A Trip Leaders Handbook* provides helpful information on leading successful group trips.

Group Size

Groups come in various shapes and sizes. A group may be comprised of children, teenagers, or adults led by camp counselors, teachers, scout masters, professional guides, or responsible, experienced adults. A group may also be an informal gathering of friends. The following recommendations apply to all groups.

Group Size Guidelines for Day Hikes

GMC strongly discourages group sizes in excess of twenty, including leaders, on day hikes in most areas. In fragile areas, such as exposed alpine summits, pond shorelines, high-use areas, and designated wilderness areas, the recommended group size is ten. These numbers have been endorsed by the National Outdoor Leadership School, Appalachian Trail Conference, Green Mountain National Forest, and Vermont Department of Forests, Parks, and Recreation.

Larger groups should hike in less frequented areas off the Long Trail. Large groups may break into smaller parties and use different trails to get to the same destination; or hike on the same trail but leave at staggered times.

Overnight Use

Most Long Trail campsites were originally intended for solitary hikers or small, informal groups. Overall annual use of the trail in the 1930s is easily exceeded in a single weekend in the twenty-first century. Over the past thirty-five years, trail use has soared, putting incredible pressure on the Long Trail's shelter system and threatening water quality and the viability of backcountry camping throughout the Green Mountains. "Blast zones," where vegetation ceases to grow, have expanded around shelters, increasing soil erosion and causing damage to waterways. To prevent further blast-zone damage, groups should carry tents and/or tarps and use them at designated tent sites, using tent platforms where available.

Group Size Guidelines for Overnight Trips

On overnight trips the recommended maximum group size is ten, although six to eight is more appropriate. Do not plan to use shelters unless tenting is not permitted. Come prepared with tarps and tents for everyone in your group.

Group Trip Planning

When planning a trip during a busy time of year, particularly weekends, holidays, or during the college orientation season (the weeks before and after Labor Day), GMC strongly recommends using a state park as a base camp instead of overcrowding a Long Trail backcountry campsite. Vermont state parks are equipped to handle large groups for overnights and can provide other amenities. Find out more about camping in state parks by visiting their Web site at www.state.vt.us/anr/fpr/parks/index.htm.

The following table will help you plan your group trip. It includes recommended group campsites, their group capacity, the guidebook division in which they are located, and if an overnight camping fee is required. **Note:** This is not a permit fee, which is separate.

DIVISION	CAMPSITE*	CAPACITY	FEE
1	Seth Warner Shelter tenting area	16	no
1	Congdon Shelter tenting area	16	no
1	**GMNF Red Mill Campground**		yes
1	**Woodford State Park Campground**		yes
2	Caughnawaga Shelter tenting area	12	no
2	Story Spring Shelter tenting area	16	no
2	**GMNF Grout Pond Campground** (includes 2 lean-tos)		yes
3	Stratton Pond North Shore tenting area and platforms	24	yes
3	Spruce Peak Shelter tenting area	10	no
3	**GMNF Hapgood Pond Campground**		yes
3	Bromley Mtn. ski area warming hut (contact GMC to confirm availability)	10	no
4	Griffith Lake tenting area and platforms	20	yes
4	Old Job Shelter tenting area	12	no
4	Lost Pond Shelter tenting area	10	no
4	Big Branch Shelter tenting area	12	no
4	**Emerald Lake State Park Campground**		yes
4	Little Rock Pond tenting area and platforms	28	yes
5	Minerva Hinchey Shelter tenting area	10	no
5	Clarendon Shelter tenting area	20	no
5	Cooper Lodge tent platforms	10	yes
5/AT 1	**Gifford Woods State Park Campground**	48	yes
6	Rolston Rest tenting area	10	no
6	David Logan Shelter tenting area	10	no
6	**GMNF Chittenden Brook Campground**		yes
7	USFS primitive campsite at Sucker Brook Trail trailhead	10	no
7	Worth Mtn. Lodge (lodge only; no tenting)	18	no
7	USFS primitive campsite at Skylight Pond Trail trailhead	10	no

DIVISION	CAMPSITE*	CAPACITY	FEE
7	Emily Proctor Shelter tent platforms	10	no
7	USFS primitive campsite at Clark Brook Trail trailhead	20	no
7	USFS primitive campsite at Cooley Glen Trail trailhead	10	no
7	Cooley Glen Shelter tenting area	10	no
8	Stark's Nest, Mad River Glen warming hut (contact GMC to confirm availability)	20	no
8	Birch Glen Camp tenting area	14	no
9	Hump Brook tenting area and platforms	20	yes
9	Bamforth Ridge Shelter tent platforms	15	no
9	**Little River State Park Campground**		yes
9	Duck Brook Shelter tenting area	10	no
9	Buchanan Shelter tenting area	10	no
10	Taylor Lodge tenting area and platforms	10	no
10	Twin Brooks tenting area and platforms	24	no
10	**Underhill State Park Campground**		yes
10	Taft Lodge (lodge only; no tenting)	24	yes
10	**Smugglers Notch State Park Campground**		yes
10	Sterling Pond (on ski slope)	14	yes
10	Bear Hollow Shelter tenting area	10	no
10	Beaver Meadow Lodge tenting area	8	no
10/11	**Elmore State Park Campground**		yes
11	Corliss Camp tenting area	10	no
11	Spruce Ledge Camp tenting area	10	no
11	Tillotson Camp tenting area	10	no
12	Hazen's Notch Camp tenting area	10	no
12	Jay Camp tenting area and platforms	10	no
12	Laura Woodward Shelter tenting area	10	no
AT 2	Happy Hill Shelter tenting area	10	no
AT 2	**Silver Lake State Park Campground**		yes

* *Campgrounds listed in bold charge per site, not per person.*

High-use sites on the Long Trail are staffed by caretakers during the hiking season to assist and educate hikers, help maintain local trails and campsites, and compost sewage to protect water quality. Additionally, caretakers work with volunteers, including groups, on needed trail projects. The per-person site fee is charged for overnight use to help fund the GMC's caretaker and site maintenance programs, and covers only a fraction of the program's annual cost. GMC encourages prepayment for group use; contact the group outreach coordinator at GMC or visit www.greenmountainclub.org.

Note: Prepayment does not constitute a reservation and does not imply exclusive rights or access to a site, which cannot be guaranteed. Overnight use fees are separate from use permit fees.

GMC encourages groups to use the voluntary Group Notification System to prevent overcrowding at Long Trail campsites. Whether visiting a summit for an afternoon or planning a multiday backpacking adventure, groups should notify GMC of their itineraries at least two weeks in advance of their trips.

This system enables GMC to track backcountry use and assist caretakers with effective site management. And it allows us to recommend alternate routes or destinations to limit overcrowding and minimize negative impacts to backcountry resources.

Green Mountain Club caretakers are trained by Leave No Trace master educators. Caretakers provide written feedback on group skills and performance. Feedback forms include observations of group strengths and suggestions for improvements in the areas of preparedness, practice of Leave No Trace skills, and leadership. A copy of this form is sent to your organization with a letter containing seasonally updated resource information. Caretaker feedback aids groups in evaluating their impacts and helps GMC measure the effectiveness of its education programs.

Before You Go

- Use resources like the latest edition of the *Long Trail Guide* to plan your trip;

- Evaluate your skills and seek instruction or refresher courses if needed.
- Contact GMC for trail updates and seasonal information.
- Determine if you need an agency permit for your hike.
- Call the GMC group outreach coordinator to use the Group Notification System.
- Be well prepared to enjoy your hike!

Permits

Most of the Long Trail lies within the public lands of the Green Mountain National Forest or Vermont Department of Forests, Parks, and Recreation, and both agencies require permits for day or overnight use by certain groups on their lands. Permit requirements are different for federal and state lands; fees may be charged. Permits are not required on private land, but please respect landowners and camp only at designated overnight sites.

To determine whether or not you need a permit, first you need to know where you plan to hike. To apply for a permit, contact the appropriate land managing agency listed below.

Federal Lands: Green Mountain National Forest

The Long Trail between Massachusetts and Mount Ellen (with the exception of some trail corridor over Killington Peak) and nearly all the Appalachian Trail east to Norwich, lies within the Green Mountain National Forest. Although the Appalachian Trail is actually part of the national park system, in Vermont it is managed by the U.S. Forest Service. You may need an out-fitter-guide permit if you or the organization you work for is:

- charging a fee for profit above the cost of basic trip expenses (i.e., food, travel). *Note:* if the leader is paid, then it is considered a fee-for-profit operation;
- providing equipment for profit as part of the trip (any fee for equipment rental is considered fee for profit); or
- collecting plants, animals, historic artifacts, or other items.

Permits are required regardless of trip length. No outfitter-guide use may occur in the national forest without a valid permit. Processing permits takes time, especially during the hiking season, so obtain permits well in advance of your trip.

Contact Green Mountain National Forest at (802) 747-6700 or visit www.fs.fed.us/r9/gmfl for information on outfitter-guide permits on the National Forest. Their mailing address is:

Realty Specialist
Green Mountain National Forest
231 North Main Street
Rutland, VT 05701

State Lands: Vermont Department of Forests, Parks, and Recreation

The Long Trail north of Mount Ellen to Canada is mostly on state forest or state park land, as are the exceptions to the Green Mountain National Forest listed above. Group use of state lands may require a commercial use permit if the use:

• is organized or publicized;

• involves a fee to participants (or requests a donation);

• alters the site in any way; or

• could conflict with other established uses.

Permit applications are available by mail:

ANR Lands Director
Vermont Department of Forests, Parks, and Recreation
103 South Main Street, Building 10 South
Waterbury, VT 05671-0601
Phone: (802) 241-3693
Or visit www.anr.state.vt.us/../anrtextonly.htm

Trip Planning

When planning your hike, consider the experience and conditioning of all members of your group, the terrain you plan to cover, the season, the weather, and available hours of daylight. Leave a copy of your itinerary with a reliable person.

Try out your equipment at home, new or old; it's always better to learn you need to fix something before you carry it into the woods. Learn basic first aid and how to deal with emergencies. Most important, use your best judgment to prevent problems from escalating.

For long hikes, plan conservatively, allowing at least one day's leeway in case of unforeseen weather conditions. Start your hike slowly to get accustomed to your pack and strengthen your legs.

Volumes of books have been written about hiking, backpacking, equipment, clothing, and trail food. Pages 248 to 252 list a number of references. Please, be safe. Most important, enjoy your hike!

Going light is critical to a pleasant backpacking trip. Beginning hikers tend to take along more than they need. Few hikers can comfortably carry more than one-fourth of their own weight. On the other hand, even experienced hikers often forget something they wished they remembered to pack. Below are some basic items to make a hike safe and comfortable.

Day Hikes for Spring, Summer, and Fall

- guidebook or map
- lunch, snacks, water (and plenty of it)
- sturdy boots or hiking shoes (some of us now use "hiking sandals")
- wind jacket or rain gear with a breathable shell (remember it's colder on summits than in valleys)
- warm layer (wool or synthetic fleece)
- hats and mittens
- flashlight or headlamp (extra bulb and batteries)
- compass
- first-aid kit
- waterproof matches
- insect repellent and sunscreen
- toilet paper and trowel
- whistle

Overnight Hikes

Add the following items to those carried on a day hike:

- backpacking stove and fuel
- cook kit and eating utensils
- additional food
- sleeping bag and pad (in a waterproof sack)
- tent and ground cloth or tarp
- extra clothes and socks (in a waterproof sack)
- garbage bags
- water filter or purifier
- repair kit (include duct tape)

Reduce pack weight on long-distance hikes by forwarding parcels marked "General Delivery, hold for Long Trail hiker, arriving about [date]" to post offices near the trail (see list of post offices on page 245), or by caching supplies out of sight in critter-proof containers near road crossings. People making an extended backpacking trip on the Long Trail may want to purchase GMC's *Long Trail End-to-Ender's Guide*.

Safety

Simply put, it is safer to hike with others. There are risks associated with hiking the Long Trail, but considering how many people hike each year and how few bad things happen, the risks are small. Hikers should be aware of their surroundings and exercise a degree of caution when dealing with strangers. If you're not comfortable with someone you meet on the trail or at a campsite, pack up and move on.

Most Long Trail campsites are at least two miles in from the nearest road. Some of the older sites were established before four-wheel-drive all-terrain vehicles, and encroaching development made them accessible to inappropriate use. The further in from a road, the less likely you are to find nonhikers at your campsite.

Unless you are a hunter, carrying a gun on the trail is unnecessary. Plus, they are really heavy!

Staying Found

Should the next blaze ahead not be visible within a ten-minute walk at a brisk pace, stop, look, and backtrack if necessary. It is better to lose a moment looking for the correct route than to forge ahead on the wrong route. We recommend carrying a topographic map and compass if you are not familiar with the trail. The guidebook maps serve only for reference and are not suitable for map and compass work.

Weather

Although summers in the Green Mountains are usually pleasant, hot humid days are common. Never underestimate the variability of Vermont weather. Conditions along the crest of the Green Mountains are not the same as in the lowlands; temperatures often vary dramatically, sometimes as much as 5 degrees Fahrenheit per 1,000 feet. There is also a marked increase in the amount of precipitation at higher elevations. The annual average precipitation in Vermont is 38 inches. Other conditions such as rain, fog, and sudden drops in temperature can occur at any time, even in the summer. Always carry a warm layer, a hat, and wind gear when hiking to higher elevations. On the higher peaks the annual precipitation exceeds 100 inches. Summer nights can be cool, so hikers should always carry layers and be prepared for rain.

Hypothermia

Hypothermia is a dangerous and potentially deadly condition; the threat of it exists year-round. Hypothermia is the cooling of the body core temperature caused by heat loss and the body's inability to keep the internal temperature constant. This condition can occur at any time of year, not just in winter. In fact, what is often referred to as "hypothermia weather" is a rainy, windy 40- to 50-degree Fahrenheit day, which can occur any time of the year in Vermont's mountains.

Hypothermia symptoms include poor judgment, forgetfulness, and confusion. Motor control may suffer, leading to problems with coordination (such as inability to fasten one's buttons or zippers), an unsteady gait, or even slurred speech. Other warning signs include inability to keep fingers and toes warm, uncontrollable shivering, or extreme unexpected fatigue. If untreated, hypothermia can result in lethargy, coma, and death.

Prevention is the key to avoiding hypothermia. Body heat is lost by radiation from uncovered surfaces (such as a bare head); from direct contact, such as sitting on frozen ground; from wind blowing away the warm air in clothing; and from evaporation through breathing or sweating.

Adequate food, water, clothing, and pacing are critical. Always eat and drink plenty while hiking, and bring along extra food in case of emergency. Dress in layers, including, as needed, wicking underwear, an insulating layer, and a wind and waterproof shell. Wear wool or synthetics like polypropylene or pile, or if it's warm, keep some of these in your pack just in case. Be sure to peel layers as you hike to prevent excessive sweating, which can soak your clothing.

Remember: Mountain weather can change suddenly and unexpectedly. Keep your pace steady. When it's cold, keep rest stops brief so as not to cool off too much. Carry some emergency gear such as a foam pad to sit on, a tarp or a tent fly or a bivy sack for an emergency shelter, waterproof matches, and possibly a stove, and consider packing at least one sleeping bag per group on a day hike.

When spotted early, hypothermia is easy to treat. Immediately get the chilled person out of the wind and into dry, warm clothing, including a hat. Provide something to eat and drink, and get moving again. This is usually all it takes to warm up. Remember, if the chilled person is walking, keep walking. If this doesn't work, then you must try to rewarm him or her. Put the chilled person in a prewarmed sleeping bag, and put either chemical hot packs or bottles filled with warm water heated on a stove around the person's neck, armpits, and groin. Build a fire, if you can. If the person becomes unconscious (fortunately a rare occurrence), then very gently and quickly effect an evacuation.

Lightning

Injury from lightning, although rare, is a serious risk to hikers. Don't provide a tempting target! Whenever you feel there is a threat: (1) Avoid summits and ridges where strikes are most apt to occur. If you are stuck on a ridge and can't get off quickly, go for the middle rather than the end of a ridge. (2) Avoid open fields. (3) If in the forest, seek an area amid shorter trees. (4) Avoid wet gullies and crevices, and stay out of small depressions where ground currents may travel. (5) Stay out of small caves (large, dry ones are usually good, however). (6) Sit or crouch on insulating objects such as a dry sleeping bag or mattress, making yourself as small as possible. (7) Set aside exposed metal objects (things inside a pack are usually all right).

About 70 percent of people hit by lightning survive. If a person is struck and is still conscious and breathing, the chance of survival is excellent. Even if a lightning victim is not breathing or has no pulse, prompt and effective CPR may be lifesaving. Continue CPR as long as possible — the chance of survival in this situation is much greater than in most other cases of cardiac arrest.

Consider taking a class in wilderness first aid for more in-depth training and practice dealing with hypothermia, lightning strikes, and other backcountry emergencies. The Green Mountain Club offers backcountry first-aid courses on a regular basis throughout the year. To report an emergency in Vermont, dial 911. Remember that cellular phone reception is not dependable in the backcountry, and in any event, rescue may be several hours away.

Bug Season

Blackflies and mosquitoes can make hiking in the Green Mountains uncomfortable and at times unbearable. Blackflies breed in running water and are most abundant in early summer. They usually fade away by mid-July. Mosquitoes buzz around most of the summer. A headnet is helpful. Be sure your tent has no-see-um-proof netting. Almost nothing works against blackflies, but long-sleeved shirts and pants can help. Although insect repellent containing Deet is most effective, there is some concern about its safety. If you do choose to use it, apply it to clothing rather than directly to the skin and avoid using it on children. Alternative repellents are available.

Lyme disease is making its way north, so hikers should be on the lookout for deer ticks and should protect themselves from bites with clothing or repellent.

If you are allergic to bees, carry the appropriate medication prescribed by your doctor and know how to use it.

Rabies

Like other areas in the Northeast, rabies exists in Vermont. Although at present human cases are rare and the danger of the disease remains greater at home than on the trail, it is best to take precautions. Stay away from animals. Beware of any animal that is acting strangely. Leave dead animals alone.

If bitten by an animal, wash the wound thoroughly with soap and water and get to a doctor as soon as possible. Rabies today is preventable as long as medical treatment is received soon after contact; otherwise, it is 100 percent fatal.

Snakes

There are no poisonous snakes on the Long Trail or Appalachian Trail in Vermont.

Winter Use

Winter hiking can be rewarding, filled with solitude, challenge, clear skies, and breathtaking views. It can also be dangerous. A winter trip must be planned and conducted with caution — the margin for error is small.

The Long Trail and its shelters are not designed for winter use. The white blazes that mark the Long Trail are usually painted four to five feet from the ground, a height that could be at knee-level or even completely buried under snow during the winter. Overhanging branches, well out of reach during summer hiking, may obstruct the winter hiker's way.

Vermont winters are severe and prolonged, with abrupt temperature changes. Unpredictable and changing weather conditions, deep snow, short daylight, and the need to carry extra warm clothing and safety gear all need to be considered. Breaking trail is strenuous and exhausting. Conditions at higher elevations will be much more severe, and wind may make winter travel impossible. On open ridges and summits hikers may encounter icy, windswept conditions. Crampons may be needed. Hypothermia, always a threat, is especially dangerous in winter. (See more about hypothermia on page 21.) Carry a map and compass and know how to use them. Be prepared to spend the night in the woods, if necessary.

Long Trail shelters are uninsulated and unheated. All Long Trail hikers should be prepared to spend the night in a shelter without a stove for warmth. The presence of a stove at a shelter on a summer trip is not a guarantee it will be there on a winter trip. Shelters may be covered or filled with snow. An open-faced lean-to provides little protection against the elements. A winter tent and below-zero rated sleeping bags are far better.

Winter conditions occur from October to May in the Green Mountains, with snow lasting until early June at higher elevations just below treeline. At 3,800 feet snow can linger for eight to twelve weeks longer than at 1,800 feet. Maximum snow depth usually occurs in March.

If you are new to winter outings, gain some experience before you set out. Go on winter hikes with friends who have experience, take a class, or join a guided hike. Green Mountain Club offers volunteer and staff-led winter trips as do many outdoor gear stores. There are a number of books available on the subject of winter hiking and camping (see page 251).

Each trail division includes a note about winter use. Some divisions are better suited for snowshoeing and require more technical equipment, while the rolling terrain of other sections make them ideal for cross-country skiing. Always give yourself extra time; the estimated hiking times in the guidebook do not apply during the winter months.

USE SKIS OR SNOWSHOES. Please think of other hikers and those who come after you. Avoid post-holing through the snow. These knee-deep holes can make it unpleasant, unenjoyable, and even dangerous for the person who comes next. Post-holing is also exhausting and time consuming, potentially turning a pleasant hike into a cold, wet, miserable outing. Wear snowshoes or skis on all winter treks.

WINTER SANITATION. Carry a shovel and dig out the outhouse door whenever possible. Be aware of the locations of streams and avoid making pit stops near them.

CATAMOUNT TRAIL. The Catamount Trail provides a full range of skiing opportunities. Fashioned after the Long Trail, it traverses the length of Vermont from Massachusetts to Canada, linking cross-country ski areas with stretches of backcountry trail. For more information about the Catamount Trail and its latest guidebook (7th edition as of August 1999), contact the Catamount Trail Association, 1 Main Street, Rm. 308A, Burlington, Vermont 05401; (802) 864-5794; www.catamount trail.org.

Trail Access

The Long Trail is easily reached from many major roads. This guide gives directions to all Long Trail road crossings at the beginning of each division. Directions to side trails are included in side trail descriptions. For a road map, hikers may request the Official Highway Map of Vermont from the Vermont Department of Travel and Tourism, 6 Baldwin Street, Drawer 33, Montpelier, Vermont, 05633; (802) 828-3237.

Access to the trail is also shown in many road atlases. *Vermont Road Atlas and Guide* and *The Vermont Atlas and Gazetteer* are excellent resources and can be useful for locating routes to the Long Trail as well as side trails.

Transportation

BUS. Public transportation in the vicinity of the Long Trail is provided primarily by Vermont Transit Lines, a component of the Greyhound bus system. Vermont Transit buses travel parts of the following highways — crossing or closely paralleling the Long Trail: U.S. 7, Vt. 9, Vt. 103, U.S. 4, U.S. 2, I-89, Vt. 15, and Vt. 100. Timetables are available from Vermont Transit Company, 345 Pine Street, Burlington, Vermont, 05401; (802) 862-9671; www.vermonttransit.com.

AIR. The Burlington International Airport and Manchester Airport in New Hampshire are served by several major carriers, while smaller companies provide air service to Rutland.

RAIL. Amtrak provides passenger rail service to Rutland and central Vermont from Washington, D.C., New York, and many other cities. Although Amtrak crosses the trail at Jonesville, it does not stop closer than Waterbury or Essex Junction.

PARKING. There are many small and some larger parking areas at trailheads on both the Long Trail and its side trails. Parking information is included with road directions to trailheads. When parking vehicles at trailheads, take special care to avoid obstructing traffic or blocking access to homes, farms, or woodlots.

Vandalism

Vandalism is a problem at some trailheads. The best option is to find a way to avoid leaving your vehicle at a trailhead overnight. If possible, leave your vehicle in town, or arrange to be shuttled to and from the trail. Police and service stations will usually provide a place to park (in the case of the latter, for a small fee), and the Long Trail may then be reached by walking, taxi, or other public transportation. The *Long Trail End-to-Ender's Guide*, updated annually, lists available shuttle services.

Leave valuables at home, or, at the very least, keep them locked in the trunk or otherwise hidden. Remove your stereo if possible. Don't leave a note on the car advising of your plans. Some folks empty their glove compartment and leave it open. If you do that, remember to unscrew the glove box light, or you may return to a dead battery. Park in the open in plain view. If you have a problem at a trailhead, call the local or state police immediately. We would like to be notified at GMC as well, but your highest priority is to notify law enforcement as soon as possible.

Public Campgrounds near the Trail

State and U.S. Forest Service campgrounds make ideal base camps for hikers. They are inexpensive and often located near trailheads. Many are on lakes or ponds with excellent swimming. For a list of campgrounds and the closest trailheads, see pages 241 to 242.

The Green Mountain Club and the Long Trail

I n 1910 the Green Mountain Club began building the Long Trail, with the mission "to make the mountains of Vermont play a larger part in the life of the people." Although GMC's mission philosophically remains the same as when the club was founded, its responsibilities have grown. In the twenty-first century we face the escalating pressures of encroaching development and damage to natural resources from overuse. Providing hiking opportunities now involves more than building and maintaining trails. Today, the Green Mountain Club and its over 9,000 members are involved in all aspects of protecting and managing the trails and facilities of the Long Trail System in coordination with the State of Vermont, the Green Mountain National Forest, and the Appalachian Trail Conference. The GMC is governed by a volunteer board of directors.

Membership

Green Mountain Club membership is an important way to support hiking opportunities in Vermont. The club welcomes anyone with an interest in hiking or supporting hiking opportunities in Vermont. Annual membership dues fund trail protection and maintenance, corridor management, education, and publications.

Those wishing to participate in outings and organized trail maintenance activities may choose to join a GMC section. Sections provide four-season schedules of outings, including hiking, biking, cross-country skiing, and canoeing. They also maintain specific sections of the Long Trail and shelters.

The club offers an at-large membership category for those who wish to support the work of GMC but are not interested in affiliating with a local section. Both section and at-large members enjoy the same benefits, including a subscription to the club's quarterly newsletter, the *Long Trail News*, which provides up-to-date information on trail and shelter conditions, hiking, statewide trails, club history, and a club activities calendar. Members receive discounts on club publications and items carried in the GMC bookstore and discounts on admission to most GMC events. Section members also receive their section's newsletters and activity schedules.

There are fourteen Green Mountain Club sections. Twelve are based in Vermont: Bennington, Brattleboro, Bread Loaf (Middlebury), Burlington, Killington (Rutland), Laraway (Northwestern Vermont), Manchester, Montpelier, Northern Frontier, Northeast Kingdom, Ottauquechee (Woodstock), and Sterling (Stowe-

Morrisville). Two sections are based out of state: Connecticut and Worcester (eastern Massachusetts). Turn to pages 30 to 31 for a description of section maintenance responsibilities.

To join GMC, send payment for annual dues ($30 individual, $40 family) to the Green Mountain Club, 4711 Waterbury-Stowe Road, Waterbury Center, Vermont 05677; or call (802) 244-7037 or visit www.greenmountainclub.org and charge it. Thank you!

Publications

The Green Mountain Club publishes a number of books, maps, and brochures, including the *Day Hiker's Guide to Vermont*, which contains descriptions of trails that are not part of the Long Trail system. A list of GMC publications appears on page 248.

Headquarters

The Green Mountain Club headquarters is located on Vt. 100 in Waterbury Center, Vermont, midway between Waterbury and Stowe. To reach GMC from I-89 in Waterbury (exit 10), head north on Vt. 100 for four miles. Headquarters are in the red barn and office building on the west (left) side of Vt. 100. From the intersection of Vt. 108 and 100 in Stowe, GMC is six miles south on Vt. 100 on the right. Safest access is via Cabin Lane, a few hundred yards south of headquarters.

Information and Education

The Marvin B. Gameroff Hiker Center houses the club's information services, educational displays, and store. The Hiker Center is open seven days a week (9:00 A.M. to 5:00 P.M.) from Memorial Day to Columbus Day. During the cold months, information services are located in GMC's administrative offices in the Herrick Office Building across the driveway from the Gameroff Hiker Center. Business hours are Monday through Friday from 9:00 A.M. to 5:00 P.M. year-round.

Hikers are encouraged to stop by the club for trail information. The GMC will also gladly respond to written, e-mailed (gmc@greenmountainclub.org), or telephone inquiries. During the winter months, the club hosts the James P. Taylor Winter Series — a slide show and lecture series celebrating outdoor recreation.

End-to-End

Approximately 150 people hike the Long Trail end-to-end each year. Although many people hike the trail in one continuous trip, the majority complete it in sections, one person having taken as long as fifty-two years to finish. Many have hiked the trail more than once.

Any hiker who has completed the Long Trail — in one season or many — is entitled to an end-to-ender's certificate. Guidelines for certification are available from the GMC office or on line.

Long Trail History

The Early Years: 1910 to 1920

The Long Trail is the oldest long-distance hiking trail in the United States. It was conceived by James P. Taylor as he waited for the mist to clear from Stratton Mountain. The trail took its first step from dream to reality when twenty-three people gathered in Burlington on March 11, 1910 to found the Green Mountain Club.

Taylor, headmaster of Vermont Academy for Boys at Saxtons River, was frustrated by the lack of suitable hiking trails in the state. Unlike the mountains in neighboring states, the Green Mountains remained largely unappreciated and unused for recreation until Taylor promised that the new organization would "make the Vermont mountains play a larger part in the life of the people."

Work began almost immediately in the Camel's Hump and Mount Mansfield areas; by the end of 1912 Burlington members had cleared a path from Sterling Pond to Camel's Hump. Early the following season, a Forestry Department crew cut a route from Killington Peak to Brandon Gap, and from Camel's Hump south to Lincoln Gap. Later that summer trail builders were busy between Lincoln and Brandon Gaps. Concurrently, the trail expanded in the north from Johnson to Sterling Pond.

In 1914 the slogan was "Killington to Massachusetts," and by 1917 that goal had been reached. Also that year the first *Guide Book of the Long Trail* was published. It listed fourteen overnight accommodations, including private camps, the Mount Mansfield Hotel, abandoned lumber camps, and five new GMC shelters. Nine farmhouses near the trail were available for lodging and meals.

The second edition of the guidebook, published in 1920, showed the trail running from Johnson to the Massachusetts line, with another nine GMC shelters and twelve more farms or other lodgings along the way. Thus, in the first decade members built 209 miles of trail and provided forty-four overnight facilities, fourteen of which were built by GMC.

Completion of the Long Trail

The next decade saw the extension of the Long Trail north from Johnson, culminating at Jay Peak in 1927. Many club members felt Jay was "almost to Canada" and far enough, but Bruce Buchanan of Brattleboro vowed, "We better get rid of the 'almost'." Two years later Bruce and his brother, Roy O. Buchanan, professor of electrical engineering at the University of Vermont, marked the remaining ten-odd miles to the Canadian border. In 1930 Charles G. Doll and Phillips D. Carleton cut the final link to Canada.

On its twenty-first birthday Green Mountain Club could celebrate the completion of Taylor's footpath from Massachusetts to Canada. The occasion was marked by a large gathering at the club's headquarters, the Long Trail Lodge at Sherburne Pass. The lodge was a gift from the Proctor family, early and dedicated supporters of the Long Trail. The highlight of the celebration was the lighting of flares from mountaintop to mountaintop along the spine of the Green Mountains.

Besides regularly updating the *Guide Book of the Long Trail*, GMC began publishing a bimonthly newsletter, the *Green Mountain News*, in 1922. It was later retitled the *Long Trail News*. Today, this membership quarterly continues to inform members and hikers about the Long Trail and club issues.

Many GMCers belong to local sections whose members maintain designated parts of the trail and overnight shelters.

The oldest is the Burlington Section, first known as the Mount Mansfield Section when it was formed in 1910. Other sections have also existed for many decades, while still others have come and gone as local interest waxed and waned.

Long Trail Patrol and End-to-End

With the trail completed, the club continued to expand its network of shelters. A prime mover in this effort was Roy Buchanan. In 1930 the club's board of trustees authorized formation of a salaried Long Trail Patrol (LTP) with Buchanan taking on the role as crew leader in 1931. Each summer through the mid-1960s he assembled groups of students and worked with them on trail maintenance, construction of new shelters, and repairs to existing ones. From 1930 to 1940, the LTP, sections, and other groups built or rebuilt twenty-nine shelters and lodges.

Not surprisingly, the World War II years saw reductions in trail use and trail work. One GMC program, however, began during this period. In 1942 the club trustees authorized formal recognition of GMCers who had tramped the full length of the trail and awarded thirty-two special certificates that began the long roster of end-to-enders.

Back to the Woods

Shelter construction and reconstruction resumed at a modest rate through the 1950s, then accelerated in the next decade. The reason for the renewed activity was a significant increase in the number of hikers, especially young people, who sought recreation in the backcountry as part of a new back-to-the-land movement. Between 1966 and 1975, responding to heavy trail traffic, the club launched a variety of initiatives, including removal of dumps at shelters and promotion of a "carry-in, carry-out" policy; dissemination of information on responsible trail and camping practices; and stationing caretakers at popular shelters and ranger-naturalists (now called summit caretakers) on the fragile alpine summits of Mount Mansfield and Camel's Hump. The caretaker program was the revival of an informal program from the 1920s and 1930s when caretakers were stationed at Taft Lodge, Butler Lodge, and Killington Peak's Porky Lodge.

During most of its history GMC has chosen not to become involved in national conservation causes, concentrating its energy on preserving the wilderness character of the Long Trail. In the mid-1930s, however, when a scenic highway, called the Green Mountain Parkway (similar to Shenandoah National Park's Skyline Drive), was proposed for the length of the Green Mountain Range, the club mounted energetic opposition. Vermonters ultimately rejected the idea in a statewide referendum. Similarly in 1958, when the U.S. Air Force dropped its plan to erect a missile communications facility on the Chin of Mount Mansfield, it was, in part, due to GMC objection.

Founder, Sponsor, Defender, and Protector

On Green Mountain Club's fiftieth anniversary in 1960 the Vermont General Assembly adopted a resolution "expressing its gratitude and recognition to the Green Mountain Club" for its role in establishing and maintaining the Long Trail. In 1971 the Legislature passed yet another resolution, recognizing the club as "the founder, sponsor, defender, and protector" of the Long Trail System and delegating to it responsibility for developing policies and programs for "the preservation, maintenance, and proper use of hiking trails for the benefit of the people of Vermont."

Although the General Assembly's continued recognition has meant very different challenges to different generations of GMCers — from pioneer trail blazing to environmental stewardship and land acquisition — the club's fundamental responsibility remains the same: to maintain and protect the Long Trail for all, now and in the future.

Protecting Vermont's Mountain Lands

Perhaps the largest endeavor for the Green Mountain Club in recent years has been Long Trail Protection.

The Long Trail protection effort began in the 1980s when the Green Mountain Club learned that land crossed by almost thirty miles of the Long Trail in northern Vermont was up for sale, threatening the future of the trail. An additional thirty miles were in private ownership and potentially at risk due to rapidly changing ownership patterns, development, clear-cutting, and log-skidding on the trail and posting by some private landowners. A protracted economic slump in the timber industry made it unprofitable for forest owners to hold onto their land, and large landholdings were coming onto the market at an alarming rate.

For the first time in the history of the Long Trail, a simple handshake wasn't enough to ensure passage for hikers or permanence of the trail corridor. Much of the southernmost 200 miles of the trail had been protected through acquisition for the Green Mountain National Forest and the Appalachian Trail. But between Mount Ellen and the Canadian border, in areas outside the Camel's Hump, Mount Mansfield, and Jay State Forests, over 60 miles of the Long Trail and 22 miles of side trail were unprotected.

In 1986, GMC launched the Long Trail Protection Campaign in an ambitious effort to acquire land or easements where the trail crossed private land. By 2001 GMC had protected 54 miles of the Long Trail and 14 miles of side trails through more than seventy willing buyer/willing seller acquisitions. Over 22,400 acres of backcountry land with important wildlife habitat and recreational value had been safeguarded. This effort was made possible in large part through state legislative appropriations for Long Trail acquisitions totaling $4 million.

Much of the acquired land has gone into state ownership. During the early years of the campaign, the Vermont field office of the Nature Conservancy assisted GMC with real estate closings and interim capital when needed. Hundreds of GMC members, friends, schools, businesses, organizations, foundations, and the Vermont Housing and Conservation Board have generously supported the cause of protecting the country's oldest long-distance hiking trail.

As of early 2003, about 6 miles of the Long Trail and 4.5 miles of side trail remain in private ownership without permanent protection. The GMC thanks the private landowners who have generously allowed the Long Trail to cross their land since club volunteers cut the first section of trail in 1910, and the twenty landowners who continue to allow it to do so.

265-Mile Club

The success of the Green Mountain Club's 265-Mile Club, named for the length of the Long Trail prior to the recent relocations, which have increased the trail's length, reflects the depth of passion that many people have for the trail. Over 650 people, foundations, businesses, civic groups, and GMC sections are members of the 265-Mile Club, having pledged $1,000 or more apiece to the Long Trail Protection Campaign. Since 1992, three permanent plaques have been unveiled at the club headquarters in Waterbury Center. Additional plaques are planned as membership in the 265-Mile Club continues to grow.

Anyone wishing to support the club's protection effort should contact the development office at GMC. Donating to the Long Trail Protection Campaign is a special way to commemorate a hike on the Long Trail, to honor a family member or friend, and to help protect the Green Mountains forever.

A Place of Our Own

When Green Mountain Club adopted its first vision statement in 1990, it could not foresee that one goal, owning its own headquarters, would become reality within two years. In 1992 the club bought the former 1836 May Farm on Vt. 100, a popular tourist route into the Green Mountains, in Waterbury Center. After leaving its original clubhouse in Sherburne Pass and renting office space for many years, first in Rutland, then in downtown Montpelier, GMC was at last its own landlord again.

With the club's relocation to Waterbury Center, wide support for the Long Trail Protection Campaign, and continued public interest in outdoor activities, membership in the club has climbed steadily. The club's long-range plan reaffirms the GMC's original mission statement and calls for GMC to play a leadership role in protecting, managing, and maintaining hiking trails throughout Vermont.

Management of the Long Trail

A Private-Public Partnership

Managing the 445-mile Long Trail System is a complex task, involving club volunteers and staff, federal and state agencies, organizations and businesses. Over the years, as use of the Long Trail and outside pressures such as development have increased, management of the trail has expanded from trail building and maintenance to include protecting natural resources from overuse, upholding landowner rights, protecting the trail from development, safeguarding special natural areas, and educating hikers.

The Long Trail is maintained by the Green Mountain Club in cooperation with the Vermont Department of Forests, Parks, and Recreation, the U.S. Forest Service, the National Park Service, the Appalachian Trail Conference, and private landowners. The cooperation and assistance of these agencies, organizations, and individuals are indispensable. In the Green Mountain National Forest, the U.S. Forest Service actively manages the Long

Trail and its side trails with GMC, providing funding for trail crews, managerial expertise, and staff support. On state lands, the Vermont Department of Forests, Parks, and Recreation works in a similar way on matters pertaining to the Long Trail System. The department provides grants from the Vermont Recreational Trails Fund. The GMC is a maintaining club of the Appalachian Trail Conference and, together with the ATC, U.S. Forest Service, and National Park Service, is working to secure a permanent route for the Long/Appalachian Trail in Vermont (the southern 100 miles of the Long Trail.)

The GMC also works with private landowners to ensure access to the trail on their land and with Vermont ski areas, who, in some instances, provide financial and logistical support for Long Trail projects.

Volunteers

Volunteers are the backbone of the Green Mountain Club. Without them the Long Trail would never have been built nor would it be managed as it is today. Volunteers serve as board members, on committees, as section officers, leaders of maintenance outings and other trips, trail and shelter adopters, and corridor monitors. These committed people blaze not only the trail itself, but the club's spirit as well.

The Green Mountain Club welcomes volunteers, members or not. Newcomers are always welcome. To volunteer or learn about club skills workshops, contact GMC.

Each GMC section maintains a portion of trail, side trails, and shelters. They host work parties throughout the year. Anyone wishing to join a section or its maintenance activities may contact GMC. Portions of the Long Trail maintained by GMC sections are listed below.

Bennington	Harmon Hill to Glastenbury Mountain
Brattleboro	Winhall River to Vt. 11 and 30
Bread Loaf	Sucker Brook Shelter to Emily Proctor Shelter
Burlington	Jonesville to Smugglers Notch
Connecticut	Glastenbury Mountain to Stratton-Arlington Road

Killington	Vt. 140 to U.S. 4
Laraway	Vt. 15 to Vt. 118
Manchester	Vt. 11 and 30 to Mad Tom Notch
Montpelier	Camel's Hump to Jonesville and Smugglers Notch to Chilcoot Pass
Northeast Kingdom	Bald Mountain*
Northern Frontier	Hazen's Notch to Canada
Ottauquechee	U.S. 4 to Maine Junction and Appalachian Trail: Maine Junction to Vt. 12
Sterling	Chilcoot Pass to Vt. 15
Worcester	Stratton-Arlington Road to Winhall River

With Vermont Leadership Center and Westmore Trails Association.

Section maintenance efforts are supplemented by the club's Trail and Shelter Adopter Program. Adopters agree to care for a shelter or portion of the trail and work independently to do inspections, basic maintenance, and cleanup. Volunteers also assist GMC field staff throughout the hiking season as site and summit caretakers, with trail maintenance, and on special projects.

Caretaker Program

The Green Mountain Club works to minimize hiker impacts through education, maintenance, and trail design. Since the late 1960s GMC has posted site and summit caretakers at a number of high-use sites and vulnerable natural areas along the Long Trail.

These caretakers educate hikers about Leave No Trace practices, maintain trails and shelters, compost sewage to protect water quality, and assist hikers. To help support this important program, an overnight use fee is charged at caretaker sites.

At the core of GMC's caretaker program is the belief that education will enlighten generations of hikers to travel in the backcountry without harming the trail, its natural resources, or the backwoods experiences of other hikers.

Long Trail Patrol

The Long Trail Patrol (LTP) is the Green Mountain Club's professional trail crew. Directed by University of Vermont

Professor Roy O. Buchanan nearly from its inception in 1930 until the mid-1960s, the LTP is GMC's oldest continuous non-volunteer program. Patrol crews, supported primarily by the U.S. Forest Service and Vermont Department of Forests, Parks, and Recreation, concentrate on trail relocation and reconstruction projects such as installing rock waterbars and steps. Crews typically live under primitive conditions for five days per week near the work sites.

From midsummer to early fall, the Volunteer Long Trail Patrol spends an intensive five days per week doing trail maintenance and construction. This successful program draws volunteers from far and wide, as well as local GMCers.

Appalachian National Scenic Trail

Vermont and the Long Trail hold a prominent place in the history of the Appalachian Trail. It may have been on or near the summit of Stratton Mountain, after construction of the Long Trail was begun, that the idea of an extended footpath linking the scenic ridges of the East crystallized in the mind of AT visionary Benton MacKaye.

First proposed in 1921 by MacKaye, a forester, author, and philosopher, the Appalachian Trail was completed in 1937. It extends for 2,150 miles from Katahdin in Maine to northern Georgia's Springer Mountain. The Appalachian Trail Conference, founded in 1925, works with its member clubs and federal and state agencies to preserve and maintain the Appalachian Trail, the world's longest linear national park.

In Vermont, the Appalachian Trail coincides with the Long Trail from the Massachusetts border to Maine Junction near Sherburne Pass, and then swings east to cross the Connecticut River near Hanover, New Hampshire, a distance of 149.5 miles. The GMC maintains the AT from the Massachusetts border to Vt. 12. From there to Norwich, the AT in Vermont is maintained by the Dartmouth Outing Club. For more information about the Appalachian Trail, contact the Appalachian Trail Conference, 799 Washington Street, P.O. Box 807, Harpers Ferry, WV 25425-0807; (304) 535-6331; Fax: (304) 535-2667; www.appalachiantrail.org.

DIVISION 1

Massachusetts–Vermont
State Line to Vt. 9

DIVISION 1 PROFILE

Distance (in miles)

Elevation (in feet)

MASS. 2, N. ADAMS, MA

SO. TERMINUS, LONG TRAIL

PEAK 3025

CONSULTATION PEAK

HARMON HILL

VT. 9

Massachusetts–Vermont State Line to Vt. 9

miles north-bound	▲ NORTH	elevation at Long Trail (feet/meters)	miles south-bound
14.3	**Vt. 9**	1360/415	0.0
12.5	**Harmon Hill**	2325/709	1.8
10.6	**Old Bennington–Heartwellville Road**	2220/677	3.7
10.0	**Congdon Shelter**	2080/634	4.3
8.4	**Sucker Pond Outlet Brook**	2180/665	5.9
7.0	**Consultation Peak**, northwest summit	2810/857	7.3
5.8	**Roaring Branch** bridge	2470/753	8.5
4.2	**Ed's Spring**, 100 ft E via spur	2890/881	10.1
3.1	**County Road**	2290/698	11.2
2.8	**Seth Warner Shelter**, 900 ft W via spur	2200/671	11.5
2.6	**Broad Brook Trail** to White Oaks Road, 4.0 mi. SW	2130/649	11.7
0.0	**Massachusetts-Vermont state line**, southern terminus of **Long Trail**	2330/710	14.3

WILLIAMSTOWN APPROACH VIA PINE COBBLE AND APPALACHIAN TRAILS

3.3	**Massachusetts-Vermont state line**, southern terminus of **Long Trail**	2330/710	0.0
2.5	**Eph's Lookout**	2254/687	0.8
2.1	**Appalachian Trail** to Mass. 2, 2.6 mi S	2010/613	1.2
1.5	**Summit of Pine Cobble** (1894 ft/577 m), 0.1 mi S via spur	1850/564	1.8
0.0	**Pine Cobble Road** in Williamstown	630/192	3.3

NORTH ADAMS APPROACH VIA APPALACHIAN TRAIL

3.8	**Southern terminus** of **Long Trail**	2330/710	0.0
3.0	**Eph's Lookout**	2254/687	0.8
2.6	**Pine Cobble Trail** to **Pine Cobble Road**, 2.1 mi W	2010/613	1.2
1.4	**Pete's Spring, Sherman Brook Primitive Campsite**, 0.1 mi W via spur	1300/396	2.4
0.0	**Mass. 2** in **North Adams**	660/201	3.8

SOUTH
▼

Division 1
Massachusetts–Vermont State Line to Vt. 9

Massachusetts: 0.0 miles   *Canada: 272.7 miles*

The south terminus of the Long Trail is at the Massachusetts-Vermont boundary, northwest of North Adams, Mass. The Appalachian Trail and Pine Cobble Trail provide access to the start of the Long Trail. The Appalachian Trail approach description begins on page 47. The Pine Cobble Trail is found on page 49.

The Long Trail and the Appalachian Trail coincide throughout this division.

Suggested Hikes

Pine Cobble. This pleasant climb on the Pine Cobble Trail leads to a vista of the tri-state region's rugged terrain. Round trip, 3.2 mi., 2¼ hr.

Harmon Hill. A steep climb on the Long Trail south from Vt. 9, this hike boasts expansive hilltop views. A steep rock staircase may be challenging to some hikers. Round trip, 3.6 mi., 2¾ hr.

Roaring Branch. This hike on the Long Trail north from County Road out of Stamford leads to a sizable beaver dam beneath Scrub Hill. County Road may not be passable all the way to the LT so some walking along the road may be necessary. Round trip, 5.4 mi., 3½ hr.

CAMPING AND FIRES

Although this division's Long Trail crosses the Green Mountain National Forest and the Stamford Meadows Wildlife Management Area, it follows a narrow publicly owned trail corridor surrounded by private property. Camping is limited to shelters. Small wood fires, although discouraged, are permitted at the shelters' established fire rings. Refer to Leave No Trace principles (pages 9 to 11) to minimize your impact.

Note: Camping at Sucker Pond is prohibited to protect the city of Bennington public water supply.

GROUP USE

Groups hiking on this division of the Long Trail may need an Outfitter–Guide Permit from the Green Mountain National Forest. Group tenting space is available at both Seth Warner and Congdon Shelters. Woodford State Park and GMNF Red Mill Campgrounds are available east of the Long Trail on Vt. 9 for base camp hiking. Refer to group use guidelines (pages 11 to 17) to determine your need for a permit and to minimize your group's impact.

WINTER USE

Harmon Hill via the Long Trail and Bald Mountain via the Bald Mountain Trail from Woodford provides rewarding snowshoe destinations with good views. The Appalachian Trail and Pine Cobble Trail out of Williamstown also make good snowshoe hikes.

ACCESS TO THE LONG TRAIL

COUNTY ROAD. Turn west onto Mill Road from Vt. 8 and 100, 0.5 mi. north of Billmont's Country Store in Stamford, or 6.8 mi. south of the junction of Vt. 8 and 100 in Readsboro. Follow the paved and then gravel road 2.0 mi. to a left turn onto County Road. Follow County Road beyond the last residences at 3.3 mi. where it becomes an unimproved gravel road. In dry conditions the road is passable another 0.9 mi. west to the Long Trail where there is parking for four cars on the south side just beyond the Trail. If the road is not passable, park cars so that no woods roads are blocked. This road is not passable from the Pownal side where it is also known as County Road. The last mile to the Long Trail is not plowed in winter.

VT. 9. This Long Trail crossing is 5.0 mi. east of U.S. 7 in downtown Bennington or 8.8 mi. west of the junction of Vt. 9 and Vt. 8 South. There is a U.S. Forest Service parking lot on the north side of the highway just west of the Trail.

APPROACH TRAILS

APPALACHIAN TRAIL (North Adams Approach). This trail begins on Mass. 2 opposite Phelps Ave. at a traffic light 3.0 mi. east of the U.S. 7/Mass. 2 traffic circle in Williamstown, and 2.4 mi. west of the center of North Adams. There is no parking at the trailhead, so hikers should obtain permission to park at the Greylock Community Club 0.1 mi. east of the trail on Mass. 2 or at the Holy Family Catholic Church adjacent to the AT.

Proceed north on the white-blazed Appalachian Trail from **Mass. 2 in North Adams (0.0 mi.)** opposite Phelps Ave. east of the church, and cross over the railroad and Hoosic River on a footbridge. Turn right and follow the AT along Massachusetts Ave. east. Just before a stone bridge, turn left off the road and cross two footbridges before reaching a small reservoir on **Sherman Brook (0.2 mi.).** Follow Sherman Brook upstream, and then climb away from the brook. Descend to **Pete's Spring (1.4 mi.)** and a **spur** leading west 0.1 mi. to **Sherman Brook**

WINTER HIKING?

- The Long Trail is marked with white blazes, which are very difficult to see against a snowy background and frequently buried beneath the snow.

- Deep snow may obscure all signs of the trail. Topographical maps and a compass are helpful.

- Daylight is short in the winter. Darkness may come suddenly.

- Stay alert to the dangers of hypothermia and frostbite. Know the signs and how to treat them.

- Keep group size between four and ten people.

- Be prepared to keep warm and sheltered with nothing more than the equipment you carry. Never count on a campfire or wood stove to keep you warm.

- You may encounter winter weather at higher elevations during the fall and spring.

- Use skis or snowshoes. Post-holing makes the trail unpleasant and dangerous for the next person.

Primitive Campsite and continuing another 0.1 mi. to loop back to the Appalachian Trail.

Continue on the AT and return to Sherman Brook at some old bridge abutments. Pass the north end of the campsite spur. Ascend and join an old woods road (1.7 mi.). Follow the woods road before swinging to the west and climbing through an old rock slide from which there are views to the south and east (2.3 mi.). There is a bad weather alternate route around the rockfall to the west. Skirt a boggy pond and climb a rocky knoll where the **Pine Cobble Trail (2.6 mi.)** enters from the west.

This junction is located near the south end of an extensive area on East Mtn. that is recovering from old forest fires. There are views of the Berkshire Hills to the south, including the Hoosac Range (left), the Taconics (right), and, between them, Mt. Greylock (3,491 ft.), the highest peak in Massachusetts. Bear right at the Pine Cobble junction and ascend to the north along the ridge to another rocky clearing, **Eph's Lookout (3.0 mi.)**, named after Ephraim Williams, founder of Williams College. Reenter the woods and continue north to the Class of 98 Trail, which leads west to the Pine Cobble Trail near Bear Spring, and then pass a blue diamond-blazed trail that also leads west. Follow the AT north to the **south terminus of the Long Trail (3.8 mi.) at the Massachusetts-Vermont state line. Mass. 2 to LT, 3.8 mi., 6.1 km., 2⅔ hr. (Rev. 2 hr.).**

PINE COBBLE TRAIL (Williamstown Approach). From its junction with U.S. 7 in Williamstown, follow Mass. 2 east 0.6 mi. to Cole Ave. Turn left and follow Cole Ave. 0.8 mi. to its end at North Hoosac Road. Turn right onto this road and proceed 0.3 mi., then take a left onto Pine Cobble Road. Follow this road 0.2 mi. to the trailhead. Pine Cobble Road is 2.1 mi. west of the AT on Massachusetts Ave./North Hoosac Road. Parking is available opposite the trail.

From **Pine Cobble Road in Williamstown (0.0 mi.)**, follow the blue-blazed Pine Cobble Trail up the hillside and into the woods. After passing a side trail on the right leading 350 ft. to Bear Spring, ascend steadily to the ridge where a **spur (1.5 mi.)** leads south 0.1 mi. to the **summit of Pine Cobble**. Here there is a wide view of the Hoosic Valley with Mt. Greylock and other Berkshire and Taconic peaks.

Continuing from the junction, follow gentle grades through scrub oak, pitch pine, and stunted white pines to a rocky knob and the **junction with the Appalachian Trail (2.1 mi.)**. From here follow the Appalachian Trail (described in the North Adams Approach) north (left) to the **south terminus of the Long Trail (3.3 mi.) at the Massachusetts-Vermont state line. Pine Cobble Road to LT, 3.3 mi., 5.3 km., 2½ hr. (Rev. 1¾ hr.).**

LONG TRAIL DESCRIPTION

From the **Massachusetts–Vermont state line (0.0 mi.)**, descend to a brook crossing (0.4 mi.). Climb to the east side of a low ridge, pass over a bedrock ridge (1.7 mi.), and continue to a woods road (2.4 mi.). Cross the road and proceed to a dirt road **(2.6 mi.)**, which to the west is the **Broad Brook Trail**. This trail leads southwest 4.0 mi. to White Oaks Road out of Williamstown.

Cross the road and ascend to the junction with a **spur (2.8 mi.)** leading 900 ft. west to **Seth Warner Shelter**. This frame lean-to was built by carpenter trainees of the Manpower Development Training Act in 1965, and has space for eight. A brook, which may fail in dry seasons, is 450 ft. to the west. A primitive tenting area is located 400 ft. south of the shelter. **North Adams to Seth Warner Shelter, 6.7 mi., 10.8 km., 4¼ hr. (SB 3½ hr.). Pine Cobble Road to Seth Warner Shelter, 6.2 mi., 10.0 km., 4 hr. (SB 3¼ hr.).**

Hike north from the shelter spur, crossing **County Road (3.1 mi.)** just beyond a power line. Under favorable conditions this road may be driven 4.2 mi. east to Vt. 8 and 100 in Stamford.

Begin a steady ascent from the road and, after passing a view south to Mt. Greylock and a **spur (4.2 mi.)** leading 100 ft. east to **Ed's Spring**, continue to the south summit of a nameless ridge (4.5 mi.). Here there are views to the south and west. Return to the woods and continue north along the ridge. After passing under a power line (4.9 mi.), descend to an old beaver pond, where there is a view of nearby Scrub Hill. Cross **Roaring Branch (5.8 mi.)** on a log bridge built by the Vermont Youth Conservation Corps (VYCC) just below the beaver dam.

Beyond the brook crossing, pass over several minor knobs and, remaining on or just below the ridge most of the way, continue to the wooded northwest summit of **Consultation Peak (7.0 mi.)**, so named by volunteer trail workers because of its strategic location for planning maintenance activities. Descend to a well-traveled woods road (8.0 mi.), which leads 0.1 mi. west to a clearing on the east shore of Sucker Pond. *Note:* To protect the Bennington public water supply, no swimming or camping is allowed at Sucker Pond.

From the woods road crossing, descend gently and cross the **Sucker Pond Outlet Brook (8.4 mi.)**. Then, after passing over puncheon through a wetland in Stamford Meadows, climb a wooded knoll, passing the stone foundation of a nineteenth-century tavern (8.9 mi.). Continue uphill to the ridge and, after crossing a woods road, descend to picturesque Stamford Stream (9.4 mi.), following it downstream before bearing left to **Congdon Shelter (10.0 mi.)**.

This open-front frame cabin, with bunks for eight, was built by the Long Trail Patrol in 1967 and modified by Pioneer Valley Section volunteers in 1994. It is named for Herbert Wheaton Congdon, a Long Trail pioneer, trail builder, guide book editor, and cartographer, and was a gift of the Congdon family. A small brook east of the shelter furnishes water; overflow campsites are located on the ridge above the outhouse. **Seth Warner Shelter to Congdon Shelter, 7.4 mi., 11.9 km., 4½ hr. (SB 4½ hr.).**

Continue north from the shelter to ascend the ridge, skirt an area of beaver activity, and then arrive at the **Old Bennington–Heartwellville Road (10.6 mi.)**. This woods road can be followed west 4.0 mi. to Vt. 9 via Burgess Road, 1.0 mi. east of U.S. 7 in Bennington. To the east, this road leads to Stamford Stream and the woods roads of Dunville Hollow.

From the woods road, cross a small stream, climb steadily past two more woods roads, and then traverse a small clearing (11.4 mi.). Beyond this point, after fairly level going, cross a brook and climb to the open summit of **Harmon Hill (12.5 mi.)**, where controlled burns are used as a management tool by the U.S. Forest Service to retain vistas and provide wildlife clearings. There is a view to the west including Mt. Anthony, the historic village of Bennington, and the monument that commemorates the American Revolution's Battle of Bennington. To the north are views of Bald Mtn. and Glastenbury Mtn.

From the summit, bear east across the clearing, enter the woods, and begin to descend. The descent steepens (13.7 mi.), following extensive rock staircases, ending at a pullout on the south side of **Vt. 9 (14.3 mi.)**. *Use caution when crossing Vt. 9; traffic moves at high speeds.*

Vt. 9 leads west 5.0 mi. to U.S. 7 in Bennington. Old Bennington, the town center of colonial days, is a mile west of the present center. Many historical buildings and sites, including the Bennington Museum and the Bennington Battle Monument, are located there. To the east it is 2.8 mi. to Woodford and 4.8 mi. to Woodford State Park.

SIDE TRAIL

BROAD BROOK TRAIL. This trail begins on White Oaks Road in Pownal, Vt., near the state line. Refer to the Pine Cobble Trail directions in this division to the junction of Cole Ave. and North Hoosac Road. From there, proceed 0.8 mi. west on North Hoosac and Bridges Road to White Oaks Road. Continue on White Oaks Road 1.2 mi. north to the Vermont border and the crossing of Broad Brook. The parking lot is on the east side of the road just beyond the Mass.–Vt. state line. Long-term parking is not recommended.

From the east side of the parking lot, skirt the south side of the North Adams waterworks. Once past the waterworks follow an old woods road east and north. Parallel Broad Brook, and cross it several times. These crossings can be challenging in the spring. Ascend northeasterly to a dirt road (3.7 mi.), and follow it east to the Long Trail. **White Oaks Road to LT, 4.0 mi., 6.4 km., 2½ hr. (Rev. 2 hr.).**

DIVISION 2

Vt. 9 to Stratton–Arlington
(Kelley Stand) Road

DIVISION 2 PROFILE

Vt. 9 to Stratton–Arlington
(Kelley Stand) Road

miles north-bound	▲ NORTH	elevation at Long Trail (feet/meters)	miles south-bound

miles north-bound	▲ NORTH	elevation at Long Trail (feet/meters)	miles south-bound
22.6	**Stratton–Arlington (Kelley Stand) Road**, Stratton Mtn. parking lot	2230/680	0.0
22.5	**Kelley Stand Road**, south junction	2240/683	0.1
21.7	**Black Brook bridge**	2220/677	0.9
20.6	**USFS Road 71** to Kelley Stand Road and Stratton Pond Trail, 0.75 mi N	2380/726	2.0
19.0	**Story Spring Shelter**	2810/857	3.6
18.1	**South Alder Brook**, crossing	2600/793	4.5
15.1	**Lydia's Rest**	3300/1006	7.5
14.4	**Caughnawaga Shelter**	2800/854	8.2
14.2	**Kid Gore Shelter**, 0.1 mi E via loop trail	2800/854	8.4
13.7	**Big Rock**	3250/991	8.9
10.4	**Glastenbury Mtn. fire tower**	3748/1143	12.2
10.1	**Goddard Shelter: West Ridge Trail** to Woodford Hollow via Bald Mtn. Trail east branch, 9.7 mi S; to Branch Street in Bennington via Bald Mtn. Trail west branch, 11.3 mi S	3560/1085	12.5
7.6	**Glastenbury Lookout**	2920/890	15.0
5.8	**Little Pond Lookout**	3060/933	16.8
4.4	**Porcupine Lookout**	2815/858	18.2
3.2	**Hell Hollow Brook bridge**	2350/716	19.4
2.1	**Maple Hill**	2630/802	20.5
1.6	**Melville Nauheim Shelter**, 250 ft E via spur	2300/701	21.0
0.7	**Split Rock**	1900/579	21.9
0.0	**Vt. 9; William D. MacArthur Memorial bridge** over **City Stream**	1360/415	22.6

SOUTH
▼

DIVISION 2
Vt. 9 to Stratton–Arlington (Kelley Stand) Road

Massachusetts: 14.3 miles   *Canada 258.4 miles*

The Long Trail and the Appalachian Trail coincide throughout this division.

SUGGESTED HIKES

SPLIT ROCK. This short hikes leads to a large glacial erratic on the Long Trail north of Vt. 9. Round trip, 1.4 mi., 1 hr.

PORCUPINE LOOKOUT. A full day's trip on the Long Trail north from Vt. 9 to a lookout that offers fine views. Round trip, 8.8 mi., 5½ hr.

CAMPING AND FIRES

This division's Long Trail crosses the Green Mountain National Forest. Primitive off-trail camping with small wood fires is allowed. Refer to Leave No Trace principles (pages 9 to 11) to minimize your impact.

Note: Camping between Maple Hill and Porcupine Lookout is prohibited to protect the city of Bennington public water supply (Hell Hollow Brook).

GROUP USE

Groups hiking this division's Long Trail may need an Outfitter-Guide Permit from the Green Mountain National Forest. Group tenting space is available at both Caughnawaga and Story Spring Shelters. Woodford State Park and GMNF Red Mill Campgrounds are available east of the Long Trail on Vt. 9 for base camp hiking. GMNF Grout Pond Campground is also available east of the Long Trail on the Stratton-Arlington Road for base camp hiking. Refer to group use guidelines (pages 11 to 17) to determine whether you need for permit and to minimize your group's impact.

WINTER USE

The remoteness of this section of trail cannot be overemphasized. Snowshoeing north from Vt. 9 provides views south to Harmon Hill.

ACCESS TO LONG TRAIL

VT. 9. Refer to directions on page 47 in Division 1.

STRATTON–ARLINGTON (KELLEY STAND) ROAD. *Western approach via U.S. 7:* From U.S. 7 take exit 3 (Arlington) and proceed 0.1 mi. west on Vt. 313 to a right turn onto South Road. Follow South Road 0.6 mi. to its end on Kansas Road. Turn right and proceed 0.7 mi. to a fork just after crossing a bridge. The right-hand fork is the Kelley Stand Road, which continues east 10.8 mi. to the Long Trail. Parking is on the north side of the road just beyond the bridge over the East Branch of the Deerfield River.

Western approach via Vt. 7A: From Vt. 7A, follow East Arlington Road east for 1.0 mi. and turn right just before a bridge onto Old Mill Road. Follow Old Mill Road, which becomes Kansas Road at the Sunderland town line, 2.4 mi. to a fork just after crossing a bridge over Roaring Brook. The right-hand fork is the Kelley Stand Road, which continues east 10.6 mi. to the

Long Trail. Parking is available on the north side of the road just beyond the bridge over the East Branch of the Deerfield River.

Eastern approach: From Vt. 100 in West Wardsboro, 0.5 mi. south of the post office, 8.5 mi. south of Vt. 30 in East Jamaica and 13.6 mi. north of Wilmington, follow the Stratton–Arlington Road west 3.4 mi. to the town of Stratton and another 3.4 mi. farther to the Long Trail parking lot on the north side of the road just before crossing the bridge over the East Branch of the Deerfield River.

Kelley Stand Road maintenance is a contract service paid by the Green Mountain National Forest to the Town of Sunderland; regular maintenance begins June 1 and ends on November 1. The road is unplowed between a major snowmobile parking lot just west of Roaring Brook and another snowmobile parking lot east of the Long Trail parking lot. The unmaintained portion of the road is a snowmobile trail.

LONG TRAIL DESCRIPTION

Cross **Vt. 9 (0.0 mi.).** *Use caution when crossing Vt. 9; traffic moves at high speeds.* North of the highway, follow the Long Trail past a spur leading west to a paved parking lot with a trailhead privy and cross the **William D. MacArthur Memorial Bridge over City Stream**. The bridge, built by the U.S. Forest Service, honors the memory of a dedicated volunteer trail maintainer with the Pioneer Valley and Bennington Sections.

From the bridge, follow City Stream's north bank downstream, and then turn right to begin a steady climb with several switchbacks to a lookout with a view to the northwest. Above the lookout, pass between the upright halves of **Split Rock (0.7 mi.).** After crossing a woods road, ascend at an easier grade, cross another woods road, and then continue to a **spur (1.6 mi.)** leading east 250 ft. to **Melville Nauheim Shelter**. This frame shelter, constructed in 1977, has bunk space for eight. It was built with funds contributed by Mrs. Melville Nauheim of New York City in memory of her husband. The stream the LT crosses just north of the spur junction provides water. A GMC roving caretaker may be on duty to assist and

educate hikers and help maintain the local trails and shelters.
**Congdon Shelter to Melville Nauheim Shelter, 5.9 mi., 9.5
km., 3¾ hr. (SB 4 hr.).**

Continue north, crossing the stream and then climbing
gradually, crossing a power line on **Maple Hill (2.1 mi.)**. Here
there are views of Bennington and Mt. Anthony to the west and
of Mt. Snow, Haystack Mtn., and the north end of the Hoosac
Range to the east. After cresting a rise, descend to cross a small
stream, and then continue with little change in elevation to
cross the **Hell Hollow Brook bridge (3.2 mi.)**. Just beyond,
cross the original route of the Long Trail (circa 1920), long
since obliterated, which followed Hell Hollow Brook upstream
from Woodford Hollow. *Camping is prohibited in this area to
protect the city of Bennington public water supply.*

North of the brook, climb gradually and, after passing
through a balsam and spruce swamp on puncheon, climb
steadily to a ridge leading to **Porcupine Lookout (4.4 mi.)**,
with views to the east and south, and then drop to the first of
several sags in the ridge. After some gradual climbing, ascend
moderately to the wooded summit of **Little Pond Mtn.
(5.5 mi.)**, descend a short distance, and then continue along a
narrow ridge to Little Pond Lookout (5.8 mi.) with a view east
over the pond. Proceed with only minor elevation changes, and
then climb steadily to a point just below the summit (3,331 ft.)
of an unnamed peak. Remaining somewhat below the ridge to
the west, descend steadily, and then continue on easier grades
for nearly a mile before regaining the ridge a short distance
south of **Glastenbury Lookout (7.6 mi.)**, from which there is
a view of Glastenbury Mtn. and West Ridge.

Beyond the lookout, drop to a shallow sag and cross an old
woods road (8.1 mi.). From the woods road, ascend gradually,
then climb steadily to a large rectangular boulder (8.8 mi.) near
an unnamed summit (3,150 ft.). Continue along the ridge with
little change in elevation before beginning a moderate ascent.

IN CASE OF EMERGENCY, CALL 911.
KNOW WHERE YOU ARE!

Climb steadily over rock and log stairs, and then level off and pass a spring just before entering the clearing for **Goddard Shelter (10.1 mi.)**, where there is a view of Mt. Greylock to the south.

This log lean-to, with space for twelve, was built by the Bennington Section and the U.S. Forest Service in 1985. Some of the materials were airlifted to the site by the Air National Guard. The name honors Ted Goddard, former president and treasurer of the GMC, and past president of the Bennington Section. The spring just to the south on the Long Trail provides water. A GMC roving caretaker may be on duty to assist and educate hikers and help maintain the local trails and shelters. **Melville Nauheim Shelter to Goddard Shelter, 8.5 mi., 13.7 km., 4¾ hr. (SB 5 hr.).**

Beyond the west wall of the shelter, the **West Ridge Trail** enters the woods and follows Glastenbury Mtn.'s southwest ridge 11.3 mi. to Bennington and 9.7 mi. to Woodford Hollow. Combined with one of the branches of the **Bald Mtn. Trail**, this is an alternate route to the summit of Glastenbury Mtn. from the south.

Ascend north of Goddard Shelter past the remains of the old fire warden's cabin to the densely wooded summit of **Glastenbury Mtn. (10.4 mi.)**. Here, a **fire tower** built in 1927 and renovated by the U.S. Forest Service in the 1970s now serves as an observation deck for hikers. It affords a 360-degree view, which includes more wild forest than can be seen from any other point on the Long Trail. Beyond the nearby ridges are the Berkshires to the south, the Taconics to the west, Mt. Equinox and Stratton Mtn. to the north, and Somerset Reservoir, Mt. Snow, and Haystack Mtn. to the east.

From the tower, descend gently, crossing a snowmobile trail one mile north of the summit, and then follow the rugged ridge with minor changes in elevation to **Big Rock (13.7 mi.)**. Drop steadily to the south end of a loop trail **(14.2 mi.)** leading east 0.1 mi. to **Kid Gore Shelter**. Pass the north end of the loop in Glen Haven. Via the north loop it is 180 ft. to Kid Gore Shelter. Just beyond and to the west is **Caughnawaga Shelter (14.4 mi.)**. Kid Gore Shelter is a log lean-to with bunks for eight. It was built by Connecticut Section volunteers and Camp

Najerog alumni in 1971 and is named in memory of Harold M. (Kid) Gore, who ran Camp Najerog. Its water source is a spring 30 ft. north of the shelter (unreliable in dry seasons). Caughnawaga Shelter, a small log shelter, was built by Camp Najerog volunteers in 1931. It has bunks for five, and there is a reliable brook in front of the shelter. A GMC roving caretaker may be on duty to assist and educate hikers and help maintain the local trails and shelters. **Goddard Shelter to Kid Gore and Caughnawaga Shelters, 4.2 mi., 6.8 km., 2½ hr. (SB 3 hr.).**

Turn right just south of Caughnawaga Shelter, drop sharply to cross the brook, ascend to a small ridge, and then descend to a brook. Beyond the brook crossing, begin to climb and bear to the west of an unnamed summit (3,412 ft.), passing a vista to the west near **Lydia's Rest (15.1 mi.).** Descend to the west side of the ridge, and follow gentle terrain before descending to cross two adjacent branches of **South Alder Brook (18.1 mi.).** Then, after passing several beaver ponds, climb a hill to **Story Spring Shelter (19.0 mi.).** This frame lean-to with space for eight was built by the U.S. Forest Service in 1963. It is named in honor of George F. Story, for many years an active trail worker in the Worcester Section. The spring beside the Trail 135 ft. north of the shelter provides water. A GMC roving caretaker may be on duty. **Caughnawaga Shelter to Story Spring Shelter, 4.6 mi., 7.4 km., 3 hr. (SB 3 hr.).**

Pass the spring, and then following a rugged climb from the shelter, descend gradually through an old logged-over area to reach **USFS Road 71 (20.6 mi.),** 0.75 mile south of Kelley Stand Road and the Stratton Pond Trail parking lot. After crossing the road, pass a series of beaver ponds, ascend a low knoll, and descend to a woods road. Cross **Black Brook bridge (21.7 mi.),** rebuilt by the Volunteer Long Trail Patrol in 2002

SIGN IN AND OUT OF TRAIL REGISTERS

It builds support for funding for maintenance on public lands.

---

and follow a woods road to a clearing with a view of Little Stratton Mtn. After bearing northeast across the clearing and entering the woods, continue along a low ridge above the Deerfield River. Cross another brook and gradually ascend to the gravel **Kelley Stand Road (22.5 mi.)**. Turn right to follow the road east over the East Branch of the Deerfield River. Just beyond the river is trailhead parking on the north side of the **Stratton-Arlington (Kelley Stand) Road (22.6 mi.)**.

2

West along the Kelley Stand Road it is 0.9 mi. to Stratton Pond Trail parking, 2.1 mi. to the Branch Pond Trailhead, 4.9 mi. to the site of Kelley Stand, an eighteenth-century overnight stagecoach stop, and 13.0 mi. to Arlington on Vt. 7A. To the east it is 3.4 mi. to Stratton village, and 6.7 mi. to West Wardsboro (store has a public phone) and Vt. 100.

SIDE TRAILS

WEST RIDGE TRAIL. This trail links the Bald Mtn. Trail to Glastenbury Mtn. and the Long Trail. From its junction with the Bald Mtn. Trail (0.0 mi.), follow the West Ridge Trail over the summit of Bald Mtn. (0.1 mi.) with views north to Glastenbury Mtn., Mt. Equinox, and Dorset Peak. Descend from the summit, and then continue north on or near the ridge toward Glastenbury Mtn. Swinging to the west of an unnamed summit (3,423 ft.), descend to an old woods road (5.3 mi.), and follow it a short distance south. Reenter the woods, pass a beaver pond, and after climbing near another unnamed summit (3,365 ft.), slab the southwest slope of Glastenbury Mtn. to arrive at the Long Trail (7.8 mi.) at Goddard Shelter. **Bald Mtn Trail to LT, 7.8 mi., 12.6 km., 4¾ hr. (Rev. 4¼ hr.).**

BALD MTN. TRAIL. *West trailhead:* The west branch of this trail begins at a power line crossing of Branch Street Extension in Bennington. Follow U.S. 7 north from the junction of U.S. 7 and Vt. 9 in Bennington. At 1.0 mi. turn east on Kocher Drive, then continue straight past a traffic light about 1.0 mi. to the power line crossing (blue-blazed utility pole). The parking space is minimal.

From Branch Street (0.0 mi.) ascend on old woods roads, cross a brook (0.6 mi.), then bear left off the road (0.9 mi.). Cross and follow several brooks for the next mile before turning right to begin a steady climb out of the hollow (1.9 mi.). Ascend on several long switchbacks, and cross some old rock slides before reaching White Rocks (2.6 mi.) with a view to the west. Continue climbing, passing a spring (3.1 mi.), to the junction with the West Ridge Trail (3.5 mi.) just below the summit of Bald Mtn. **Branch Street to West Ridge Trail, 3.5 mi., 5.6 km., 2¾ hr. (Rev. 1¾ hr.).**

East trailhead: To reach the east branch of the Bald Mtn. Trail, continue 1.0 mi. west of the LT crossing on Vt. 9. From here turn north onto Harbour Road in Woodford Hollow. Follow the road 0.8 mi. north just past a large water storage tank. There is limited parking near the trail sign. Care should be taken not to block any access roads. The trail follows a woods road west uphill beyond the water tank. From the road (0.0 mi.), ascend a series of old woods roads to a spur (1.6 mi.) leading 0.1 mi. to a spring at Bear Wallow, then climb switchbacks to the junction with the West Ridge Trail (1.9 mi.). **Woodford Hollow trailhead to West Ridge Trail, 1.9 mi., 3.1 km., 1½ hr. (Rev. 1 hr.).**

Additional distances: Branch Street in Bennington to Woodford Hollow via the Bald Mtn. Trail is 5.4 mi.; Branch Street in Bennington to Goddard Shelter on the LT via the Bald Mtn. (west branch) and West Ridge Trails is 11.3 mi.; and Woodford Hollow to Goddard Shelter on the LT via the Bald Mtn. (east branch) and West Ridge Trails is 9.7 mi.

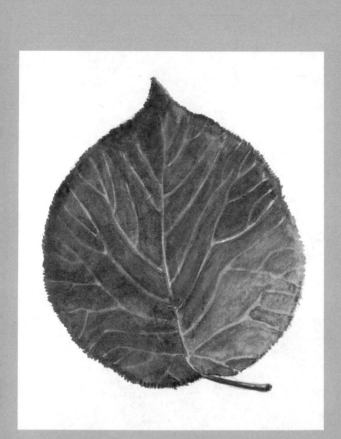

DIVISION 3

Stratton-Arlington
(Kelley Stand) Road to
Mad Tom Notch

DIVISION 3 PROFILE

Stratton–Arlington (Kelley Stand) Road to Mad Tom Notch

miles north-bound	▲ NORTH	elevation at Long Trail (feet/meters)	miles south-bound
22.7	**USFS Road 21** at **Mad Tom Notch**	2446/746	0.0
20.7	**Bromley Mtn.**, north summit	3120/951	2.0
20.2	**Bromley Mtn.**, observation tower, 100 ft E	3260/994	2.5
18.2	**Bromley Brook bridge; Bromley Tenting Area**	2080/634	4.5
17.5	**Vt. 11** and **30**	1800/549	5.2
15.1	**Spruce Peak**, 300 ft W via spur	2040/622	7.6
14.7	**Spruce Peak Shelter**, 0.1 mi W via spur	2200/671	8.0
12.6	**Prospect Rock**, 150 ft W via spur; Old Rootville Road: to paved public road, 1.8 mi W	2150/655	10.1
11.7	**Branch Pond Trail** to **William B. Douglas Shelter**, 0.5 mi S; to **Bourn Pond Shelter**, 4.0 mi S; to Kelley Stand Road, 8.3 mi S	2280/695	11.0
8.9	**Winhall River bridge**; Lye Brook Wilderness east boundary	2175/663	13.8
7.1	**North Shore Trail** to **North Shore Tenting Area**, 0.5 mi W; to **Lye Brook Trail**, 0.7 mi W	2555/779	15.6
7.0	**Willis Ross Clearing** at **Stratton Pond; Lye Brook Trail** to **Bourn Pond Shelter**, 2.4 mi W; to Manchester, 9.7 mi W	2555/779	15.7
6.9	**Stratton Pond Trail** to **Stratton Pond Shelter**, 450 ft S via Stratton Pond Trail and spur; to Kelley Stand Road, 3.7 mi S	2620/799	15.8
3.8	**Stratton Mtn. fire tower; Stratton Mtn., north peak** (3875 ft/1181 m), 0.7 mi N via old service road	3936/1200	18.9
1.4	**IP Road**, south intersection	2520/768	21.3
0.0	**Stratton–Arlington (Kelley Stand) Road**; Stratton Mtn. parking lot	2230/680	22.7

SOUTH

▼

Division 3

Stratton–Arlington (Kelley Stand) Road to Mad Tom Notch

Massachusetts: 36.9 miles   *Canada: 235.8 miles*

From the Winhall River to the Branch Pond Trail, the Long Trail crosses the Lye Brook Wilderness. Refer to wilderness information on page 7.

Mad Tom Shelter was removed in 1996. The GMC is working with the U.S. Forest Service to relocate the Long Trail on the south side of Bromley Mtn., including a new shelter.

Bromley Ski Area has generously allowed hikers to use their ski patrol warming hut on the summit; this use depends on respect for the facility, and its availability is subject to change.

The Long Trail and the Appalachian Trail coincide throughout this division.

Suggested Hikes

Spruce Peak. This rock outcrop with views of the Battenkill Valley, Mt. Equinox, and Dorset Peak is located on a spur off the Long Trail south from Vt. 11 and 30. Round trip, 4.8 mi., 2½ hr.

BROMLEY MTN. This summit, reached from either the south or the north via the Long Trail, features 360-degree views from its observation tower. LT north from Vt. 11 and 30: round trip, 5.4 mi., 3½ hr.; LT south from Mad Tom Notch: round trip, 5.0 mi., 3 hr.

STRATTON MTN. This summit also offers a 360-degree view from its fire tower. Round trip via Long Trail north from Kelley Stand Road, 7.6 mi., 4⅔ hr.

LYE BROOK WILDERNESS. The LT/AT and its side trails offer a number of day hike and backpack loop opportunities featuring highland ponds, wetlands, and scenic views. One such hike is a circuit from Kelley Stand Road north to Stratton Pond, then west to Bourn Pond, then south back to Kelley Stand Road using the Stratton Pond, Long, Lye Brook and Branch Pond Trails. It requires a 1.2 mi. road walk on the Kelley Stand Road between the Stratton Pond Trail and Branch Pond Trail. This loop can be done as a day hike or a backpack. Round trip, 11.7 mi., 6 hr.

CAMPING AND FIRES

This division's Long Trail is within the Green Mountain National Forest. Primitive off-trail camping with small wood fires is allowed. Refer to Leave No Trace principles (pages 9 to 11) to minimize your impact.

Exceptions: Camping at Stratton Pond is limited to designated sites and prohibited on Stratton Mtn. to protect vulnerable vegetation and soils. Wood fires are prohibited at Stratton Pond Shelter to protect the surrounding vegetation; wood fires are permitted at Stratton Pond's North Shore Tenting Area.

GROUP USE

Groups hiking this division's Long Trail may need an Outfitter-Guide Permit from the Green Mountain National Forest. Group tenting space is available at Stratton Pond's North Shore Tenting Area, Spruce Peak Shelter, and, if available, at Bromley's ski patrol warming hut. GMNF Grout Pond Campground is available east of the Long Trail on the Stratton-Arlington Road for base camp hiking. GMNF Hapgood Pond Campground is also available (refer to Long Trail access directions for USFS Road 21) for base camp hiking. Refer to group use guidelines (pages 11 to 17) to determine your need for a permit and to minimize your group's impact.

WINTER USE

Much of the terrain between Stratton Pond and Vt. 11 and 30 is suitable for intermediate level cross-country skiing. Both Stratton Mtn. and Bromley Mtn. make challenging snowshoe trips. Spruce Peak via the LT from Vt. 11 and 30 is also a good winter destination. It offers fine views without exposing winter hikers to the more severe conditions of the high summits. The Long Trail intersects the Catamount Trail (a crosscountry ski trail that runs the length of Vermont) at Stratton Pond. See Catamount Trail information on page 26.

ACCESS TO LONG TRAIL

STRATTON–ARLINGTON (KELLEY STAND) ROAD. Refer to directions on page 58 in Division 2.

VT. 11 AND 30. This Long Trail crossing is 5.9 mi. east of Vt. 7A in Manchester Center, 4.5 mi. east of the U.S. 7 interchange east of Manchester Center, and 0.5 mi. west of the junction of Vt. 11 and 30 South. There is a large paved parking lot on the north side of the road. *Use caution when crossing this highway.*

USFS ROAD 21 AT MAD TOM NOTCH. This Long Trail intersection is 4.0 mi. west of Peru. From Peru's J. J. Hapgood Store (0.3 mi. north of Vt. 11, 3.5 mi. east of the junction of Vt. 11 and 30 South or 4.4 mi. west of the junction of Vt. 11 and 100 South), follow the Hapgood Pond Road 1.0 mi. to North Road. Take the initially paved North Road 0.5 mi. beyond the end of the pavement to the second left, which is the gravel-surfaced Mad Tom Notch Road. Follow this road 2.1 mi. to the height-of-land in Mad Tom Notch and the LT. A gravel parking lot on the south side of the road is just beyond the trail crossing. USFS Hapgood Pond campground, a good base for day hikes in the region, is on Hapgood Pond Road, 0.7 mi. north of North Road.

The last mile of USFS Road 21 to the Long Trail is not plowed in winter. A large parking lot is maintained at the end of the plowed portion of the road. It is a popular snowmobile trailhead and is open for all winter recreation activities.

LONG TRAIL DESCRIPTION

From the parking lot on the north side of **Stratton-Arlington (Kelley Stand) Road (0.0 mi.)**, at the site of Grout Job, an old lumber camp; head north into the woods and travel over gently rolling terrain toward Stratton Mtn. After crossing the gravel **International Paper (IP) Road (1.4 mi.)**, begin to climb gradually, then ascend switchbacks to a vista to the south (2.0 mi.).

Climb to the col (2.7 mi.) between Stratton and Little Stratton Mtns., and then ascend another series of switchbacks. Pass a spring (3.2 mi.), and continue to climb to the **fire tower** on the **south peak of Stratton Mtn. (3.8 mi.)**. Straight ahead from the tower, the old service road follows the ridge 0.7 mi. to the **north peak of Stratton Mtn.** and provides access to Stratton Ski Area. Stratton Mtn. claims a unique role in hiking trail history. James P. Taylor was on this mountain when the idea of the Long Trail was born, and the Appalachian Trail was conceived by Benton MacKaye near its summit.

The fire tower on the summit provides views of the surrounding mountains and countryside. Somerset Reservoir and Mt. Snow are to the south, Glastenbury Mtn. is southwest, and the Taconics, including Mt. Equinox, the highest peak of the range, lie to the west. Mt. Ascutney is to the northeast and Grand Monadnock in New Hampshire is to the southeast. To the north is Stratton's north peak with its gondola station. On clear viewing days, Killington Peak is visible to the north. A GMC summit caretaker may be on duty to assist hikers. *Camping is prohibited on Stratton Mtn. to protect its vulnerable vegetation and soils.*

At the summit, bear left beyond the tower. Descend a series of switchbacks, pass a short spur (4.0 mi.) to a spring and continue to a view (4.5 mi.) west to Stratton Pond, the Lye Brook Wilderness and Mt. Equinox. Continue downhill at a gradual grade to the IP Road (5.8 mi.). Beyond the road, descend gently to cross a bridge (6.4 mi.) over a brook.

Beyond the brook, ascend past a beaver pond, then level out before reaching a junction with the **Stratton Pond Trail (6.9 mi.)**. This trail leads 150 ft. south to a **spur** and 3.7 mi. south to Kelley Stand Road, and provides an alternate route between Kelley Stand Road and Stratton Pond. The spur leads 300 ft. east to **Stratton Pond Shelter**. This post-and-beam structure, built by Erik and Laurel Tobiason and the Worcester Section in 1999, is dedicated to the memory of Robert Humes, longtime Worcester Section volunteer and past GMC president. Wood fires are prohibited at Stratton Pond Shelter to protect the surrounding vegetation. There is a composting privy on the shelter spur. The water source is Bigelow Spring, just west of Willis Ross Clearing on the Lye Brook Trail. **Story Spring Shelter to Stratton Pond Shelter, 10.6 mi., 17.1 km., 6¼ hr. (SB 6 hr.).**

Descend from the junction to reach **Willis Ross Clearing** and the junction with the Lye Brook Trail at the southeast shoreline of **Stratton Pond (7.0 mi.)**. The foundation stones of Willis Ross Camp, which burned in 1972, are visible at the east end of the clearing. To the south of the clearing, the Lye Brook Trail follows the south shore of the pond to piped **Bigelow Spring** (unreliable in drought) and continues west 2.4 mi. to **Bourn Pond** and ultimately 9.7 mi. to Manchester.

Stratton Pond is the largest body of water on the Long Trail. It also receives the most annual overnight use of any location on the Trail. This heavy use was once concentrated at the pond's shoreline, which is particularly prone to erosion, adding sediment to the pond. A GMC caretaker stays near Willis Ross Clearing during the hiking season to assist and educate hikers, help maintain the local trails and campsites, and compost sewage to protect water quality. Hikers are strongly urged to safeguard this natural area by using the shelter and designated campsites. A fee is charged for overnight use at the shelter and campsites near the pond.

From Willis Ross Clearing, head north, pass an intermittent spring on the right, and reach a junction with the **North Shore Trail (7.1 mi.)**. This trail leads west 0.5 mi. to the **North Shore Tenting Area**, which has tent platforms and a composting privy, and 0.7 mi. to the Lye Brook Trail. From the junction, bear right and leave the shoreline on the Catamount Trail following a woods road. After a short distance, bear left from the woods road and continue with minor changes in elevation, before descending to the **Winhall River (8.9 mi.)**. Cross the river on a bridge, enter the Lye Brook Wilderness, and proceed, again with little change in elevation, along the northeast edge of the plateau above the Winhall River Valley. The Long Trail may be more challenging to follow in the Wilderness Area due to minimal brushing and blazing. Continue to the junction with the **Branch Pond Trail (11.7 mi.)**, at the north boundary of the Lye Brook Wilderness. The Branch Pond Trail leads 0.5 mi. south to **William B. Douglas Shelter** and 8.3 mi. south to **Kelley Stand Road**. Douglas Shelter is a log lean-to, built by the Brattleboro Section in 1956, and has bunks for 10. There is a spring 50 ft. south of the shelter on the Branch Pond Trail. **Stratton Pond Shelter to William B. Douglas Shelter, 5.4 mi., 8.7 km., 2¾ hr. (SB 2¾ hr.).**

From the junction, cross a brook over a bridge and turn left into a clearing. After following the unimproved Old Rootville Road for nearly a mile, arrive at a **spur (12.6 mi.)** leading west 150 ft. to **Prospect Rock**, perched high above Downer Glen. It offers a view of Manchester below and Mt. Equinox. Turn right at the spur, climbing a rock staircase out of the roadbed, and proceed north. The **Old Rootville Road** continues downhill 1.8 mi. to a paved public road, which leads 0.2 mi. to Vt. 11 and 30, 1.8 mi. east of Manchester Center.

After passing west of a summit (14.3 mi.), descend to a **spur (14.7 mi.)** leading west 0.1 mi. to **Spruce Peak Shelter**. This enclosed log structure, with bunk space for 16, was built by the Brattleboro Section in cooperation with the U.S. Forest Service in 1983. A reliable piped spring is located 100 ft. beyond the shelter. A composting privy is just northwest of the shelter. **William B. Douglas Shelter to Spruce Peak Shelter, 3.6 mi., 5.8 km., 2¼ hr. (SB 2¼ hr.).**

From the shelter spur, travel to a junction where a **spur (15.1 mi.)** leads west 300 ft. to **Spruce Peak**. From here is a view of the Taconic Range and valley below. Continue north from the junction, drop to a brook, cross a power line (15.6 mi.) and, just beyond, a woods road. After a gradual ascent, crest the top of a ridge, pass two vistas to the west and begin a winding descent to a stream crossing. A short distance beyond, cross abandoned Old Vt. 30, and a bridge over a stream (17.1 mi.), and then pass through large boulders to **Vt. 11 and 30 (17.5 mi.)**. From here it is 5.8 mi. west to Vt. 7A in Manchester Center and 4.1 mi. east to Peru. *Use caution when crossing Vt. 11 and 30; traffic moves at high speeds.*

Cross the highway and bear right through a large, paved parking lot to follow abandoned Old Vt. 11, before turning sharply left (17.6 mi.) to enter the woods. Cross a brook over an I-beam bridge, pass under a power line, and climb gently to **Bromley Brook**. Cross over a bridge and arrive at **Bromley Tenting Area (18.2 mi.)** to the east. Two tent platforms are located here. Nearby Bromley Brook is the water source.

Beyond the tenting area, ascend gradually staying to the east of a ridge. Then, just before reaching a brook (19.3 mi.) turn sharply left and climb steadily. Upon reaching a ski trail (20.0 mi.), bear left and follow it to the **south summit of Bromley Mtn. (20.2 mi.)**. It is 100 ft. east to the facilities of Bromley Mtn. Ski Area including a warming hut and an **observation tower** that offers views in all directions, notably of Stratton Mtn. and Mt. Equinox. Camping at the warming hut may be allowed.

Continuing straight ahead along the west edge of the clearing, the Trail turns sharp left, passing to the right of an outhouse. Descend to a col, then climb over **Bromley's north summit (20.7 mi.)**. Descend steadily, passing a vista near the north summit, and then continue downhill to **USFS Road 21 (Mad Tom Notch Road)** at **Mad Tom Notch (22.7 mi.)**. A parking area is located just west of the Trail. The U.S. Forest Service maintains a water pump at the trail crossing, however occasional breakdowns make it unreliable as a water source. To the south it is 4.0 mi. to a small store and public phone in the village of Peru.

SIDE TRAILS

STRATTON POND TRAIL. This trail provides an alternate lowland route between the Kelley Stand Road and Stratton Pond. Refer to Long Trail access directions for the Stratton–Arlington (Kelley Stand) Road on page 58. There is parking for the Stratton Pond Trail opposite USFS Road 71, 0.9 mi. west of the LT parking lot and 1.2 mi. east of the Branch Pond Trailhead and 12.1 mi. east of East Arlington. In winter the Kelley Stand Road is not plowed west of the LT crossing.

Gradually ascend from the Kelley Stand Road (0.0 mi.), passing through wet areas on puncheon and cross a gravel road (2.2 mi.), which is also the Catamount Trail. From the road travel northeast with little change in elevation over more puncheon to the spur to Stratton Pond Shelter, and just beyond, the junction (3.7 mi.) with the Long Trail, 0.1 mi. east of Stratton Pond. **Kelley Stand Road to Long Trail, 3.7 mi., 6.0 km., 2 hr. (Rev. 2 hr.).**

LYE BROOK TRAIL. Linking Manchester and Bourn Pond to the Long Trail, this trail is within the Lye Brook Wilderness from near its trailhead in Manchester to its crossing of the Winhall River west of Stratton Pond. From Vt. 7A in Manchester Center follow Vt. 11 and 30 1.9 mi. east and then turn right onto East Manchester Road. Follow the road 1.2 mi. to Glen Road and turn left. Continue straight on a short access road to the trailhead where Glen Road bears left at 0.1 mi. A parking lot and the trailhead are about 0.4 mi. from that junction. This access road is not plowed in winter.

From the parking lot (0.0 mi.) travel east and enter the Lye Brook Wilderness (0.5 mi.), following old railroad grades and woods roads uphill along the west side of Lye Brook Hollow. Shortly after entering the wilderness the trail traverses a large blowdown area associated with a wind shear event from a 1997 thunderstorm; GMC and GMNF are minimally clearing this area to minimize human alteration of the landscape. A spur (2.3 mi.) leads south 0.4 mi. to a small stream and one of the higher waterfalls in Vermont. From the waterfall to Bourn Pond this trail may be more challenging to follow as it is minimally maintained in the Wilderness Area. A compass and topographic map (USGS) are strongly recommended. From the spur, continue along an old woods road; the grade eases, crossing a series of low ridges. Pass some beaver ponds, and reach the junction with the Branch Pond Trail (7.3 mi.) at a stream crossing just beyond South Bourn Pond Shelter. This shelter, a frame lean-to with space for eight, was built by the U.S. Forest Service in 1966 on a low bluff overlooking the south shore of Bourn Pond. Water is supplied by the stream and a boxed spring located on a spur leading east 250 ft. from the shelter. **Manchester to South Bourn Pond Shelter, 7.3 mi., 11.8 km., 4½ hr. (Rev. 3½ hr.).**

From Bourn Pond, pass over a low ridge and cross a shallow ford of the headwaters of the Winhall River (8.5 mi.), Lye Brook Wilderness's east boundary. Turn left onto the Catamount Trail, cross the outlet stream of Stratton Pond, and turn right, leaving the Catamount Trail. Ascend along the stream to a junction (9.1 mi.) with the North Shore Trail at Stratton Pond. Bearing right to cross the pond's outlet on puncheon, follow the south shore of Stratton Pond to piped Bigelow Spring and, just beyond, the GMC caretaker tent platform and the junction (9.7 mi.) with the Long Trail at Willis Ross Clearing. **Manchester trailhead to Long Trail, 9.7 mi., 15.6 km., 6¼ hr. (Rev. 5¼ hr.).**

NORTH SHORE TRAIL. This trail links the Lye Brook Trail near the outlet at the west end of Stratton Pond with the Long Trail at the east end, and together with the Lye Brook and Long Trails completes a 1.4 mi. loop around the pond. Bear east from the Lye Brook Trail (0.0 mi.) and follow the shoreline past a clearing (0.1 mi.), the former site of Stratton View Shelter, with a view of Stratton Mtn. Paralleling the shoreline, a spur turns left at a beaver-dammed stream to follow puncheon to its headwaters, Stratton View Spring.

Continuing to hug Stratton Pond's shoreline, arrive at a spur (0.2 mi.) leading north 200 ft. to the North Shore Tenting Area, which has tent platforms and a composting privy. Stratton View Spring is the site's water source. Follow the increasingly rugged shore, crossing an arm of the pond on a massive double log bridge, to the junction (0.7 mi.) with the Long

Trail, where the Catamount Trail enters Stratton Pond on a woods road from the east. **Lye Brook Trail to Long Trail 0.7 mi., 1.1 km., ½ hr. (Rev. ½ hr.).**

BRANCH POND TRAIL. Traversing the east half of the Lye Brook Wilderness, this trail connects Branch and Bourn Ponds with the Long Trail near the Old Rootville Road. Refer to Long Trail access directions for the Stratton–Arlington (Kelley Stand) Road on page 58. The trailhead is 1.2 mi. west of the Stratton Pond parking lot, 2.1 mi. west of the LT crossing, and 11.0 mi. east of East Arlington. There is space for one car on the north side of the road at the trailhead and space for four cars further west on the north side of the road. In winter the Kelley Stand Road is not plowed west of the LT parking lot.

From the Kelley Stand Road (0.0 mi.), travel north over rolling terrain to a spur (1.8 mi.) leading west 0.3 mi. to USFS Road 70 where there is a boat access ramp to Branch Pond. Continue east of Branch Pond, and enter the Lye Brook Wilderness (2.5 mi.). The trail may be more challenging to follow in the Wilderness Area due to minimal brushing and blazing. Traverse Lye Brook Meadows on an old railroad grade, and reach the junction (4.3 mi.) with the Lye Brook Trail at South Bourn Pond Shelter just south of Bourn Pond. **Kelley Stand Road to South Bourn Pond Shelter, 4.3 mi., 6.9 km., 2¼ hr. (Rev. 2¼ hr.).**

Passing below the shelter, follow the west shore of Bourn Pond, reaching a spur (4.8 mi.) leading east 300 ft. to North Bourn Pond Tenting Area. From there a path leads to the shoreline where there is a view of Stratton Mtn. Continuing north from the spur junction, skirt an area of beaver activity and follow an old lumber railroad grade to a ford (5.6 mi.) of Bourn Brook. This crossing can be difficult during snowmelt or heavy rains. After crossing an overgrown clearing (7.0 mi.), arrive at William B. Douglas Shelter (7.8 mi.). **South Bourn Pond Shelter to William B. Douglas Shelter, 3.5 mi., 5.6 km., 1¾ hr. (Rev. 1¾ hr.).**

Follow a old, sunken woods road from the shelter to the junction (8.3 mi.) with the Long Trail at the Lye Brook Wilderness's north boundary. **Kelley Stand Road to Long Trail, 8.3 mi., 13.4 km., 4½ hr. (Rev. 4¾ hr.).**

DIVISION 4

Mad Tom Notch to
Vt. 140

DIVISION 4 PROFILE

Mad Tom Notch to Vt. 140

miles northbound	▲ NORTH	elevation at Long Trail (feet/meters)	miles southbound
20.6	**Vt. 140; Roaring Brook bridge**	1160/354	0.0
19.8	**Keewaydin Trail** to White Rocks Picnic Area, 0.4 mi N	1380/421	0.8
19.1	**Greenwall Shelter** (2020 ft/616 m), 0.2 mi E via Greenwall Spur	2300/701	1.5
18.6	**White Rocks Cliff Trail** to vista, 0.2 mi W	2400/732	2.0
15.6	**Homer Stone Brook bridge**	1900/579	5.0
14.7	**Little Rock Pond Shelter**, 100 ft E via spur	1820/555	5.9
14.6	**Green Mtn. Trail** to USFS Road 10, 4.1 mi N; **Little Rock Pond Tenting Area**, 100 ft E via spur	1854/565	6.0
14.3	**Little Rock Pond; Little Rock Pond Loop** to **Green Mtn. Trail**, 0.4 mi N; **Little Rock Pond Tenting Area**, 100 ft E via spur	1854/565	6.3
14.0	**Lula Tye Shelter**, 100 ft E via spur	1865/569	6.6
12.3	**Big Black Branch; USFS Road 10**, west junction	1500/457	8.3
12.1	**USFS Road 10**, east junction	1530/466	8.5
11.0	**Big Branch Shelter**	1470/448	9.6
10.9	**Big Branch** suspension bridge	1500/457	9.7
10.8	**Old Job Trail**, north junction to **Old Job Shelter**, 1.1 mi SE; to USFS Road 30, 2.0 mi SE	1525/465	9.8
9.3	**Lost Pond Shelter**, 100 ft W via spur	2150/655	11.3
7.3	**Baker Peak**	2850/869	13.3
7.2	**Baker Peak Trail** to South End Road via Lake Trail, 2.9 mi W	2760/841	13.4
5.4	**Lake Trail** to South End Road, 3.3 mi W	2620/799	15.2
5.3	**Old Job Trail**, south junction to USFS Road 30, 3.4 mi NE	2600/793	15.3
5.1	**Griffith Lake; Griffith Lake Tenting Area**	2600/793	15.5
4.6	**Peru Peak Shelter**	2550/777	16.0
3.3	**Peru Peak**	3429/1045	17.3
1.6	**Styles Peak**	3394/1034	19.0
0.0	**USFS Road 21** at **Mad Tom Notch**	2446/746	20.6

SOUTH
▼

DIVISION 4
Mad Tom Notch to Vt. 140

Massachusetts: 59.6 miles   *Canada: 213.1 miles*

4

From Mad Tom Notch to USFS Road 10, the Long Trail traverses Peru Peak Wilderness and Big Branch Wilderness. Refer to wilderness information on page 7.

From Mad Tom Notch to Bully Brook, the Long Trail passes through the White Rocks Recreation Area, where the U.S. Forest Service emphasizes management of the forest to provide recreation opportunities.

The GMC and the U.S. Forest Service are working to relocate the trailhead for the Homer Stone Brook Trail ¼ mi. south of its current location.

The Long Trail and the Appalachian Trail coincide throughout this division.

SUGGESTED HIKES

STYLES PEAK. This climb on the Long Trail north from Mad Tom Notch provides views of southeast Vermont from the summit rock outcrop. Round trip, 3.2 mi., 3¼ hr.

GREEN MOUNTAIN AND LITTLE ROCK POND. A loop using the Long, Green Mtn. and Green Mtn. Connector Trails from USFS Road 10 combines scenic Little Rock Pond with views from the ledges of Green Mtn. Round trip, 7 mi., 4¾ hr.

BAKER PEAK. This loop hike from U.S. 7 follows the Lake, Baker Peak, and Long Trails, and features views from the open summit. Round trip, 8.1 mi., 5 hr.

BIG BRANCH WILDERNESS. The Old Job Trail and the Long Trail create a loop hike to Griffith Lake, Baker Peak, Big Branch, and Old Job. This circuit is suitable for a day hike or a backpack. Round trip, 10.4 mi., 6 hr.

CAMPING AND FIRES

This division's Long Trail crosses the Green Mountain National Forest. Primitive off-trail camping with small wood fires is allowed. Refer to Leave No Trace principles (pages 9 to 11) to minimize your impact.

Note: Camping at Griffith Lake and Little Rock Pond is limited to designated sites to protect vulnerable vegetation and soils.

GROUP USE

Groups hiking this division's Long Trail may need an Outfitter-Guide Permit from the Green Mountain National Forest. Group tenting space is available at Griffith Lake and Little Rock Pond Tenting Areas, and Lost Pond, Old Job, and Big Branch Shelters. GMNF Hapgood Pond Campground is available (refer to Long Trail access directions for USFS Road 21) for base camp hiking. Emerald Lake State Park Campground, south of Danby on U.S. 7, is also available for base camp hiking. Refer to group use guidelines (pages 11 to 17) to determine your need for a permit and to minimize your group's impact.

WINTER USE

Many of the trails in this division, in combination with the unplowed USFS roads, provide good cross-country ski opportunities. A suggested loop includes USFS Roads 10 and 30 with the Old Job Trail (north branch) and the Long Trail.

Little Rock Pond via the Homer Stone Brook Trail makes a fine snowshoe destination. Styles Peak from Mad Tom Notch provides good views for a 5.2 mi. round trip from the winter parking lot on USFS Road 21.

ACCESS TO LONG TRAIL

USFS ROAD 21 AT MAD TOM NOTCH. Refer to directions on page 71 in Division 3.

USFS ROAD 10. Long Trail parking is available at two trailheads, 0.2 mi. apart. From U.S. 7 in Danby, follow USFS Road 10 3.2 mi. to the primary parking lot (paved) at the west trailhead or continue to a smaller, pull-off parking area at the east trailhead. Because of the risk of vandalism, parking lots in this area are not recommended for long-term parking.

These sites are also accessible from Peru to the east. Refer to Long Trail access directions for Mad Tom Notch, USFS Road 21 on page 71 in Division 3. From Peru's J. J. Hapgood General Store follow the Hapgood Pond/Landgrove Road 3.6 mi. to an intersection. Turn left and follow USFS Road 12 0.6 mi. to USFS Road 10 on the right. USFS Road 10 leads 10.6 mi. west to the Trail.

USFS Road 10 between the bridge over Big Black Branch (0.9 mi. east of Danby) and the Long Trail is not plowed in winter, a distance of 2.3 mi. The road is also not plowed between the LT and Landgrove to the east.

VT. 140. The Long Trail intersects this highway 2.7 mi. east of Wallingford and U.S. 7, and 3.3 mi. west of Vt. 103 and 155 in East Wallingford. The parking lot is off a steep driveway on the north side of Vt. 140, 0.2 mi. east of the Trail crossing.

LONG TRAIL DESCRIPTION

From **USFS Road 21 at Mad Tom Notch (0.0 mi.)**, enter the Peru Peak Wilderness and the White Rocks National Recreation Area (0.1 mi.). The Long Trail may be more challenging to follow in the Wilderness Area due to minimal brushing and blazing. Climb steadily to the summit of **Styles Peak (1.6 mi.)**, with views extending from the northeast to the south. Follow the ridge passing over several knobs, to the summit of P**eru Peak (3.3 mi.)**, where a short spur leads east to a lookout.

Beyond the summit, descend past a piped spring (3.7 mi.) and then leave the Peru Peak Wilderness. Just beyond is **Peru Peak Shelter (4.6 mi.)**. This log structure, with space for 10, was built by the Civilian Conservation Corps in 1935 and re-built by the Youth Conservation Corps and U.S. Forest Service in 1979. The shelter was rebuilt by the Long Trail Patrol with the assistance of the U.S. Forest Service to replace rotten logs in 2000. Water is found at the nearby brook. There is a composting privy to the north of the shelter. **Spruce Peak Shelter to Peru Peak Shelter, 12.7 mi., 20.4 km., 8 hr. (SB 7¾ hr.).**

Proceed west from Peru Peak Shelter and cross three bridges before arriving at the shore of **Griffith Lake (5.1 mi.)**, and follow extensive puncheon to **Griffith Lake Tenting Area** with tent platforms and a composting privy. To protect this shoreline and preserve its natural beauty, all camping in the vicinity of Griffith Lake is limited to tent platforms. A GMC caretaker is in residence to assist and educate hikers, help maintain the local trails and campsites, and compost sewage to protect water quality. A fee is charged for overnight use at these designated sites and at Peru Peak Shelter.

Follow more puncheon north, paralleling the shore of the lake, to the south junction with the **Old Job Trail (5.3 mi.)**, which leads northeast 3.4 mi. to USFS Road 30. From the trail junction, continue straight ahead and leave the shoreline of Griffith Lake. Enter Big Branch Wilderness, where the Long Trail may be more challenging to follow due to minimal brushing and blazing. Pass the **Lake Trail (5.4 mi.)**, which descends 3.3 mi. west to South End Road, 0.5 mi. east of U.S. 7.

Follow the ridge northward and descend to cross an old woods road (6.2 mi.). Cross another woods road, and begin to ascend Baker Peak. Reach the junction with the **Baker Peak Trail (7.2 mi.)**, which joins the Lake Trail to lead 2.9 mi. west to South End Road. Bear right for the final scramble up the ex-posed ledges to the summit of **Baker Peak (7.3 mi.)**. Should adverse weather conditions make the ascent over open rocks treacherous, there is a parallel by-pass route to the east. Baker Peak offers views of the valley below. Danby and the north-flowing Otter Creek are directly below. Across the valley is Dorset Peak with its famous marble quarry. Emerald Lake and Mt. Equinox are to the south, and the fire tower on Stratton Mtn. can be seen just behind the ridge of Peru Peak. Pico and Killington Peaks are to the north, and the Adirondacks are visible on a clear day, to the northwest.

Leave the summit of Baker Peak, enter the woods, and bear north, keeping east of a ridge. After crossing over a height-of-land (7.8 mi.), descend along the west side of the ridge. Reach a wide, grassy woods road (9.1 mi.) and follow the road to the right for 250 ft., before turning left into the woods. Continue north on an old woods road to a **spur (9.3 mi.)** leading west 100 ft. to Lost Pond Shelter. The original **Lost Pond Shelter**, built by Louis (Sandy) Stare, Jr. in 1965, burned in November 2001. It was rebuilt by Tom Abbott and GMC volunteers co-ordinated by Marge Fish in 2002. The water supply is a stream in the ravine west of the shelter. **Peru Peak Shelter to Lost Pond Shelter, 4.7 mi., 7.6 km., 2¼ hr. (SB 2¾ hr.).**

Continue north from the shelter spur along the woods road. Descend steadily to Big Branch and the north junction with the **Old Job Trail (10.8 mi.).** This trail leads southeast 1.1 mi. to Old Job Shelter and 2.0 mi. to USFS Road 30. Turn left to follow the river downstream, and then cross the **Big Branch suspension bridge (10.9 mi.).** Continue following the river on an old road, pass a stone mill foundation, and arrive at **Big Branch Shelter (11.0 mi.).** This frame lean-to, with floor space for eight, was built by the USFS in 1963. Big Branch furnishes water. The outhouse is up the hill behind the shelter. **Lost Pond Shelter to Big Branch Shelter, 1.7 mi., 2.7 km., 1 hr. (SB 1¾ hr.).**

TRAIL CHANGES? LET GMC KNOW!

Contact GMC to report trail updates for the next edition of this guidebook.

PLEASE DO YOUR PART TO ENSURE THE FUTURE OF THE LONG TRAIL: JOIN THE GREEN MOUNTAIN CLUB!

Your membership or gift will:

- Conserve Vermont's high-mountain country.
- Supports trail and shelter maintenance.
- Educates hikers
- Sustain hiking opportunities for you and for generations to come.

To join or make a gift to the GMC, contact:

Green Mountain Club
4711 Waterbury-Stowe Road
Waterbury Center,
Vermont 05677
(802) 244-7037
gmc@greenmountainclub.org
www.greenmountainclub.org

Thank you!

From the shelter follow Big Branch downstream for a short distance, and then turn right and ascend gradually, crossing the north boundary of the Big Branch Wilderness. Continue a gentle ascent to **USFS Road 10 (12.1 mi.)** and a small parking area. To the east it is 10.6 mi. to Landgrove via USFS Road 10. Descend on the road west to the crossing of **Big Black Branch (12.3)**. Turn north to reenter the woods at the trailhead just beyond the bridge. A paved parking lot is to the south of the trailhead. USFS Road 10 continues west down the mountain 3.2 mi. to U.S. 7 in Danby.

Leave the pavement and follow an old woods road north. Cross Little Black Branch (12.9 mi.) over an I-beam bridge, then recross it over large rocks (13.1 mi.). Travel over numerous puncheon to a **spur (14.0 mi.)** leading east 100 ft. uphill to **Lula Tye Shelter**. This frame lean-to, with room for 8, was built by the U.S. Forest Service in 1962. It was moved to its present location from the current site of the caretaker platform on the east shore of Little Rock Pond in 1972. It is named in memory of Miss Lula Tye, who was corresponding secretary for the Green Mountain Club from 1926 to 1955. Water is available from Little Rock Pond's spring on the LT just north of the caretaker tent platform. **Big Branch Shelter to Lula Tye Shelter, 3.0 mi., 4.8 km., 2 hr. (SB 1¾ hr.).**

Proceed to the south end of **Little Rock Pond (14.3 mi.)** and the **Little Rock Pond Loop Trail**. The loop trail follows the former route of the Long Trail 0.4 mi. around the west side of Little Rock Pond and rejoins the LT north of the pond. Just beyond lies the GMC caretaker tent platform and the Little Rock Pond Tenting Area with tent platforms and a composting privy on a low shelf 100 ft. east of the pond. This popular pond is one of the most visited sites on the Long Trail, and careful management is required to preserve its beauty and fragile shoreline. Camping in the vicinity of the pond's shoreline is limited to designated sites. A GMC caretaker is in residence to assist and educate hikers, help maintain the local trails and campsites, and compost sewage to protect water quality. A fee is charged for overnight use at these designated sites, as well as at Lula Tye and Little Rock Pond Shelters.

Hug the east shore of the pond and pass the spring (14.4 mi.), which is the water source for all campsites in the vicinity of Little Rock Pond. Arrive at the trail junction near the pond's outlet with the **Green Mtn. Trail (14.6 mi.)**, which ascends Green Mtn. and continues south 4.1 mi. to USFS Road 10. It also leads west 2.3 mi. to South Wallingford via the Homer Stone Brook Trail. From the junction, descend an old woods road to a **spur (14.7 mi.)** leading east 100 ft. to **Little Rock Pond Shelter**. Built by the U.S. Forest Service in 1962, this frame lean-to has space for eight. It was moved to its present location from its original site on Little Rock Pond's small island in 1972. **Lula Tye Shelter to Little Rock Pond Shelter, 0.8 mi., 1.1 km., ⅓ hr. (SB ½ hr.).**

North of the shelter, continue with little change in elevation to the long-abandoned Aldrich Job clearing (15.4 mi.). Cross the **Homer Stone Brook bridge (15.6 mi.)**, before intersecting with the old South Wallingford-Wallingford Pond Road. Begin a steady ascent, passing just to the west of the summit of White Rocks Mtn. (17.8 mi.), then descend to the **White Rocks Cliff Trail (18.6 mi.)**, which leads west downhill 0.2 mi. to a vista from the top of the cliffs. Continue north to the **Greenwall Spur (19.1 mi.)**, which descends east 0.2 mi. to **Greenwall Shelter** just outside the north boundary of the White Rocks National Recreation Area. This frame lean-to, with floor space for eight, was built by the U.S. Forest Service in 1962. A spur leads 600 ft. northeast behind the shelter to a spring, which may fail in droughts. **Little Rock Pond Shelter to Greenwall Shelter, 4.6 mi., 7.4 km., 3 hr. (SB 2¾ hr.).**

From the Greenwall Spur, continue downhill to a trail junction with the **Keewaydin Trail (19.8 mi.)** which leads north 0.4 mi. to the White Rocks Picnic Area. At the junction, turn right and cross Bully Brook (19.9 mi.). Leave the White Rocks National Recreation Area just past the brook. Descend beside a dramatic gulch to Sugar Hill Road (20.5 mi.), cross the road and drop to cross the **Roaring Brook bridge (20.6 mi.)**, built by the Volunteer Long Trail Patrol in 2000, and then reach **Vt. 140**. To the east, it is 3.3 mi. to Vt. 103 and Vt. 155 in East Wallingford; to the west, 2.7 mi. to U.S. 7 in Wallingford.

SIDE TRAILS

OLD JOB TRAIL. Formerly the route of the Long Trail, this trail provides an alternate lowland route between Griffith Lake and Big Branch. An old woods road, this trail links the Long Trail at both Griffith Lake and Big Branch with USFS Road 30. Follow USFS Road 10 for 6.9 mi. east out of Danby, passing the Long Trail crossing, and turn right onto USFS Road 30 for 2.3 mi. to its end. USFS Road 30 and most of USFS Road 10 are not plowed in winter.

South branch: From the end of USFS Road 30, bear south (left) onto a gated woods road. From the gate (0.0 mi.), ascend gradually, paralleling the east side of Lake Brook, to cross two tributary brooks on snowmobile bridges (0.6 mi. and 2.1 mi.) before crossing Lake Brook (2.4 mi.) on a large bridge. Follow a woods road around Long Hole, and join the Long Trail (3.4 mi.) at the north end of Griffith Lake. **USFS Road 30 to Long Trail at Griffith Lake, 3.4 mi., 5.5 km., 2 hr. (Rev. 1¾ hr.).**

North branch: From the end of USFS Road 30, travel north (right) and descend the road embankment (0.0 mi.). Follow Lake Brook, which leads to Old Job Shelter (0.9 mi.) in an extensive clearing where the village of Griffith once stood. The shelter is a log structure with space for 8, built by the Civilian Conservation Corps in 1935. Lake Brook provides water. Cross Lake Brook on a suspension bridge and head northwest through the clearing, passing first a large sawdust pile and then an old jeep road on the right (1.1 mi.). The trail can be difficult to follow in the late summer when the meadow is overgrown. Continue west, entering the Big Branch Wilderness, and parallel Big Branch to the Long Trail junction (2.0 mi.), 0.1 mi. south of the Big Branch suspension bridge. **USFS Road 30 to Long Trail at Big Branch, 2.0 mi., 3.2 km., 1 hr. (Rev. 1¼ hr.). Griffith Lake to Big Branch via the Old Job Trail is 5.4 mi., 8.7 km., 2¾ hr. (Rev. 3¼ hr.).**

LAKE TRAIL. Take U.S. 7 south from Danby. At 2.1 mi., turn east onto South End Road and follow it 0.5 mi. east to a parking lot and the trailhead. This trail was once a bridle path leading from the valley to Griffith Lake (formerly Buffum Pond).

Enter the woods (0.0 mi.) from the parking lot and gently ascend the old road. Switch back to the left and enter the Big Branch Wilderness (0.9 mi.) where the climb steepens. Cross a bridge (1.5 mi.) anchored to a rock face where the old trestle supports are still visible. Reach a spur to the right, which climbs to an open rock with views of Dorset Peak and the valley. Ascend to cross McGinn Brook at the junction with the Baker Peak Trail (1.9 mi.). From the junction, the climb moderates, leading to the Long Trail (3.3 mi.) just north of Griffith Lake. **South End Road to Long Trail, 3.3 mi., 5.3 km., 2½ hr.).**

BAKER PEAK TRAIL. This trail connects the Lake Trail with the Long Trail near the summit of Baker Peak. From its junction with the Lake Trail (0.0 mi.), gradually ascend an old woods road before climbing a steeper grade over ledges to join the Long Trail (0.9 mi.), 0.1 mi. south of the summit of Baker Peak. **Lake Trail to Long Trail, 0.9 mi., 1.5 km., 1 hr. (Rev. ½ hr.). South End Road to Baker Peak via the Lake, Baker Peak and Long Trails is 2.9 mi., 4.7 km., 2½ hr. (Rev. 1½ hr.).**

LITTLE ROCK POND LOOP TRAIL. This shoreline trail, formerly the Long Trail, follows the west side of Little Rock Pond. From the Long Trail (0.0 mi.) at the south end of Little Rock Pond, bear left and skirt the south shore of the pond. Climb away from the shore to pass above the ledges of the west shore and

HUNTING

Hunting seasons are underway in Vermont from September 1 through mid-December. Deer rifle season is from mid- to late November. Wear bright colors, preferably fluorescent orange. For more information, contact: Vermont Department of Fish and Wildlife; 103 South Main St., Waterbury, VT, 05671-0501; (802) 241-3700; www.anr.state.vt.us/fw/fwhome/index.htm.

reach the Green Mtn. Trail junction (0.4 mi.), 0.1 mi. west of the Long Trail at the north end of the pond. **Long Trail to Green Mtn. Trail, 0.4 m., 0.6 km., ¼ hr. (Rev. ¼ hr.).**

GREEN MOUNTAIN TRAIL. This trail links USFS Road 10 with the Long Trail at the north end of Little Rock Pond. Follow USFS Road 10 2.7 mi. east from Danby to the USFS Big Branch Picnic Area. USFS 10 is plowed in winter only to the silver bridge, 1.8 mi. west of this trailhead.

Enter the woods opposite the picnic area (0.0 mi.), and ascend to the junction (0.1 mi.) with the Green Mtn. Connector, which leads east paralleling the road 0.6 mi. to the LT parking lot at Big Black Branch. Take a sharp right and climb to a lookout (0.3 mi.) to the west. Continue to ascend on an old woods road, traverse an impressive, mature stand of hemlock and white pine, before joining another woods road and crossing a brook (1.3 mi.). Cross a shallow saddle (2.1 mi.) before climbing a spruce-covered ridge to a spur leading east 50 ft. to a lookout near the summit of Green Mtn. Cross ledges and reach another spur, which leads east 200 ft. to an outlook with limited views. From the spur, descend steadily to the Little Rock Pond Loop Trail junction (4.0 mi.), and then the junction with the Homer Stone Brook Trail, before continuing over the pond outlet to the north end of Little Rock Pond (4.1 mi.) and the Long Trail. **Big Branch Picnic Area to Long Trail, 4.1 mi., 6.6 km., 2½ hr. (Rev. 2¼ hr.).**

HOMER STONE BROOK TRAIL. *Note:* The GMC and U.S. Forest Service plan to relocate the trailhead for the Homer Stone Brook Trail ¼ mi. south of the schoolhouse. This trail provides an alternate route from the Otter Creek Valley to Little Rock Pond. From U.S. 7 in South Wallingford, just north of Charlie's Market or 4.2 mi. south of Vt. 140 in Wallingford, turn east onto the south end of Hartsboro Road and cross Otter Creek and the railroad tracks, then bear right onto Homer Stone Road. Park at the old schoolhouse lot to the left.

From the schoolhouse, follow the paved road south and leave it just after the bridge crossing to climb a private driveway (0.0 mi.) to the left, and follow the driveway to a woods road just to the left of a garage. Climb steadily, and keeping to the right at all forks, follow the old South Wallingford–Wallingford Pond Road until it reaches a ford of Homer Stone Brook (1.7 mi.). This ford can be challenging in high water. From the brook crossing, ascend an old woods road southeast to its junction with the Green Mtn. Trail (2.3 mi.) which leads west uphill to Green Mtn. and east over the pond outlet to the Long Trail just north of Little Rock Pond. **Homer Stone Road to Long Trail, 2.3 mi., 3.7 km., 1¾ hr. (Rev. 1¼ hr.).**

WHITE ROCKS CLIFF TRAIL. This path descends west from the Long Trail to an outlook on the very brink of White Rocks Cliff. **Long Trail to White Rocks Cliff, 0.2 mi., 0.3 km., 10 min. (Rev. 5 min.).**

KEEWAYDIN TRAIL. This trail links the USFS White Rocks Picnic Area with the Long Trail near its crossing of Bully Brook. From Wallingford, travel 2.3 mi. east on Vt. 140, turn south on Sugar Hill Road for 0.1 mi., then turn right onto USFS Road 52. Continue on this road 0.6 mi. to the picnic area and parking. Overnight parking at the picnic area is not permitted. USFS Road 52 is not maintained in winter.

From the far end of the picnic area and parking lot, climb steadily to the Long Trail, 0.1 mi. from Bully Brook. **USFS White Rocks Picnic Area to LT, 0.4 mi., 0.6 km., ½ hr. (Rev. ¼ hr.).** Other hiking trails from the picnic area include the White Rocks Trail leading 0.2 mi. to a viewpoint on a knoll below White Rocks Cliff and the 0.8 mi. Ice Bed Trail.

DIVISION 5
Vt. 140 to U.S. 4

LONG TRAIL 5

SCALE IN MILES

1   0   1   2

DIVISION 5 PROFILE

Elevation (in feet)

Distance (in miles)

VT. 140

CLARENDON GORGE

COLD RIVER RD.

KILLINGTON SPUR

JUNGLE JUNCTION

U.S. 4

Vt. 140 to U.S. 4

miles north-bound	▲ NORTH	elevation at Long Trail (feet/meters)	miles south-bound
23.7	**U.S. 4** west of Sherburne Pass	1880/573	0.0
21.8	**Churchill Scott Shelter**, 0.1 mi W via spur	2560/780	1.9
21.5	**Mendon Lookout**	2890/881	2.2
19.9	**Jungle Junction, Sherburne Pass Trail** south end to **Pico Camp**, 0.4 mi N; to Sherburne Pass, 2.9 mi N	3480/1061	3.8
17.6	**Bucklin Trail** to Wheelerville Road, 3.3 mi W	3770/1149	6.1
17.4	**Killington Spur** to **Killington Peak** (4235 ft/1291 m), 0.2 mi. E; **Cooper Lodge**, 100 ft north via Long Trail	3850/1173	6.3
15.8	**Shrewsbury Peak Trail** to **Shrewsbury Peak** (3720 ft/1135 m), 2.0 mi E; **CCC Road**, 4.0 mi. E	3500/1067	7.9
13.1	**Governor Clement Shelter**	1850/564	10.6
11.7	**Upper Road**	1630/497	12.0
11.0	**Gould Brook** ford	1480/451	12.7
10.2	**Cold River (Lower) Road**	1400/427	13.5
7.8	**Beacon Hill**	1740/530	15.9
7.3	**Clarendon Shelter**, 400 ft E via spur	1350/412	16.4
6.3	**Vt. 103**	860/262	17.4
6.2	**Clarendon Gorge** suspension bridge over Mill River	800/244	17.5
5.5	**Airport Lookout**, 50 ft W via spur	1400/427	18.2
4.2	**Spring Lake Clearing**	1600/488	19.5
3.6	**Minerva Hinchey Shelter**, 200 ft E via woods road	1530/466	20.1
2.7	**Patch Hollow**	1800/549	21.0
1.0	**Domed ledge** vista, 300 ft W via spur	1575/480	22.7
0.0	**Vt. 140**	1300/396	23.7

SOUTH
▼

Division 5
Vt. 140 to U.S. 4

Massachusetts: 80.2 miles   *Canada: 192.5 miles*

Tenting near Pico Camp is very limited. Do not plan to camp near the site if the shelter is full.

The Long Trail and the Appalachian Trail coincide throughout this division.

Suggested Hikes

Airport Lookout. This hike south on the Long Trail from Vt. 103 crosses Clarendon Gorge over a suspension bridge and climbs to a lookout with views to the west. Round trip, 1.6 mi., 1¾ hr.

Beacon Hill. This hike on the Long Trail north of Vt. 103 passes Clarendon Lookout, then leads to views from an old hilltop pasture. Round trip, 3.0 mi., 2 hr.

Shrewsbury Peak. This hike at the south end of the Coolidge Range combines the Shrewsbury Peak Trail and Black Swamp Trail with a 1.5 mi. walk on the CCC Road for a loop hike over the summit of Shrewsbury Peak, one of the high peaks of the range. Round trip, 5.4 mi., 3½ hr.

PICO CIRCUIT. This trip combines the Sherburne Pass Trail, the former, historic route of the Long Trail, south from U.S. 4 at Sherburne Pass with the Long Trail south of U.S. 4. The full circuit requires a one mile road walk on the highway where traffic may be heavy; walk on the far side of the guardrails. This destination features views from the ski slopes and the summit of Pico (an optional destination). Round trip, 7.9 mi., 5 hr. Add 0.8 mi. and ¾ hr. if summiting via the Pico Link.

KILLINGTON PEAK. With sweeping views from its rocky summit, this peak is directly accessed by the Bucklin Trail and Killington Spur. Round trip, 7.2 mi., 5¼ hr. A longer hike with an optional climb of Pico Peak follows the Sherburne Pass Trail south from U.S. 4 at Sherburne Pass. Round trip, 11.2 mi., 7 hr.

CAMPING AND FIRES

This division's Long Trail traverses a mix of both state and federally owned Appalachian Trail corridor land, with two campsites on private property. Camping is limited to shelters. Small wood fires, although discouraged, are permitted at the shelters' established fire rings, with the exception of Cooper Lodge, due to its sensitive high-elevation location, and Churchill Scott Shelter, owing to permit guidelines. Camping is prohibited in the vicinity of Clarendon Gorge. Refer to Leave No Trace principles (pages 9 to 11) to minimize your impact.

GROUP USE

Groups hiking this division's Long Trail may need an Outfitter-Guide Permit from the Green Mountain National Forest. Groups planning to camp at Cooper Lodge may need a Commercial Use Permit from the Vermont Department of Forests, Parks & Recreation. Group tenting space is available at Minerva Hinchey and Clarendon Shelters and Cooper Lodge. Gifford Woods State Park Campground, east of Sherburne Pass on Vt. 100, is available for base camp hiking. Refer to group use guidelines (pages 11 to 17) to determine your need for a permit and to minimize your group's impact.

WINTER USE

A ll suggested hikes in this division make good winter trips, except for the Shrewsbury Peak loop owing to the CCC Road's unmaintained winter condition. The challenging terrain is suitable only for advanced cross-country skiers.

ACCESS TO LONG TRAIL

VT. 140. Refer to directions on page 85 in Division 4.

VT. 103. The Long Trail crosses this highway just north of Clarendon Gorge. The road crossing is 2.4 mi. east of U.S. 7, and 6.0 mi. west of East Wallingford and Vt. 155. There is a parking lot on the south side of the highway, just west of the railroad crossing. Long term parking is not recommended.

COLD RIVER (LOWER) ROAD. Take Lincoln Hill Road north from Vt. 103, 0.7 mi. east of the LT crossing. Follow this road 2.5 mi. to Shrewsbury and continue 2.8 mi. more to North Shrewsbury where the Cold River Road turns left opposite an old store. Proceed on Lower Cold River Road (the Upper Road is to the right just beyond the fire station) 2.4 mi. west to the Long Trail. It is another 7.3 mi. west to U.S. 7 in Rutland. There is limited parking on the north side of the road just east of a bridge.

U.S. 4. This trail crossing is 8.6 mi. east of U.S. 7 in Rutland, and 1.0 mi. west of the crest of Sherburne Pass. A large unpaved lot on the south side of the highway provides ample parking. The Catamount Trail shares this highway crossing. This parking lot is not always plowed in winter; however another area about 0.3 mi. east is always plowed. *Use extreme caution when crossing this highway.*

LONG TRAIL DESCRIPTION

C ross **Vt. 140 (0.0 mi.)**, climb past boulders to a large asphalt parking lot (0.1 mi.), and then gently ascend a woods road to abandoned hillside pastures separated by stone walls.

Turn right, join the abandoned Bear Mtn. Road (0.6 mi.) and follow it 50 ft. east. Turn right to leave the road, pass through an old orchard, and ascend by switchbacks to a **spur (1.0 mi.)** leading 300 ft. west to a **domed ledge vista** of White Rocks Mtn. and Dorset Peak. Continue the steady ascent; near the crest of Bear Mtn.'s ridge, the grade moderates. Pass west of a springtime vernal pool, and reach the trail's height-of-land (2.1 mi.) on Bear Mtn. Follow switchbacks downhill to a former homesite at **Patch Hollow (2.7 mi.)**, at the north end of a beaver pond. Continue to descend on an abandoned road, which the trail shares with a cross-country ski trail, and then bear north to cross under a power line. Turn left to follow a grassy woods road before turning left to ascend the ridge. Here the **woods road (3.6 mi.)** continues east 200 ft. to **Minerva Hinchey Shelter**.

This frame structure, with bunk space for eight, was constructed by Sandy Stare and members of the Killington Section in 1969. It is named for Minerva Hinchey in tribute to her twenty-two years of service as GMC corresponding secretary, 1955–1977. Water can be found at a small spring 150 ft. south. **Greenwall Shelter to Minerva Hinchey Shelter, 5.3 mi., 8.5 km., 3¼ hr. (SB 3¼ hr.).**

Climb to the ridge and then descend to **Spring Lake Clearing (4.2 mi.)**, where the forest is reclaiming a highland meadow and there are limited views. Reenter the woods, pass the airport beacon power line (4.3 mi.), and follow a narrow ridge for over a mile before reaching a spur leading west 50 ft. to **Airport Lookout (5.5 mi.)**. Drop off the ridge to the head of picturesque **Clarendon Gorge (6.2 mi.)**. Cross the suspen-

---

KEEP YOUR DRINKING WATER CLEAN

Proper disposal of human and pet waste prevents the spread of *Giardia* and other diseases. If an outhouse is not available, bury waste in a six-inch deep hole at least 200 feet from water and 50 feet from trails.

---

sion bridge over Mill River. The bridge was built in 1974 to replace a similar structure swept away in the 1973 flood. It is dedicated to the memory of Robert Brugmann. Follow the old road uphill to the parking lot on Vt. 103 (6.3 mi.). *Use caution when crossing Vt. 103; traffic moves at high speeds.*

Cross the highway and the Green Mountain Railroad, and then traverse a small pasture, climbing over stiles to negotiate its barbed wire fences. Turn left and follow a woods road uphill to a power line, and then climb up through a boulder-filled ravine. At the top of the ravine, bear right and rise gradually along the ridge to Clarendon Lookout (6.7 mi.) with views to the south and west, and then continue along the ridge before dropping gradually to an abandoned town road. Just beyond that road, a **spur** descends east 400 ft. to **Clarendon Shelter (7.3 mi.)**. This frame building, with bunks for 12, was constructed by the Killington Section in 1952. A brook 50 ft. east furnishes water. **Minerva Hinchey Shelter to Clarendon Shelter, 3.7 mi., 6.0 km., 2½ hr. (SB 2½ hr.).**

From the spur, continue east to cross a brook, briefly following it before climbing to the partially open summit of **Beacon Hill (7.8 mi.)**, where there is a view of the nearby countryside. Turn north to drop down through a sugarbush, traverse a pasture, pass through a gate (please keep the gate closed so the cows don't escape) and cross Lottery Road (8.2 mi.) west of the village of Shrewsbury. Reenter the woods (8.3 mi.) and pass Hermit Spring (8.6 mi.), unreliable in dry seasons. Ascend a ridge, drop through another old pasture, and continue to the gravel Kieffer Road (9.9 mi.). Bear left on Kieffer Road, and then enter a field to the right with views of the Coolidge Range, and descend to the west bank of Cold River (10.1 mi.), which you follow downstream to the paved **Cold River (Lower Road) (10.2 mi.)**, 2.4 mi. west of North Shrewsbury.

Turn right on the road to cross a bridge over the Cold River, then bear left onto a woods road to pass through a clearing. Reenter the woods to follow the woods road a short distance, then bear right (10.4 mi.) to ascend a ridge high above the brook. Traversing this ridge and passing a vista of the Coolidge Range, the Trail then drops to the **Gould Brook ford**

Hiker Safety Is Hiker Awareness

Although the trail is safer than most places, problems can occur. Hiker awareness is one of your best lines of defense.

HIKING WITH OTHERS IS SAFER. If you encounter a stranger or a situation that makes you feel uncomfortable, move on.

DON'T CAMP NEAR ROAD CROSSINGS, even at established campsites. If tenting away from an established campsite, camp out of sight of the trail.

ELIMINATE OPPORTUNITIES FOR THEFT. Don't leave gear on the trail or in a shelter unattended. Don't leave anything in vehicles parked at trailheads.

USE TRAIL AND SHELTER REGISTERS. Please sign them. Doing so will help rescuers find you in an emergency. Be sure your at-home contact knows your trail name, if you use one.

(11.0 mi.), which can be challenging in high water. Parallel Gould and Sargent Brooks to the unpaved **Upper Road (11.7 mi.)**, 2.4 mi. west of North Shrewsbury.

Cross the Upper Road and continue paralleling the stream to another road (12.3 mi.). Turn left onto the road to cross a bridge over Sargent Brook, and, in 150 ft., turn right into the woods. After ascending a ridge, pass through an overgrown clearing (12.7 mi.), the site of the former Haley Farm. The GMC's 1920 *Guide Book of the Long Trail* described the farm as providing, "good beds and board; telephone." Follow the brook, crossing it on a bridge, and immediately cross a woods road before reaching **Governor Clement Shelter (13.1 mi.)**, located on a dirt road in an overgrown field. This stone structure was built by the family of William H. Field of Mendon in 1929 and is named for Percival W. Clement, governor of Vermont, 1919 to 1921. There is bunk space for ten. Abundant water is available at the brook 200 ft. to the east. There have been problems over the years with partying on this spot, and GMC is working with the Green Mountain National Forest to limit inappropriate use. Move on if your encounter problems. **Clarendon Shelter to Governor Clement Shelter, 5.8 mi., 9.3 km., 3½ hr. (SB 3 hr.).**

Follow the road behind the shelter to the north, then bear left into the woods (13.4 mi.), and, sometimes following woods roads, climb steadily to two small brook crossings (15.3 mi.). Slab the steep south slope of Little Killington to the north end of the **Shrewsbury Peak Trail (15.8 mi.)**, which leads 2.0 mi. east to Shrewsbury Peak. From the junction, ascend through stunted evergreens to a view of Mendon Peak to the west. From the height-of-land on Little Killington (16.2 mi.), pass mossy conifers and continue by easy grades along the west flank of Killington Peak to **Killington Spur (17.4 mi.)**, which leads uphill steeply east 0.2 mi. to the summit of **Killington Peak**. Bear left at the spur and proceed downhill 100 ft. to **Cooper Lodge**. There are tent platforms at the spur junction's clearing, the site of a steel camp that preceded the lodge.

Cooper Lodge, of stone and wood construction with bunks for twelve, was built by the Vermont Forest Service and CCC in 1939. It is located on land given to the state by Mortimer R.

Proctor, former president of the Green Mountain Club and later governor of Vermont, and named in honor of Charles P. Cooper, president of the Club when a considerable portion of the Long Trail was completed. It is the highest shelter (3,850 ft.) on the LT. There is a composting privy to the east of the lodge, and a spring 100 ft. west on the Long Trail. A GMC caretaker may be present during the hiking season to assist and educate hikers, help maintain the local trails and campsites, and compost sewage to protect water quality. An overnight fee may be charged. **Governor Clement Shelter to Cooper Lodge, 4.3 mi., 6.9 km., 3¼ hr. (SB 2¼ hr.).**

From the lodge, descend past the spring, passing just above the barely discernable site of the nineteenth-century summit hotel, and then diverge to the right from the abandoned Killington carriage road in a swampy glade. Reach the top of the **Bucklin Trail (17.6 mi.),** which leads 3.3 mi. downhill east to the Wheelerville Road, and bear right to slab through an area of many seeps and brooklets, before reaching the trail's height-of-land on Snowden Peak (18.4 mi.). Descend to the east of the Killington-Pico ridge before crossing back to the west side of the ridge (18.8 mi.), and then remain nearly level to Jungle Junction and the south end of the **Sherburne Pass Trail (19.9 mi.).** The name originated with the Long Trail's former junction with Pico's abandoned West Side Trail where the 1938 hurricane left behind a "jungle" of blowdowns. The Sherburne Pass Trail, the former route of the Long Trail, leads north 0.4 mi. to **Pico Camp** and 3.1 mi. to U.S. 4 at Sherburne Pass. Pico Camp, built by the Long Trail Patrol in 1959, is a frame cabin with bunks for twelve. It has a view of Killington Peak directly south and Mt. Ascutney to the southeast. A small spring is located 100 ft. north of the camp on the Sherburne Pass Trail. A GMC caretaker may be present, and an overnight fee may be charged. **Cooper Lodge to Pico Camp, 2.9 mi., 4.7 km., 1¾ hr. (SB 2 hr.).**

From the Sherburne Pass Trail, bear left to wrap around the west flank of Pico and descend through conifers and then open white birch forest to **Mendon Lookout (21.5 mi.).** Follow a series of switchbacks down to a **spur (21.8 mi.)** leading west 0.1 mi. to **Churchill Scott Shelter.** This post-and-beam structure, with space for eight, was built by Erik and Laurel Tobiason, the Killington Section, and other GMC volunteers in 2002. It is named for a longtime leader and trail maintainer for the section and dedicated to the memory of Alice H. Ferrance, an Appalachian Trail long distance hiker, whose family donated the funds for the project. The water source is a spring located 450 ft. south of the shelter. The campsite includes a tent platform and an accessible composting privy. A GMC caretaker may be present during the hiking season to assist and educate hikers, help maintain trails and campsites, and compost sewage to protect the water quality of the Rutland City watershed. An overnight fee may be charged. **Cooper Lodge to Churchill Scott Shelter, 4.5 mi., 7.2 km., 2¼ hr. (SB 3¼ hr.).**

From the shelter spur, descend to a brook crossing (21.9 mi.), and continue downhill on easy grades to **U.S. 4 (23.7 mi.),** 1.0 mi. west of Sherburne Pass and the Inn at Long Trail.

5

Side Trails

Shrewsbury Peak Trail. This trail links the CCC Road south of the Coolidge Range with the Long Trail near Little Killington. The Trail starts at a parking lot on the CCC Road 3.0 mi. east of North Shrewsbury, and 3.5 mi. west of Vt. 100. The CCC Road leaves Vt. 100 10.7 mi. north of the junction of Vt. 100 and 103 and 3.1 mi. south of the junctions of Vt. 100 and U.S. 4. The CCC Road is not maintained in winter.

From the parking lot (0.0 mi.), climb Russell Hill (0.2 mi.), then descend into a small ravine (0.5 mi.) before ascending to the summit of Shrewsbury Peak (1.8 mi.), where there are views to the south and east. Descend to a junction with the Black Swamp Trail (1.9 mi.), and continue north to a wooded summit (2.0 mi.). Drop into a swale (3.2 mi.) and climb to the northwest, crossing three brooks before turning south to join the Long Trail (4.0 mi.) on the south slope of Little Killington. **CCC Road to Long Trail, 4.0 mi., 6.8 km., 3¼ hr. (Rev. 2½ hr.).**

Black Swamp Trail. This is an easier route from the CCC Road to Shrewsbury Peak and the Long Trail beyond. It begins at the intersection of the Black Swamp and CCC Roads, 4.5 mi. east of North Shrewsbury, 1.3 mi. east of the Shrewsbury Peak

Trail, and 2.0 mi. west of Vt. 100. Because this is a spring feed-ing area for black bears, the Black Swamp Road is gated until at least mid-July. The CCC Road is not maintained in winter.

From the CCC Road (0.0 mi.) ascend the gravel Black Swamp Road to its end (0.8 mi.). Follow the blazed trail and climb steadily on more primitive woods roads to Shrewsbury Peak Shelter (1.8 mi.), a log lean-to with space for eight, built by the Civilian Conservation Corps. Continue the ascent to the junction with the Shrewsbury Peak Trail (2.1 mi.), 0.1 mi. north of Shrewsbury Peak and 2.1 mi. south of the Long Trail. **CCC Road to Shrewsbury Peak, 2.2 mi., 3.5 km., 1½ hr. (Rev. 1 hr.).**

KILLINGTON SPUR. This trail scrambles up Killington Peak from the Long Trail near Cooper Lodge. The spur bears east from the Long Trail 100 ft. south of Cooper Lodge, and then climbs steeply to the summit.

Killington Peak (4235 ft.) is the second highest mountain in Vermont; only Mt. Mansfield is higher. It is part of the Coolidge Range, which also includes Pico Peak, Mendon Peak, Little Killington, and Shrewsbury Peak. From the summit a path descends a short distance east to the facilities of the Killington resort. The summit is on a self-guided Killington Ski Area nature trail that starts near the gondola station.

There are views in all directions from the rocky summit of Killington Peak, including all the prominent Green Mountain peaks from Glastenbury Mtn. to Mt. Mansfield. To the south-east is Mt. Ascutney and to the northeast are the White Moun-tains. To the west are the Taconics, including Bird Mtn. with its precipitous south face, Lake Champlain, and the Adirondacks. To the east is the village of Plymouth where Calvin Coolidge was born and where he was sworn in as president by his father in 1923. **Long Trail to Killington Peak, 0.2 mi., 0.3 km., ⅓ hr. (Rev. ⅓ hr.).**

BUCKLIN TRAIL. This trail ascends the west slope of Killington Peak from the town of Mendon. The trail begins at Brewers Corners on the unpaved Wheelerville Road 4.0 mi. south of U.S. 4 and 6.5 mi. east of downtown Rutland. From Sherburne Pass follow U.S. 4 west 4.3 mi. then turn south onto the

Wheelerville Road. Follow the road 4.0 mi. to a sharp turn, Brewers Corners, and the beginning of the trail. To reach Brewers Corners from Rutland, turn onto Killington Ave. east from U.S. 7 at Christ the King Church, 0.5 mi. south of the junction of U.S. 7 and U.S. 4 East. Turn right at the end of Killington Ave. onto Notch Road. Beyond the end of the pavement, turn left onto Wheelerville Road and follow it 3.1 mi. to the trail. Do not block woods roads when parking. North from Brewers Corners, the old Killington Carriage Road (gated, unmaintained) heads south, then east, joining the Long Trail 0.1 mi. west of Cooper Lodge, just above the Bucklin Trail junction with the Long Trail.

From Brewers Corners (0.0 mi.), follow a level woods road, joining the Catamount Trail, and cross a bridge over Brewers Brook (0.2 mi.). Continue east on the woods road while the Catamount Trail bears left, and follow the north side of the brook except where it ascends to a limited view west. Leave the woods road and descend to the second stream crossing (1.2 mi.) that is challenging, except in times of low water. Rejoin the woods road and follow the south side of the brook until turning right (2.0 mi.) to climb steadily out of the valley to meet the Long Trail (3.3 mi.) about 0.1 mi. north of Cooper Lodge and the Killington Spur. **Brewers Corners to Long Trail, 3.3 mi., 5.3 km., 2¾ hr. (Rev. 1¾ hr.).**

SHERBURNE PASS TRAIL (SOUTH OF SHERBURNE PASS). This trail extends north and south from U.S. 4, and is the former, historic route of the Long Trail. It connects with the Appalachian Trail on both sides of the pass, providing an alternate hiking route across U.S. 4. The Sherburne Pass Trail north of Sherburne Pass is described on page 232.

The trailhead is at Sherburne Pass, 9.3 mi. east of U.S. 7 in Rutland, and 1.4 mi. west of Vt. 100 North near the Killington Access Road. There is a large, unpaved parking lot on the south side of the highway, across from the Inn at Long Trail. *Use caution when crossing U.S. 4; traffic moves at high speeds.*

From the highway (0.0 mi.), follow an old road south from the back of the parking lot. Turn right at a trail register (0.1 mi.), enter the woods, and ascend steadily to Sink Hole Brook

(1.1 mi.), a permanent stream that disappears into a sink hole beside the trail. Continue uphill to a ski trail, with a wide view of the Green Mountains to the north. Follow the ski trail uphill 300 ft. before turning left to reenter the woods at Pico Junction (2.1 mi.). The Summit Glades and 49er ski trails lead uphill 0.4 mi. to Pico Peak. Proceed south along the rugged route with little change in elevation to pass a spring and then reach Pico Camp and Pico Link (2.5 mi.), which leads uphill to the summit of Pico. Beyond the camp, follow the contour to cross a pipeline clearing (2.7 mi.), and arrive at the Long Trail (2.9 mi.) at Jungle Junction, 2.5 mi. north of Cooper Lodge and 3.8 mi. south of U.S. 4. **Sherburne Pass south to Long Trail, 2.9 mi., 4.7 km., 2¼ hr. (Rev. 1½ mi.).**

PICO LINK. This route provides access to the summit of Pico Peak from the Sherburne Pass Trail. Enter the woods on the north side of Pico Camp and climb steeply to the pipeline clearing, and then continue uphill to the open summit of Pico Peak. Note your route carefully after entering the summit ski trails, because blazes may be hard to see when you return. An alternative descent follows the 49er ski trail down to the Summit Glades ski trail leading to the Sherburne Pass Trail at Pico Junction, 0.4 mi. below the summit. **Sherburne Pass Trail to Pico Peak, 0.4 mi., 0.6 km., ½ hr. (Rev. ¼ hr.).**

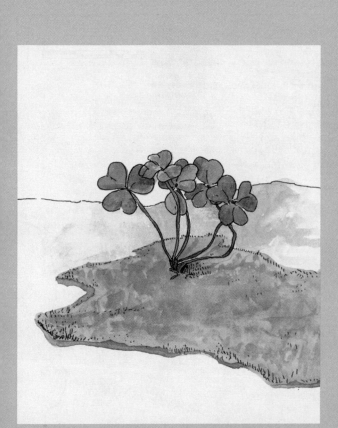

DIVISION 6
U.S. 4 to Brandon Gap

Division 6 Profile

U.S. 4 to Brandon Gap

miles north- bound	▲ NORTH	elevation at Long Trail (feet/meters)	miles south- bound
19.9	**Vt. 73** at **Brandon Gap**	2183/665	0.0
19.0	**Sunrise Shelter**	2564/782	0.9
17.6	**Chittenden Brook Trail** to **USFS** Road 45, 3.7 mi E	2951/899	2.3
16.2	**Farr Peak**, east ridge	3150/960	3.7
15.7	**Bloodroot Gap**	3110/948	4.2
14.0	**Bloodroot Mtn.**, east ridge	2900/884	5.9
13.2	**Wetmore Gap**	2600/792	6.7
12.7	**New Boston Trail** to **David Logan** **Shelter** (2620 ft/799 m), 0.2 mi W, to USFS Road 99, 1.2 mi W	2760/841	7.2
10.8	**Telephone Gap**	2300/701	9.1
8.9	**Green Road**	2500/762	11.0
5.0	**Rolston Rest Shelter**	2240/683	14.9
3.3	**Elbow Road**	1951/595	16.6
1.4	**Tucker-Johnson Shelter**	2250/686	18.5
1.0	**Maine Junction** at **Willard Gap**: **Appalachian Trail**; to **U.S. 4** via **Sherburne Pass Trail**, north branch, 1.4 mi	2250/686	18.9
0.0	**U.S. 4** west of Sherburne Pass	1880/573	19.9

SOUTH
▼

Division 6
U.S. 4 to Brandon Gap

Massachusetts 103.9 miles　　　　　　　*Canada 168.8 miles*

Water is scarce between Rolston Rest and David Logan Shelters. Hikers should take advantage of the water sources at these two sites.

South of Wetmore Gap, this division's Long Trail passes through some private lands that are managed for timber. Be prepared to encounter logging operations, and yield to logging trucks. The Long Trail and the Appalachian Trail coincide in Division 6 for 1.0 mile from U.S. 4 to Maine Junction at Willard Gap.

Suggested Hike

Chittenden Brook Trail. This hike alongside a mountain brook leads from USFS Road 45 uphill to the Long Trail. Round trip, 7.4 mi., 4⅓ hr.

Camping and Fires

This division's Long Trail crosses federal and state land with scattered private holdings. Camping is limited to shelters between Sherburne Pass and Wetmore Gap. Small wood fires, although discouraged, are permitted at the shelters' established fire rings.

From Wetmore Gap to Brandon Gap the Trail crosses the Green Mountain National Forest. Primitive off-trail camping with small wood fires is permitted.

Refer to Leave No Trace principles (pages 9 to 11) to minimize your impact.

GROUP USE

Groups hiking this division's Long Trail may need an Outfitter-Guide Permit from the Green Mountain National Forest. Group tenting space is available at Rolston Rest and David Logan Shelters. Gifford Woods State Park Campground, east of Sherburne Pass on Vt. 100, is available for base camp hiking. GMNF Chittenden Brook Campground, near the trailhead for the Chittenden Brook Trail, is also available for base camp hiking. Refer to group use guidelines (pages 11 to 17) to determine your need for a permit and to minimize your group's impact.

WINTER USE

This division loses its "green tunnel" aspect after the leaves have fallen. Much of it is suitable for intermediate cross-country skiers. A recommended trip is to follow the Long Trail from Brandon Gap to a suitable half-way point, and then follow your tracks back to Vt. 73. The trailhead parking lot on the south side of Vt. 73 is plowed in winter.

PLAN AHEAD AND PREPARE
Prepare for extreme weather and emergencies; bring appropriate clothing; carry and know how to use a map and compass; be able to purify drinking water; know local regulations.

ACCESS TO LONG TRAIL

U.S. 4. Refer to directions on page 101 in Division 5.

BRANDON GAP, VT. 73. The Long Trail crosses this highway 9.2 mi. west of Vt. 100 just south of Rochester, and 5.2 mi. east of Forest Dale and 8.2 mi. east of Brandon from U.S. 7. There is a parking lot for thirty cars on the south side of the highway just west of the Long Trail crossing.

LONG TRAIL DESCRIPTION

Cross **U.S. 4 (0.0 mi.)**. *Use caution when crossing U.S. 4; traffic moves at high speeds.* North of the highway, follow the Catamount Trail across a wet area, and after the Catamount Trail diverges west, climb gradually to a view of Pico Peak (0.8 mi.). Continue to **Maine Junction (1.0 mi.) at Willard Gap.** Here the **Appalachian Trail** bears right, toward Gifford Woods State Park and ultimately Katahdin in Maine, while the Long Trail bears left, north, to Canada. A description of the AT from here to the Connecticut River begins on page 227. The north end of the **Deer Leap Trail** begins 0.1 mi. south on the AT.

From Maine Junction follow an old woods road north on level ground to **Tucker-Johnson Shelter (1.4 mi.).** This frame shelter, with bunks for 8, was built by the Long Trail Patrol, Louis Stare, and members of the Killington Section in 1969. It is named for Fred H. Tucker of Boston, a long-time member of the GMC, and for Otto Johnson of Proctor, Vt., who bequeathed funds for its construction. Nearby Eagle Square Brook furnishes water. **Churchill Scott Shelter to Tucker-Johnson Shelter, 3.4 mi., 5.5 km., 2 hr. (SB 2¼ hr.).**

North from the shelter, cross the brook, and continue, with minor changes in elevation and occasional stretches of rough footing, to the east side of the ridge, reaching the abandoned **Elbow Road (3.3 mi.)** or Chittenden-Pittsfield Road, now an active logging road, at a three-way junction. Follow the middle logging road north, turn right to climb the embankment, and continue without much change in elevation to **Rolston Rest**

Shelter (5.0 mi.). This frame lean-to, with space for eight, was built by the Long Trail Patrol in 1966. The shelter is named for Ben Rolston, a former GMC guidebook editor and trail maintainer. The water source is a small brook that crosses the Long Trail just south of the shelter. **Tucker-Johnson Shelter to Rolston Rest, 3.6 mi., 5.8 km., 2¼ hr. (SB 2¼ hr.).**

Just north of the shelter cross a private road, which descends east to Vt. 100. Climb moderately to the top of a ridge (5.5 mi.), passing west of an unnamed summit (2,800 ft.), and continue northwest on or near the ridgeline with occasional views. Leave the crest in a shallow gap (7.2 mi.) to slab the west side of the ridge. In a small rocky gap, cross the abandoned **Green Road (8.9 mi.)** that runs from Chittenden to Pittsfield, which was used as early as 1796 and is now a snowmobile trail. There is a view west of Chittenden Reservoir just north of the road. Slab the west slope and pass about 100 ft. west of an enormous split boulder. Cross to the east side of the ridge, drop to a sag known as **Telephone Gap (10.8 mi.)** and, swinging back to the northwest, ascend to the west side of the ridge again. Follow a snowmobile trail (11.9 mi.), then ascend the south slope of Mt. Carmel, and continue with minor elevation changes along the ridge to the **New Boston Trail (12.7 mi.).**

This trail descends west 0.2 mi. to **David Logan Shelter** and 1.2 mi. to USFS Road 99. The shelter is a frame lean-to with bunks for 8. It was built with the help of 60 campers from the Vermont Camping Association under the direction of GMC's George Pearlstein in 1976, and is named in memory of David Logan, an active club member. The shelter was rebuilt by the Long Trail Patrol in 1996 with funds donated by the Logan family. A reliable spring is located 200 ft. north of the shelter

IT'S YOUR DRINKING WATER
Wash dishes and yourself away from the water source. The next person might not like secondhand oatmeal or the taste of detergent.

along the New Boston Trail. **Rolston Rest to David Logan Shelter, 7.9 mi., 12.7 m., 5¼ hr. (SB 5¼ hr.).**

Continue north from the trail junction, briefly ascend the west slope of Mt. Carmel and drop to **Wetmore Gap (13.2 mi.).** Climb the east ridge of **Bloodroot Mtn. (14.0 mi.),** and then contour around the east slope of the mountain to **Bloodroot Gap (15.7 mi.),** another snowmobile trail crossing.

From the gap, slab the east ridge of **Farr Peak (16.2 mi.),** named for Albert G. Farr of Brandon who supplied the funds to complete the LT between Lincoln and Brandon Gaps. Continue with little change in elevation around the east slope of the peak until reaching the **Chittenden Brook Trail (17.6 mi.),** which leads 3.7 mi. east to USFS Road 45. Beyond the junction, begin a gradual descent on an old woods road to **Sunrise Shelter (19.0 mi.).** This frame shelter was built by the Long Trail Patrol in 1964, a gift of Mortimer R. Proctor, governor of Vermont from 1945 to 1947, and former president of the GMC. The shelter has space for eight, and the water source is a brook 200 ft. south on the LT. **David Logan Shelter to Sunrise Shelter, 6.5 mi., 10.5 km., 4 hr. (SB 4 hr.).**

Continue downhill on the old woods road, which is maintained for cross-country skiing south of Brandon Gap. Pass a clearing with a view of the Great Cliff of Mt. Horrid, and reach **Brandon Gap at Vt. 73 (19.9 mi.).** The trailhead parking lot is just west of the LT. *Use caution when crossing Vt. 73; traffic moves at high speeds.* USFS Road 45 which leads to the Chittenden Brook Trail and a Forest Service campground is 3.7 mi. east.

SIDE TRAILS

NEW BOSTON TRAIL. From the Civil War monument in Chittenden (0.0 mi.) follow the road to Mountain Top Ski Touring Center 1.8 mi. north to a fork in the road just beyond Mountain Top Inn. Continue straight ahead on the right-hand fork on the unpaved town road to a small pullout (2.4 mi.) on the right. Here the road becomes USFS Road 99 and is passable only by high clearance vehicles. The road improves after turning left on a logging road. Continue past USFS Road 99A to a primitive campsite with a privy at the trailhead (3.7 mi.).

From the trailhead, bear left off the logging road and ascend on a woods road for 0.75 mi. to a fork. Here the Mt. Carmel snowmobile trail follows the wide woods road to the right. Continue straight, uphill, on an old woods road and climb steadily to David Logan Shelter (1.0 mi.). Just above the shelter pass a piped spring to the left, and arrive at the Long Trail (1.2 mi.). **USFS Road 99 to Long Trail, 1.2 mi., 1.9 km., 1¼ hr. (Rev. ¾ hr.).**

CHITTENDEN BROOK TRAIL. Located in the Chittenden Brook Recreation Area (named for Vermont's first governor, Thomas Chittenden), this trail offers a pleasant approach to the Long Trail as well as some good hiking and skiing loops with other trails in the recreation area. From Vt. 100 near Rochester, follow Vt. 73 west 5.5 mi. and turn south onto USFS Road 45. Continue 0.6 mi. on this road to the trailhead parking area. The USFS Chittenden Brook Campground is another 1.7 mi. up the road from the trailhead. USFS Road 45 is not maintained for winter travel.

From the trailhead lot (0.0 mi.), follow the stream on old woods roads and climb steadily through spruce and fir forest, passing a cross-country trail on the right, and reach the Beaver Pond Spur (1.7 mi.), which leads to a wetland with the chance to see beaver, tree swallows, and an occasional moose. After crossing a major branch of the brook, pass a short spur (1.9 mi.) leading left to the campground, cut across the last of the cross-country ski loops (2.2 mi.), and then climb steadily to the Long Trail (3.7 mi.). **USFS Road 45 to Long Trail, 3.7 mi., 6.0 km., 2⅓ hr. (Rev. 2 hr.).**

DIVISION 7

Brandon Gap to
Cooley Glen

DIVISION 7 PROFILE

Brandon Gap to Cooley Glen

miles northbound	▲ NORTH	elevation at Long Trail (feet/meters)	miles southbound
22.5	**Cooley Glen Trail** 3.2 mi W to USFS Road 201, **Cooley Glen Shelter**	3130/954	0.0
22.0	**Mt. Cleveland**	3482/1061	0.5
20.3	**Little Hans Peak**	3348/1020	2.2
18.5	**Clark Brook Trail** to USFS Road 55, 3.0 mi E	3390/1033	4.0
17.7	**Mt. Wilson**	3745/1141	4.8
16.8	**Emily Proctor Shelter; Emily Proctor Trail** to USFS Road 201, 3.5 mi W	3460/1055	5.7
16.2	**Breadloaf Mtn.** to vista, 0.1 mi W via spur	3835/1169	6.3
15.0	**Skylight Pond Trail** to **Skyline Lodge** (3380 ft/1030 m), 0.1 mi E; to USFS Road 59, 2.5 mi W	3420/1042	7.5
13.9	**Mt. Boyce**	3323/1013	8.6
13.0	**Boyce Shelter**	3020/920	9.5
12.4	**Burnt Hill Trail** to USFS Road 59, 2.2 mi W	2950/899	10.1
10.3	**Silent Cliff Trail** to vista, 0.4 mi E	2480/756	12.2
9.9	**Vt. 125** at **Middlebury Gap**	2144/653	12.6
9.5	**Lake Pleiad** (2128 ft/649 m), 0.1 mi. W via spur	2150/655	13.0
8.9	**Middlebury Snow Bowl; Worth Mtn. Lodge** (2450 ft/747 m), 0.2 mi W via ski slope	2640/805	13.6
7.2	**Worth Mtn.**	3234/986	15.3
5.4	**Sucker Brook Trail** to **Sucker Brook Shelter** (2420 ft/738 m), 0.1 mi W; to USFS Road 67, 1.0 mi W	2440/744	17.1
4.5	**Romance Gap**	2685/818	18.0
4.1	**Romance Mtn.**, east summit	3125/953	18.4
3.3	**Gillespie Peak**	3366/1026	19.2
1.8	**Cape Lookoff Mtn.**	3320/1012	20.7
1.3	**Mt. Horrid**	3216/980	21.2
0.7	**Great Cliff of Mt. Horrid** (2860 ft/872 m), 0.1 mi E via spur	2760/841	21.8
0.0	**Vt. 73** at **Brandon Gap**	2183/665	22.5

SOUTH
▼

DIVISION 7
Brandon Gap to Cooley Glen

Massachusetts: 123.8 miles   *Canada: 148.9 miles*

This division's Long Trail remains on or near the ridgeline. Water is scarce and hikers should take advantage of sources noted in the text.

From Middlebury Gap to Cooley Glen, this division's Long Trail traverses the Breadloaf Wilderness. Refer to wilderness information on page 7. The halfway point of the Long Trail is Burnt Hill Trail Jct., 12.4 mi. north of Brandon Gap.

SUGGESTED HIKES

LAKE PLEIAD. This hike follows the Long Trail south from Middlebury Gap and the spur to Lake Pleiad, and is especially suitable for children. Round trip, 1.0 mi., ½ hr.

MT. HORRID'S GREAT CLIFF. This climb on the Long Trail north from Brandon Gap provides a sweeping view south from its precipitous heights. The cliffs may be closed to hikers from March 15 to August 1 because they are a prime peregrine falcon nesting site. In recent years (as of 2002) the falcons have nested far to the east of the hiking trails, and the cliffs have remained open. However, if falcons return to nest near the trails, the spur to the cliff will be closed until August 1. Round trip, 1.4 mi., 1¼ hr.

Mt. Roosevelt. This trip follows the Clark Brook Trail and Long Trail into the Breadloaf Wilderness to an open ledge just north of the summit. Round trip, 6.8 mi., 4½ hr.

Camping and Fires

This division's Long Trail crosses the Green Mountain National Forest from Brandon Gap to Worth Mtn., and from Middlebury Gap to Cooley Glen. Primitive off-trail camping with small wood fires is allowed. Refer to Leave No Trace principles (pages 9 to 11) to minimize your impact.

Note: Camping within 500 ft. of Skylight Pond is limited to Skyline Lodge (tenting around the pond is prohibited) and wood fires are prohibited within 500 ft. of Skylight Pond to protect vulnerable vegetation and soils. The designated tenting area for Skyline Lodge is on the Long Trail just south of the Skylight Pond Trail junction. Campers are requested to use the composting privy for the lodge to protect water quality.

Between Worth Mtn. and Middlebury Gap, the Long Trail traverses private Middlebury College property; camping and fires are prohibited along this portion of the Trail, and hikers are asked to stay off and away from chairlift equipment and all other buildings. From May 1 to October 31, Long Trail hikers can stay at Middlebury College's Worth Mtn. Lodge, which is 0.2 mi. west of the Long Trail from the upper chairlift station of the Snow Bowl.

Group Use

Groups hiking this division's Long Trail may need an Outfitter-Guide Permit from the Green Mountain National Forest. Groups can stay at Worth Mtn. Lodge. Tenting at Middlebury College's Snow Bowl is not permitted. Group tenting space is available at Emily Proctor and Cooley Glen Shelters. Primitive campsites are also available at the trailheads for the Sucker Brook, Skylight Pond, Clark Brook, and the Cooley Glen Trails. GMNF Chittenden Brook Campground, near the trailhead for the Chittenden Brook Trail east of Brandon Gap, is available for base camp hiking. Refer to pages 11 to 17 for additional group use guidelines.

WINTER USE

All suggested hikes in this division are suitable as snowshoe treks. Most of the terrain is too rugged for beginner and intermediate cross-country skiers. The Breadloaf Wilderness' signs and blazing make winter trail navigation challenging. Map and compass skills are recommended.

ACCESS TO LONG TRAIL

VT. 73 AT BRANDON GAP. Refer to directions on page 117 in Division 6.

VT. 125 AT MIDDLEBURY GAP. This Long Trail crossing is 2.5 mi. east of Middlebury College's Bread Loaf Campus, 5.6 mi. east of Ripton, and 10.1 mi. east of the junction with U.S. 7, south of Middlebury. It is also 6.2 mi. west of Vt. 100 in Hancock. There is a large area for pull-off parking on the highway's south shoulder.

LONG TRAIL DESCRIPTION

Cross Vt. 73 at Brandon Gap (0.0 mi.). *Use caution when crossing Vt. 73; traffic moves at high speeds.* Climb up an old road, reenter the woods, and ascend steadily on a trail rebuilt by the Long Trail Patrol and Forest Service trail crews in the mid-1990s. At the top of a rock staircase, a **spur (0.7 mi.)** leads east

MINIMIZE CAMPFIRE IMPACTS
Build fires only where permitted and only in established fire rings; use a portable stove.

0.1 mi. to the **Great Cliff of Mt. Horrid**. The cliff top, 600 ft. above the road, provides a view of the gap and the mountains to the south. The spur may be closed between March 15 and August 1 to prevent disturbing nesting peregrine falcons. Continue west of the ridge to the summit of **Mt. Horrid (1.3 mi.)**, and then along the wooded ridge to **Cape Lookoff Mtn. (1.8 mi.)** and **Gillespie Peak (3.3 mi.)**. There are many vistas along this ridge.

North from Gillespie Peak (formerly White Rocks Mtn.) to Mt. Wilson, the Long Trail traverses forest land bequeathed to Middlebury College in 1915 by Colonel Joseph Battell. The college still owns 700 acres at the Snow Bowl ski area, including 1.8 mi. of the LT and Lake Pleiad; the remainder is now part of the Green Mountain National Forest. Col. Battell established the Bread Loaf Inn west of Middlebury Gap, now used as Middlebury College's Bread Loaf Campus. He also cut a trail from Mt. Abraham north to Mt. Ellen in 1901.

From Gillespie Peak, follow the ridge north, passing a spur to a view west just before reaching the east summit of **Romance Mtn. (4.1 mi.)**. Switchback down to **Romance Gap (4.5 mi.)** and continue west of the ridge to a junction with the **Sucker Brook Trail (5.4 mi.)**, which leads west 0.1 mi. to **Sucker Brook Shelter** and 1.0 mi. west to USFS Road 67. This frame shelter, which sleeps eight, was built by the U.S. Forest Service in 1963. The water source is Sucker Brook, 50 ft. further down the Sucker Brook Trail. **Sunrise Shelter to Sucker Brook Shelter, 6.4 mi., 10.3 km., 4 hr. (SB 4 ¼ hr.).**

From the Sucker Brook Trail junction, climb gradually up the ridge of Worth Mtn. passing by vistas to the south and west. Continue the moderate ascent, passing two vistas to the east, before reaching the wooded summit of **Worth Mtn. (7.2 mi.)**. From the summit, follow the ridge, passing Eastern Lookout,

---

COUNT ON YOURSELF, NOT YOUR CELL PHONE

Your cell phone doesn't replace common sense; being prepared; or carrying adequate food, water, and clothing.

then descend moderately, passing over a couple of minor summits until reaching the clearing for **Middlebury Snow Bowl's** upper chairlift station (**8.9 mi.**). There are views to the north and east. **Worth Mtn. Lodge**, 0.2 mi. west of the Long Trail down the ski slope just beyond the chairlift station, is open to the public for camping from May 1 to October 31. Camping on the ski trails is prohibited. Pass to the west of the chairlift on a ski trail and descend steadily, continuing to follow and cross ski trails several times. Pay close attention to blazes and signs. At the bottom of the descent, cross a small brook at a junction with a **spur** (**9.5 mi.**) leading west 0.1 mi. to **Lake Pleiad**.

Pass over a low ridge to **Vt. 125 at Middlebury Gap** (**9.9 mi.**). The Snow Bowl entrance is 0.7 mi. west and U.S. 7 south of Middlebury is 10.1 mi. west. Vt. 100 in Hancock is 6.4 mi. east.

Cross the highway. *Use caution when crossing Vt. 125; traffic moves at high speeds.* Climb the road embankment and enter the Breadloaf Wilderness at its south boundary. The Long Trail may be more challenging to follow in the Wilderness Area due to minimal brushing and blazing. Climb steadily to a junction with the **Silent Cliff Trail** (**10.3 mi.**), which leads east 0.4 mi. to the vista at Silent Cliff. North of the trail junction, ascend to the ridge (10.8 mi.), continue to Burnt Hill, then descend to the west side of the ridge and a junction with the **Burnt Hill Trail** (**12.4 mi.**), which descends west 2.2 mi. to USFS Road 59. From the junction, follow the rugged west slope of Kirby Peak (12.6 mi.), before descending to **Boyce Shelter** (**13.0 mi.**). This frame shelter, with space for eight, was built by the U.S. Forest Service in 1963. A small, unreliable brook 200 ft. north via the Long Trail supplies water. **Sucker Brook Shelter to Boyce Shelter, 7.7 mi., 12.4 km., 5¼ hr. (SB 5½ hr.).**

Beyond the shelter, climb **Mt. Boyce** (**13.9 mi.**) and continue along the ridge over Battell Mtn. (14.9 mi.), to reach an established tenting area with a spur leading west to a vista at Sunset Rock. Descend to a junction with the **Skylight Pond Trail** (**15.0 mi.**), which descends west 2.5 mi. to USFS Road 59 and east 0.1 mi. to **Skyline Lodge** at Skylight Pond.

Skyline Lodge, an enclosed shelter with bunk space for fourteen, was built by the GMC and U.S. Forest Service in 1987.

MUD SEASON

The Green Mountain Club encourages hikers
to avoid higher elevation trails during the spring
mud season (late March through the end of May).
Snow melt creates extremely muddy trails and makes
them vulnerable to damage from foot traffic, which
is often compounded when hikers walk beside the
trail to avoid the mud.

SPRING AND FALL HIKING GUIDELINES

- If a trail is so muddy that you need to walk on
  the vegetation beside it, turn back, and seek an
  alternative area to hike.

- Hike in the hardwood forest at lower elevations.

- The State of Vermont closes trails in the Camel's
  Hump and Mt. Mansfield areas from mid-April
  until Memorial Day
  weekend. Please do not
  hike here. Also avoid
  Stratton Mtn., the
  Coolidge Range
  (Killington to Pico
  Peaks), Lincoln Ridge (Lincoln
  Gap to Appalachian Gap),
  and Jay Peak.

- Late fall and winter thaws
  can present similar conditions.

The lodge sits on a steep hillside overlooking shallow Skylight Pond, which is not suitable for fishing or swimming. Water is available from a spring 250 ft. north of the shelter. The area around the pond is sensitive to resource damage. A caretaker is in residence during the hiking season to assist and educate hikers, help maintain trails and campsites, and compost sewage to protect water quality. A fee is charged for overnight use of the shelter. Tenting is not allowed in the vicinity of the pond, but there is an established tenting area just south of Battell Mtn. on the Long Trail. Wood fires are not allowed within 500 ft. of the pond to permit the surrounding forest to recover from years of tree and branch cutting by campers. **Boyce Shelter to Skyline Lodge, 2.1 mi., 3.4 km., 1½ hr. (SB 1¼ hr.).**

From the junction, follow the ridge north and begin a steep ascent to the top of the ridge on **Bread Loaf Mtn. (16.2 mi.).** At a sharp turn to the right, a spur leads west, 0.1 mi. to a western vista just beyond the summit of the mountain. Follow the rugged path downhill to cross a brook just before reaching **Emily Proctor Shelter** and the **Emily Proctor Trail (16.8 mi.),** which descends 3.5 mi. west to USFS Road 201 out of South Lincoln.

Emily Proctor Shelter, a log lean-to with space for 5, was built by the Long Trail Patrol in 1960 and rebuilt by the U.S. Forest Service in 1983. The shelter was rebuilt by the Long Trail Patrol to replace rotten logs in 2002. The brook crossed by the Long Trail just south of the shelter provides water and may be the most reliable water source on the Long Trail in the Breadloaf Wilderness. There are two tent platforms and a privy on spurs north of the shelter. **Skyline Lodge to Emily Proctor Shelter, 1.9 mi., 3.1 km., 1¾ hr. (SB 1¼ hr.).**

Turn sharp right at the north end of the shelter, enter the woods, and ascend steadily to the ridge. Continue along the crest to **Mt. Wilson (17.7 mi.)** where a short spur leads east to a summit vista with views to the south and east. Leave the summit and descend steadily to a sag between Mt. Wilson and Mt. Roosevelt, and then continue to a junction with the **Clark Brook Trail (18.5 mi.).** This trail leads east downhill 3.0 mi. to USFS Road 55.

7

From the trail junction, ascend Mt. Roosevelt (18.9 mi.); just beyond is a rock outcrop, Killington View, with sweeping views to the south and east. From here descend, then traverse a series of knobs along the northeast ridge of Mt. Roosevelt before dropping to a sag and crossing a small seep. Reach wooded **Little Hans Peak (20.3 mi.)** before dropping steadily and then climbing to the wooded summit of **Mt. Cleveland (22.0 mi.)**. Descend gradually to a sharp right turn, and then drop steeply to the junction with the **Cooley Glen Trail (22.5 mi.)**, which leads 3.2 mi. west to USFS Road 201 where it shares a trailhead with the Emily Proctor Trail. **Cooley Glen Shelter** is a short distance further north on the Long Trail.

A frame lean-to with room for eight, Cooley Glen Shelter was built by the U.S. Forest Service in 1965. A spring is located 600 ft. west on the Cooley Glen Trail. **Emily Proctor Shelter to Cooley Glen Shelter, 5.7 mi., 9.2 km., 3¾ hr. (SB 3¾ hr.).**

Side Trails

Sucker Brook Trail. This trailhead is at the end of USFS Road 67 (Brooks Road) 3.8 mi. south of Vt. 125. USFS Road 67 starts 3.5 mi. east of Ripton or 0.5 mi. east of Middlebury College's Bread Loaf Campus, and 8.5 mi. west of Vt. 100 in Hancock or 2.1 mi. west of the LT crossing in Middlebury Gap. The road may be gated near its beginning during spring and fall mud seasons. There is parking for several cars at a USFS primitive campsite at the end of the road where the trail begins. Follow old logging roads west, and ascend gently, then more steadily, to Sucker Brook Shelter (0.9 mi.). Beyond the shelter, climb to the Long Trail junction. **USFS Road 67 to Long Trail, 1.0 mi., 1.6 km., ¾ hr. (Rev. ½ hr.).**

Silent Cliff Trail. This spur leaves the Long Trail 0.4 mi. north of Middlebury Gap and leads east 0.4 mi. to Silent Cave and Silent Cliff. Monastery Gap and the Green Mountains beyond are visible to the south from the cliff. **Long Trail to Silent Cliff, 0.4 mi., 0.6 km., ¼ hr. (Rev. ¼ hr.).**

Burnt Hill Trail. This trail begins on the east side of USFS Road 59, 1.1 mi. north of Vt. 125. USFS Road 59 (Steam Hill

Road) is 2.7 mi. east of Ripton and 0.2 mi. west of Bread Loaf Campus. There is a small grassy parking lot just off the road at the trailhead. Follow an old woods road where the trail coincides with the Norske Ski Trail. At an intersection (0.7 mi.) at the crest of a rise, turn left and ascend on an old logging road, where the Norske Trail descends straight ahead. Enter the Breadloaf Wilderness (1.0 mi.) and climb steadily to the Long Trail. **USFS Road 59 to Long Trail, 2.2 mi., 3.5 km., 1¾ hr. (Rev. 1 hr.).**

SKYLIGHT POND TRAIL. This trail starts at a primitive campsite on the east side of USFS Road 59, 3.6 mi. north of Vt. 125. Refer to directions for the Burnt Hill Trail. There is a large gravel parking lot at the trailhead. USFS Road 59 is not plowed north of the Burnt Hill Trail in winter. From the parking lot (0.0 mi.) which is also a primitive campsite, ascend gently on an old woods road and cross two small streams (the upper crossing over a bridge), before entering Breadloaf Wilderness (0.4 mi.). Continue uphill on long, sweeping switchbacks, ascending moderately to the Long Trail (2.5 mi.), 0.1 mi. west of Skyline Lodge. Continue down the east side of the ridge 0.1 mi. to Skyline Lodge at Skylight Pond. **USFS Road 59 to Skylight Pond, 2.6 mi., 4.2 km., 2 hr. (Rev. 1¾ hr.).**

EMILY PROCTOR TRAIL. This trailhead, shared with the Cooley Glen Trail, is reached via USFS Roads 54 and 201. From the north, follow USFS Road 54 (South Lincoln Road) south off the Lincoln Gap Road, 1.2 mi. east of Lincoln and 3.5 mi. west of the LT crossing in Lincoln Gap. Continue through South Lincoln, then bear left onto USFS Road 201, 4.2 mi. from the Lincoln Gap Road. Follow USFS Road 201 east 0.3 mi. to the trailhead and a USFS primitive campsite where there is parking at a turn-around. From the south, follow USFS Road 59 north either from Ripton or near Middlebury College's Breadloaf Campus (refer to directions for the Burnt Hill Trail). From USFS Road 59 take USFS Road 54 north to USFS Road 201. USFS Road 201 is not maintained in winter. The Emily Proctor Trail and the Cooley Glen Trail share this trailhead.

From the trailhead (0.0 mi.), turn right and ascend on a logging road, cross the edge of a clear-cut, and follow an older woods road, entering Breadloaf Wilderness (0.6 mi.). Leave the old road (1.4 mi.), and stay on the west side of the New Haven River, before crossing it on some large rocks. After crossing two small streams, make a steady, rocky ascent to the clearing in front of Emily Proctor Shelter (3.5 mi.) at the Long Trail. **USFS Road 201 to Long Trail, 3.5 mi., 5.6 km., 2¾ hr. (Rev. 1¾ hr.).**

CLARK BROOK TRAIL. From Vt. 100 at the north end of Granville take USFS Road 55 (West Hill Road) west. At a gated road (0.5 mi.), bear left and continue on USFS Road 55. Follow this road 1.3 mi., ignoring three right-hand turns, before reaching the trailhead shortly after a sharp left turn over a bridge above Clark Brook. There is roadside parking adjacent to a USFS primitive campsite. USFS Road 55 is not plowed in winter. Leave the road (0.0 mi.) and ascend gently along Clark Brook, crossing it twice, and then enter Breadloaf Wilderness (1.1 mi.). After a brook crossing (2.5 mi.), the ascent becomes steeper and rockier before reaching the Long Trail (3.0 mi.). **USFS 55 to Long Trail, 3.0 mi., 4.8 km., 2¾ hr. (Rev. 1½ hr.).**

COOLEY GLEN TRAIL. This trail shares a trailhead with the Emily Proctor Trail. Refer to directions for the Emily Proctor Trail. From the turn-around (0.0 mi.), follow the extension of USFS Road 201 to a bridge crossing of the New Haven River (0.4 mi.). Pass through a clearing, and then stay on the north bank of the river. Enter the Breadloaf Wilderness (1.6 mi.) shortly after a brook crossing. Ascend the west flank of Mt. Cleveland and, after passing a spring (3.1 mi.) that provides water for Cooley Glen Shelter, reach the Long Trail (3.2 mi.) in Cooley Glen just south of the shelter. **USFS Road 201 to Long Trail, 3.2 mi., 5.1 km., 2½ hr. (Rev. 1¾ hr.).**

DIVISION 8

Cooley Glen to
Birch Glen

DIVISION 8 PROFILE

Elevation (in feet)

Distance (in miles)

COOLEY GLEN SHELTER
MT. GRANT
LINCOLN GAP
MT. ABRAHAM
MT. ELLEN
APPALACHIAN GAP
MOLLY STARK MTN.
BEANE TRAIL

Cooley Glen to Birch Glen

miles north- bound	▲ NORTH	elevation at Long Trail (feet/meters)	miles south- bound
18.9	**Beane Trail** to **Birch Glen Camp** 100 ft W, to Carse Road, 1.5 mi W	2020/616	0.0
17.6	**Molly Stark's Balcony**	2900/884	1.3
16.7	**Baby Stark Mtn.**, east slope	2807/856	2.2
16.3	**Vt. 17** at **Appalachian Gap**	2377/725	2.6
14.5	**Theron Dean Shelter**; 25 ft W via spur	3320/1012	4.4
13.8	**Stark's Nest**, Mad River Glen single chairlift station	3644/1111	5.1
13.2	**General Stark Mtn.**, highest summit	3662/1117	5.7
12.9	**Barton Trail** to **Glen Ellen Lodge** (3250 ft/991 m) 0.3 mi E	3430/1046	6.0
12.8	**Jerusalem Trail** to Jim Dwire Road, 2.4 mi W	3430/1046	6.1
11.4	**Green Mountain National Forest** north boundary	3800/1159	7.5
11.0	**Mt. Ellen**, Sugarbush Mt. Ellen upper chairlift	4083/1245	7.9
9.4	**Castlerock chairlift**	3750/1144	9.5
8.1	**Lincoln Peak**	3975/1212	10.8
7.3	**Mt. Abraham**	4006/1222	11.6
6.5	**Battell Shelter**	3240/988	12.4
6.4	**Battell Trail** to USFS Road 350, 2.0 mi W	3220/982	12.5
4.7	**Lincoln Gap Road** at **Lincoln Gap**	2424/739	14.2
3.6	**Sunset Ledge**	2811/857	15.3
0.8	**Mt. Grant**	3623/1105	18.1
0.0	**Cooley Glen Trail** 3.2 mi W to **USFS Road 201, Cooley Glen Shelter**	3130/954	18.9

SOUTH
▼

Division 8
Cooley Glen to Birch Glen

Massachusetts: 146.3 miles   *Canada: 126.4 miles*

This division's Long Trail remains on or near the ridgeline. Water is scarce and hikers should take advantage of sources noted in the text. It also crosses Mt. Abraham, one of three summits along the route with alpine plants. Please take care to do the "rock walk" and tread only on the rocks, not the plants.

From Cooley Glen to Lincoln Gap this division's Long Trail traverses the Breadloaf Wilderness. Refer to wilderness information on page 7.

The Long Trail from Lincoln Gap north to the Winooski River is called the Monroe Skyline in honor of Prof. Will S. Monroe who led the building of this section of the trail.

Mad River Glen Ski Area has generously allowed hikers to use Stark's Nest, their ski patrol warming hut; this use depends on respect for the facility, and its status is subject to change.

Suggested Hikes

Molly Stark's Balcony. This hike follows the Long Trail north from Appalachian Gap to a lookout with views to the north. Round trip, 2.6 mi., 2 hr.

Mt. Ellen. South on the Long Trail from Appalachian Gap, this wooded summit features views from its upper slopes. Round trip, 10.6 mi., 6½ hr. A shorter trip to Mt. Ellen uses the Jerusalem Trail and the Long Trail south. Round trip, 8.4 mi., 5½ hr.

Camping and Fires

This division's Long Trail crosses the Green Mountain National Forest from Cooley Glen to the forest boundary north of Mt. Ellen. Primitive off-trail camping with small wood fires is allowed.

Note: Wood fires are prohibited within 500 ft. of Battell Shelter to protect this site's high-elevation spruce-fir forest. Camping and wood fires are prohibited on the summit of Mt. Abraham to protect the alpine plant community.

North of Mt. Ellen the LT crosses state and private land. Camping is limited to shelters. Wood fires are prohibited at Glen Ellen Lodge and Theron Dean Shelter due to their sensitive, high-elevation nature. Small wood fires, although discouraged, are permitted at Birch Glen Camp.

Refer to Leave No Trace principles (pages 9 to 11) to minimize your impact.

Group Use

Groups hiking this division's Long Trail south of Mt. Ellen may need an Outfitter-Guide Permit from the Green Mountain National Forest. Groups hiking this division's Long Trail north of Stark's Nest may need a Commercial Use Permit from the Vermont Department of Forests, Parks, and Recreation. Groups can stay at Stark's Nest if available. Group tenting space is available at Cooley Glen Shelter and Birch Glen Camp. Primitive campsites are also available at the trailhead for the Cooley Glen Trail. Refer to group use guidelines (pages 11 to 17) to determine your need for a permit and to minimize your group's impact.

WINTER USE

The suggested hikes for the north end of this division make challenging snowshoe treks. The summit of Mt. Abraham is more readily accessible from the Battell Trail to the west than the Long Trail because the upper portions of the Lincoln Gap Road leading to the LT are not maintained in winter. Although the Long Trail crosses the Catamount Trail at Lincoln Gap, the rugged terrain the LT traverses is not suitable for beginner or intermediate cross-country skiers. See Catamount Trail information on page 26

ACCESS TO LONG TRAIL

LINCOLN GAP ROAD AT LINCOLN GAP. The Long Trail crosses this steep, winding road at Lincoln Gap, 4.7 mi. east of Lincoln, and 10.0 mi. east of its junction with Vt. 17 and 116 in Bristol. The crossing is also 4.7 mi. west of Vt. 100 in Warren. There is roadside parking at the crossing and a large secondary parking lot just east of the Trail on the road's south side. This trailhead is heavily used during the hiking season, however, long-term parking is not recommended. The road through Lincoln Gap is closed during winter.

VT. 17 AT APPALACHIAN GAP. The Long Trail intersects this highway at Appalachian Gap, 1.4 mi. west of Mad River Glen Ski Area, 6.0 mi. west of Vt. 100 in Irasville, and 9.5 mi. east of Vt. 116. There is a large parking lot on the north side of the road just west of the Long Trail. Vt. 17 is open year-round, subject to winter weather conditions.

LONG TRAIL DESCRIPTION

From **Cooley Glen Shelter (0.0 mi.)** to Lincoln Gap, the Long Trail traverses the Breadloaf Wilderness, where it may be more challenging to follow due to minimal brushing and blazing. Ascend northwest to the summit of **Mt. Grant (0.8 mi.)**, where there is a broad view south into the heart of the

Breadloaf Wilderness. From the summit, descend steadily along the ridge through a hardwood forest before following a series of switchbacks downhill to a sag (2.9 mi.). Climb out of the sag, cross some open areas and ledges with views to the south and east, then traverse a short ridge and drop down to another sag. After ascending to a smaller open area with views to the south, arrive at **Sunset Ledge (3.6 mi.)**, which has an expansive western vista. Continue along the ridge to Eastwood's Rise (4.3 mi.), then drop steeply to the north boundary of the Breadloaf Wilderness and cross Lincoln Gap Road at **Lincoln Gap (4.7 mi.)**.

Climb north out of Lincoln Gap, bear to the west of a knoll and begin a steady ascent, passing en route the "Carpenters" (5.9 mi.), two huge boulders named after a pair of trail workers. Soon after crossing a brook, reach a junction where the **Battell Trail (6.4 mi.)** descends west 2.0 mi. to USFS Road 350. Turn right and climb to **Battell Shelter (6.5 mi.)**. This shelter, a frame structure built by Farm and Wilderness Camp volunteers in 1967, sleeps eight. Water is from a small spring 100 ft. to the east. A caretaker may be in seasonal residence during the hiking season to help protect the alpine plants on Mt. Abraham, assist and educate hikers, help maintain trails and campsites, and compost sewage to protect water quality. A fee is charged for overnight use. Wood fires are not allowed within 500 ft. of this high-elevation site. Tenting near Battell Shelter is very limited. **Cooley Glen Shelter to Battell Shelter, 6.5 mi., 10.5 km., 4¼ hr. (SB 4¼ hr.).**

Bear north from the shelter and follow an old road for the initially gradual, then steep, ascent of Mt. Abraham. Scramble up bare ledge in places; extra care should be used in wet weather. The alpine summit of **Mt. Abraham (7.3 mi.)**, the south peak of Lincoln Mtn., offers one of the best panoramas on the entire Long Trail, ranging from nearby valley farms to New Hampshire's White Mountains, 80 miles east. Due west is Mt. Marcy and its Adirondack neighbors. To the south the Green Mountains may be visible as far south as Killington Peak. To the north, though partly hidden by nearby higher peaks, the "Greens" may be visible as far as Belvidere Mtn.

The summit of this mountain is above treeline and supports a small community of alpine vegetation, one of only three such communities along the Long Trail. These plants do not tolerate foot traffic; they have been damaged by hikers straying from the trail. *Note:* Above treeline, take care to walk only on the rocks, not the fragile alpine plants. Please leash dogs. Camping and wood fires are prohibited on the summit of Mt. Abraham.

Enter the woods and cross a sag, and ascend Little Abe (8.0 mi.), a minor summit, just beyond which is **Lincoln Peak (8.1 mi.)**. A spur leads east to an observation platform just off the trail. Built by Sugarbush Valley Resort and the U.S. Forest Service, it offers wide views.

Enter a ski trail clearing, and bear left to reenter the woods and head north, following the wooded ridge of Lincoln Mtn. After passing over Nancy Hanks Peak (8.7 mi.), continue along the ridge to the upper station of the **Castlerock chairlift (9.4 mi.)**. Turn left and pass behind the lift station, following a ski trail to Holt Hollow (9.5 mi.), where water may be found on a spur leading 200 ft. west.

Follow the skyline, and gradually ascend to Cutts Peak (10.6 mi.), where there are views. From this point it is easy going to the wooded summit of **Mt. Ellen (11.0 mi.)**, which is tied with Camel's Hump as the third-highest mountains in Vermont (4,083 ft.). Leave the summit and enter a clearing at the upper station of the Sugarbush North summit chairlift. Follow a ski trail downhill for 150 ft. before turning left to reenter the woods. Descend, steeply at first, and then more moderately, to the north boundary of the **Green Mountain National Forest (11.4 mi.)**. Wind back and forth across the ridge, passing several limited lookouts, before reaching a junction with the **Jerusalem Trail (12.8 mi.)**, which descends 2.4 mi. west to the Jim Dwire Road.

Just beyond the junction pass a spur leading west 50 ft. to Orvis Lookout, and then reach the **Barton Trail (12.9 mi.)**, which leads east 0.3 mi. downhill to **Glen Ellen Lodge**. Built by the Long Trail Patrol in 1933, the lodge is of log construction with bunks for eight. Water sources for the lodge include an unreliable spring located to the west of the Long Trail near the junction of the Barton Trail. A second intermittent water source is a brook that may be found by following the contour south beyond the lodge's composting outhouse. Wood fires are prohibited at the lodge. There are views to the east from Glen Ellen Lodge. Beyond the Mad River Valley are the Northfield Mountains, the Granite Mountains, and, on the horizon, several ridges of the White Mountains. **Battell Shelter to Glen Ellen Lodge, 6.7 mi., 10.8 km., 4 hr. (SB 4 hr.).**

The small clearing to the west of the trail junction is the site of the original Glen Ellen Lodge. From the Barton Trail junction, climb steadily to the ridge of General Stark Mtn. After passing **General Stark's highest summit (13.2 mi.)**, continue along the ridge and then join a ski trail, following it for 600 ft. to the north peak and **Stark's Nest (13.8 mi.)**, Mad River Glen Ski Area's summit warming hut and single chairlift station. Camping may be allowed here. *Wood fires are prohibited*. There are views to the east and limited views of Lake Champlain and the Adirondacks to the west.

Pass to the west of the summit building and enter Camel's Hump State Forest, following a ski trail, then reenter the woods to the left. Rejoin the ski trail, and then cut back into the woods again, before continuing along the ridge and then descending steeply, using a ladder at one point (14.3 mi.), to a **spur** leading west 25 ft. to **Theron Dean Shelter (14.5 mi.)**.

This small log shelter, with space for 5, was built by the Long Trail Patrol in 1966. It is named for Theron Dean, an energetic promoter of the GMC in its early years and a close friend

---

DISPOSE OF WASTE PROPERLY

If you packed it in, pack it out; please pick up trash others have left behind. When provided, use toilets, otherwise, bury human and pet waste in a six-inch deep hole at least 200 feet from water sources and pack out toilet paper and sanitary products.

---

of Prof. Monroe. The sole water source is a small, unreliable spring to the west of the shelter. Wood fires are prohibited at Theron Dean Shelter. **Glen Ellen Lodge to Theron Dean Shelter, 1.9 mi., 3.1 km., 1¾ hr. (SB 1¼ hr.).**

From the shelter, the spur leads back to the LT, while an alternate route leads straight ahead to Dean Panorama where there is a view north. This trail then drops and switchbacks to the right, passing through Dean Cave, before rejoining the Long Trail 150 ft. north of the shelter.

Continue the steep descent, passing the upper station of another chairlift (14.7 mi.), and then leveling out along the ridge. Drop sharply once again, pass a vista to the north, cross over a knoll, and then descend to cross **Vt. 17 at Appalachian Gap (16.3 mi.).** There is a parking lot west of the LT at the summit of the highway with a fine western vista. At "App" Gap, the Long Trail enters Camel's Hump State Park and passes in and out of it until entering it on Mts. Ira and Ethan Allen for the remainder of the route north over Camel's Hump to Duxbury Road.

At Appalachian Gap turn right and follow the highway east for 100 ft. Climb the north embankment of the road into the woods, pass a spur (16.4 mi.) to the Mad River Glen Lookout, and reach the trail's height-of-land on the **east slope** of **Baby Stark Mtn. (16.7 mi.).** Drop to a brook (16.9 mi.), and then ascend to the ridgeline. Pass over Molly Stark Mtn, (17.3 mi.) and continue to **Molly Stark's Balcony (17.6 mi.)** where there is a view of Camel's Hump, with the Worcester Range standing out to the northeast. Follow a circuitous route around the cliff below the Balcony, and descend moderately, passing west of Beane Mtn., to the **Beane Trail (18.9 mi.),** which leads west 100 ft. to **Birch Glen Camp** and 1.5 mi. to Carse Road.

This log structure was built by GMC volunteers in 1930, and renovated by the Long Trail Patrol in 1999. The renovation is dedicated to the memory of Marc von Trapp, an avid hiker. It has an open front "living room" and semi-enclosed sleeping quarters with bunk space for twelve. The water source is the brook 100 ft. south. **Theron Dean Shelter to Birch Glen Camp, 4.4 mi., 7.1 km., 2¾ hr. (SB 3¼ hr.).**

8

SIDE TRAILS

BATTELL TRAIL. From Lincoln turn north off the Lincoln Gap Road onto Quaker Street by the general store. At 0.7 mi. turn right onto USFS Road 350 (Elder Hill Rd.). Follow this road (with signs to the trail) 1.9 mi. to a left turn, which continues 0.1 mi. to the Battell Trail and a small parking lot. The final 0.1 mi. is not maintained in the winter.

From the road (0.0 mi.), climb steadily through a sugarbush for almost a mile. After crossing two small streams and an old woods road (1.0 mi.), and then another woods road (1.2 mi.), arrive at the Long Trail (2.0 mi.) just south of Battell Shelter. **USFS Road 350 to Long Trail, 2.0 mi., 3.2 km., 2 hr. (Rev. 1 hr).**

JERUSALEM TRAIL. Take the east branch of the Jerusalem Road south from Vt. 17, 6.0 mi. west of the Long Trail at Appalachian Gap and 3.5 mi. east of Vt. 116. Follow this road 1.2 mi. south and turn left onto Jim Dwire Road and follow it 0.5 mi. to the trailhead on the right. Roadside parking space is limited.

From the road (0.0 mi.), ascend easily through open hardwoods on old woods roads, cross a logging road, and then climb steeply to the Long Trail (2.4 mi.), south of the Barton Trail. Please note that much of the Jerusalem Trail crosses private land, thanks to the generosity of the landowner. **Jim Dwire Road to Long Trail, 2.4 mi., 3.9 km., 2¼ hr. (Rev. 1¼ hr.).**

BEANE TRAIL. Take Gore Road north from Vt. 17, 2.7 mi. west of the Long Trail at Appalachian Gap and 7.0 mi. east of Vt. 116. Follow this road 2.9 mi. and then take Carse Road east across a bridge, and at 0.5 mi., bear right, and then immediately left. At 1.1 mi. there is parking on the north side of the road at a large bend before the farmhouse of the old Beane Farm.

From the gate (0.0 mi.), follow a grassy road before turning right (0.4 mi.) to leave the road and climb into the woods. Continue uphill and cross two brooks before reaching Birch Glen Camp (1.4 mi.), 100 ft. from the Long Trail junction. **Carse Road to Long Trail, 1.5 mi., 2.4 km., 1¼ hr. (Rev. ¾ hr.).**

DIVISION 9

Birch Glen to
Bolton Mountain

DIVISION 9 PROFILE

Elevation (in feet): 4000, 3000, 2000, 1000

Distance (in miles): 0, 5, 10, 15, 20, 25, 30

BEANE TRAIL
HUNTINGTON GAP
BURNT ROCK MTN.
MT. ETHAN ALLEN
WIND GAP
CAMEL'S HUMP
DUXBURY ROAD
JONESVILLE BRIDGE
HARRINGTON'S VIEW
BOLTON MTN.

Birch Glen to Bolton Mountain

miles northbound	▲ NORTH	elevation at Long Trail (feet/meters)	miles southbound
30.3	**Bolton Mtn.**	3725/1136	0.0
27.6	**Harrington's View**, 150 ft E via spur	2585/788	2.7
26.6	**Buchanan Shelter**, (2180 ft/664 m), 0.3 mi E via spur	2310/704	3.7
24.3	**Bolton Notch Road**	1120/341	6.0
21.0	**Duck Brook Shelter**	670/204	9.3
19.3	**Winooski River bridge**; U.S. 2 in Jonesville	326/99	11.0
16.1	**Duxbury Road**	400/122	14.2
15.5	**Gleason Brook bridge**	580/177	14.8
13.4	**Bamforth Ridge Shelter**, 0.2 mi E via spur	1900/579	16.9
11.0	**Alpine Trail** (5) north end	2800/853	19.3
10.6	**Gorham Spring**	3400/1037	19.7
10.2	**Camel's Hump Hut Clearing**; **Burrows Trail** (6) to Camel's Hump Road, 2.1 mi W; **Monroe Trail** (7) to Couching Lion parking lot, 3.1 mi E	3800/1159	20.1
9.9	**Camel's Hump**	4083/1245	20.4
9.7	**Alpine Trail** (5), south end to **Long Trail** north of summit, 1.7 mi E	3800/1159	20.6
8.2	**Wind Gap**; **Allis Trail** (2) north end; **Deane Trail** (4) to **Hump Brook Tenting Area** (2420 ft/738 m), 0.8 mi E; to Couching Lion parking lot via **Monroe Trail** (7), 2.3 mi E	2800/853	22.1
8.0	**Forest City Trail** (3) to Camel's Hump Road, 2.2 mi W	2660/811	22.3
8.0	**Montclair Glen Lodge**	2670/814	22.3
7.8	**Allis Trail** (2), south end to **Long Trail** at Wind Gap, 0.3 mi N	2890/881	22.5
7.0	**Mt. Ethan Allen**, north peak	3680/1122	23.3
4.4	**Burnt Rock Mtn.**	3168/966	25.9
3.8	**Hedgehog Brook Trail** (1) to Big Basin Road, 2.0 mi E	2800/853	26.5
2.9	**Cowles Cove Shelter**	2520/768	27.4
1.5	**Huntington Gap**	2217/676	28.8
0.0	**Beane Trail** to **Birch Glen Camp**, 100 ft W; to Carse Road, 1.5 mi W	2020/616	30.3

SOUTH
▼

DIVISION 9
Birch Glen to Bolton Mountain

Massachusetts: 165.2 miles   *Canada: 107.5 miles*

T his division's Long Trail crosses Camel's Hump, the state's highest undeveloped mountain. It is one of three summits on the Long Trail with alpine vegetation. Please take care to do the "rock walk" and tread only on the rocks, not the plants. See page 154 for information about Camel's Hump.

Backpacking groups camping on Camel's Hump should use Hump Brook Tenting Area to reduce impact at the mountain's heavily used shelter sites.

From Lincoln Gap to the Winooski River, the Long Trail is called the Monroe Skyline in honor of Prof. Will S. Monroe who led the effort to build this section of the Trail. GMC is trying to relocate the Long Trail across the Winooski River Valley to reduce road walking, but to date has been unable to secure certain landowners permissions. Side trails in the division are numbered to correspond with both the division map (page 148) and Camel's Hump map (page 155).

SUGGESTED HIKES

MT. ETHAN ALLEN. This moderate ascent from Huntington reaches the north peak of Mt. Ethan Allen via the Forest City and Long Trails. It offers a less crowded summit with views. Round trip, 6.4 mi., 4¼ hr.

DUXBURY WINDOW. This steady climb out of the Winooski River valley provides a vista of the south face of Bolton Mountain. Round trip from Duxbury Road, 3.2 mi., 2½ hr.

HARRINGTON'S VIEW. This ascent north on the Long Trail from Bolton Notch Road leads to a blocky ledge with views of Bolton Mtn. Round trip, 6.6 mi., 3¾ hr.

CAMPING AND FIRES

This division's Long Trail south of the Winooski River primarily traverses Camel's Hump State Park. Primitive off-trail camping with small wood fires below 2500 ft. is allowed.

Tenting at Cowles Cove and Montclair Glen is permitted only if the shelter is filled to capacity. Small wood fires, although discouraged, are permitted in established fire rings at Birch Glen and at Hump Brook Tenting Area.

North of the Winooski River the Trail crosses both state land and private property. Camping is allowed only at shelters. Small wood fires, although discouraged, are permitted at the shelters' established fire rings.

Note: Fires are prohibited at Cowles Cove Shelter, Montclair Glen Lodge, and Bamforth Ridge Shelter to protect the vulnerable vegetation at these sites. Camping and wood fires at the hut clearing and above timberline on Camel's Hump are illegal, and violators are subject to fine by the State of Vermont.

Refer to Leave No Trace principles (pages 9 to 11) to minimize your impact.

PROTECT CAMEL'S HUMP'S ALPINE PLANTS. DO THE ROCK WALK!

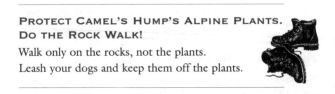

Walk only on the rocks, not the plants.

Leash your dogs and keep them off the plants.

GROUP USE

Groups hiking this division's Long Trail may need a Commercial Use Permit from the Vermont Department of Forests, Parks & Recreation. Group tenting space is available at Birch Glen Camp; Hump Brook Tenting Area; and Bamforth Ridge, Duck Brook, and Buchanan Shelters. Little River State Park Campground, east of the Long Trail off U.S. 2, is available for base camp hiking. Refer to group use guidelines (pages 11 to 17) to determine your need for a permit and to minimize your group's impact.

WINTER USE

Camel's Hump is a challenging winter ascent. Its lower slopes, particularly on the east side with open hardwood forest, are popular with skilled backcountry skiers. Both skiers and winter hikers should maintain a comfortable distance from each other: skiers should recognize the trails exist for hikers, and hikers should recognize that backcountry skiers may be descending the mountain. The Long Trail crosses the Catamount Trail at Huntington Gap.

ACCESS TO LONG TRAIL

U.S. 2. The Long Trail crosses this highway in Jonesville next to the post office opposite the bridge over the Winooski River, 3.5 mi. east of Richmond and 9.5 mi. west of Vt. 100 in Waterbury. There is limited parking opposite the post office by the railroad tracks.

DUXBURY ROAD. *Western approach:* From Jonesville, follow Cochran Road south from U.S. 2 and cross the bridge over the Winooski River (0.0 mi.). Turn left onto Duxbury Road and proceed east, passing the Honey Hollow parking lot (formerly the Long Trail lot from 1986 to 1995) across from a field at 2.1 mi., to the Long Trail parking lot (3.2 mi.) in the woods on the south side of the road.

Eastern approach: From the junction of U.S. 2 and Vt. 100 in Waterbury, follow U.S. 2 east, take the first right on Winooski Street, cross the bridge over the river (0.0 mi.), and follow River Road, which becomes Duxbury Road in Bolton, west to the Long Trail parking lot (6.5 mi.).

BOLTON NOTCH ROAD. From Jonesville, follow U.S. 2 east 1.0 mi. and turn north (left) on Bolton Notch Road. The Long Trail crossing is 2.7 mi. north of U.S. 2. From the road, the trail can be difficult to find; on the east side of Bolton Notch Road it coincides with an abandoned road that splits off from the start of a driveway. There is limited parking on the east side of the road.

CAMEL'S HUMP AREA

The summit profile of Camel's Hump makes it one of the most distinctive peaks in the Green Mountains. It is tied with Mt. Ellen (4,083 ft.) as Vermont's third highest mountain.

The Waubawakee called Camel's Hump the Tawabodi-e-wadso, meaning "the mountain that is like a seat," and Samuel de Champlain's explorers named it *le lion couchant*, translated "the couching lion" or, in more contemporary language, "the sleeping lion." Either name is more descriptive of the mountain's profile seen from the east or west than is Camel's Hump, a name amended by Zadock Thompson in 1830 from the less genteel "Camel's Rump" listed on Ira Allen's 1798 map.

Camel's Hump is the only undeveloped peak over 4,000 ft. elevation in Vermont. State land acquisition began in 1911 with a gift of 1,000 acres, including the summit, from Col. Joseph Battell of Middlebury, Vt. The present size of Camel's Hump State Park is nearly 24,000 acres. In 1965 the summit area was designated a State Natural Area; in 1968 it was designated a National Natural Landmark; and in 1969 the Vermont General Assembly expanded this protected zone, making the mountain itself the focal point of Camel's Hump Forest Reserve.

Camel's Hump is one of three high summits that supports communities of rare alpine vegetation along the Long Trail. Several of the flowers and grasses growing above treeline are listed on Vermont's endangered plant list. Although these

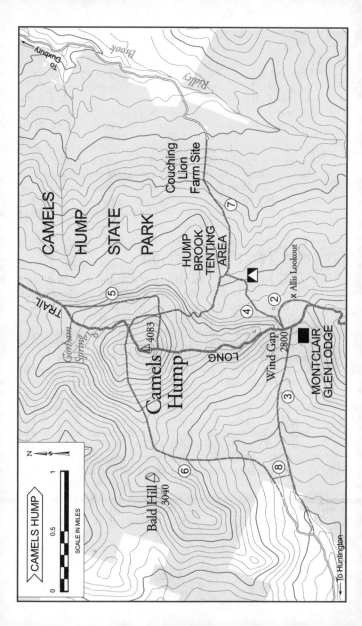

plants are hardy to the weather, they are extremely fragile to foot traffic. Please take special care to walk only on the rocks, not the plants. Above treeline, walk only on marked trails. Camping is not permitted in any of Vermont's alpine zones.

Camel's Hump is one of the most popular peaks in the Northeast. Each year over 15,000 people and hundreds of dogs visit the summit. Please leash your dog on the summit out of consideration for other visitors and to reduce impact to the alpine vegetation. GMC summit caretakers are on duty at or near the summit to assist hikers and teach about the fragile nature of the alpine area. The caretaker program on Camel's Hump is funded by the GMC and the Vermont Department of Forests, Parks, and Recreation.

Long Trail Description

Proceed north from the **Beane Trail junction (0.0 mi.)**, 100 ft. east of Birch Glen Camp, and contour around the north side of Beane Mtn., crossing two woods roads before reaching **Huntington Gap (1.5 mi.)**. Both a snowmobile trail and the Catamount Trail follow an abandoned road across the gap.

Climb northwest to the west side of the ridge, and then cross over **(2.0 mi.)** to slab the east slope through mature woods to **Cowles Cove Shelter (2.9 mi.)**. This log lean-to, with space for eight, is named for Judge Clarence Cowles of Burlington, a charter member of the GMC who helped build trails on Mt. Mansfield and the Monroe Skyline section of the Long Trail. The shelter was built by the New York Section under the direction of Prof. Roy O. Buchanan in 1956. The brook 100 ft. south on the Long Trail is a dependable water source. Wood fires are prohibited at Cowles Cove Shelter. The clearing near the brook was the site of the original Cowles Cove Shelter built in 1920. **Birch Glen Camp to Cowles Cove Shelter, 2.9 mi., 4.7 km., 1¾ hr. (SB 1½ hr.).**

From the shelter ascend gradually and, after gaining the crest of the ridge, reach the **Hedgehog Brook Trail (1) (3.8 mi.)**, which descends 2.0 mi. east to Big Basin Road (see map on page 148). Beyond the junction, the Long Trail becomes increasingly rugged. Continue to a spur (4.0 mi.) that leads west a short distance to a small glacial pothole, one of the highest of its kind in New England. Beyond the spur, emerge from the woods and begin an up-and-down scramble over bare rocks and cobbles to the summit of **Burnt Rock Mtn. (4.4 mi.)**. The summit provides views in nearly every direction. To the north are Mts. Ira and Ethan Allen and Camel's Hump, to the west lies Lake Champlain, to the east are the Northfield Mountains and Granite Mountains, and to the south stands Lincoln Mtn. Several other knobs lie north of the main summit.

Descend a ladder to drop into Ladder Ravine (4.8 mi.), and then commence a steady ascent along the "Paris Skidway," an old skid road (5.5 mi.). After some rough going reach a height-of-land on the east slope of Mt. Ira Allen (5.9 mi.) about 100 ft. below the summit, which is at the top of the cliff west of the Long Trail. Contour along the sidehill and slowly descend, passing Rock Refuge, a shallow cave in the rocks to the west of the Long Trail, one of many features named by Professor Monroe.

After more rough but relatively level scrambling, climb to the south peak of Mt. Ethan Allen (6.9 mi.) and, after a small dip, reach the **north peak of Mt. Ethan Allen (7.0 mi.)**, with a lookout facing east. Descend to a small rocky area (7.2 mi.) and drop through a birch glade to the south end of the **Allis Trail (2) (7.8 mi.)**.

At the junction, turn left, continuing downhill through more birch woods to **Montclair Glen Lodge (8.0 mi.)**, a log cabin with bunks for ten, built by the Long Trail Patrol for the New York Section in 1948. The water source is a brook 80 ft. north along the Long Trail. A GMC caretaker is in residence

9

TRAILHEAD PARKING

Please avoid obstructing traffic or blocking access to homes, farms, or woodlots. Park efficiently so others have a place to park. Remember to remove valuables from your car to minimize risk of theft and vandalism.

during the hiking season. A fee is charged for overnight use. Wood fires are prohibited at Montclair Glen Lodge. **Cowles Cove Shelter to Montclair Glen Lodge, 5.1 mi., 8.2 km., 3¼ hr. (SB 3¼ hr.).**

From the lodge, proceed north to the site of the original Montclair Glen Shelter, built in 1917, where the **Forest City Trail (3)** descends west 2.2 mi. to Huntington Center's Camel's Hump Road. Ascend north to **Wind Gap (8.2 mi.)**, where the north end of the **Allis Trail (2)** ascends to the east and, just beyond, the **Dean Trail (4)** descends east 0.8 mi. to **Hump Brook Tenting Area** and 2.3 mi. east to North Duxbury's Couching Lion parking lot via the Monroe Trail.

At Wind Gap the craggy cliffs of the mountain's south ridge loom above the trail. Turn west, then east, to steeply ascend the ridge. Break into the open and follow the east slope, with views of the beaver ponds alongside the Dean Trail below. Clamber over rocks and through thickets of spruce and balsam scrub, and reenter the woods.

Cross to the west side of the ridge and skirt two minor knobs with intermittent views. Climb steadily and steeply to the south end of the yellow-blazed **Alpine Trail (5) (9.7 mi.)** near treeline. This trail leads east 1.7 mi. to circle the mountain and rejoin the Long Trail north of the summit cone, and is a safer way around Camel's Hump in inclement weather. Above the Alpine Trail junction, bear west around the forbidding south wall of the summit cone, climb the exposed west face, and arrive at the summit of **Camel's Hump (9.9 mi.)** from the southwest.

The views from the summit are extensive and remarkable. To the south, the Green Mountains are visible to Killington Peak. To the north, Bamforth Ridge leads to the Winooski Valley. Beyond the valley Mt. Mansfield stands out, with the Sterling Range of the White Mountains and the Worcester Range to its right. Mt. Washington is a little south of east, dominating the White Mountains' Presidential Range. Mt. Marcy is somewhat south of west, surrounded by a contingent of Adirondack peaks, while Whiteface Mtn. stands alone to the north. Lake Champlain is visible for much of its length.

Descend north from the summit, skirting the exposed northwest slope before dropping down to the **Camel's Hump**

Hut Clearing (10.2 mi.). This was the site of a nineteenth-century rustic hotel (summit house), which failed financially and burned in 1875. The clearing was also the location for three metal huts managed by the Camel's Hump Club of Waterbury for hikers from 1912 until the early 1950s. Camping and wood fires are prohibited at the Hut Clearing. From the clearing, the **Burrows Trail (6)** descends west 2.1 mi. to Huntington Center's Camel's Hump Road, and the **Monroe Trail (7)** leads east 3.1 mi. to North Duxbury's Couching Lion parking area.

Reenter the woods at the north end of the clearing and descend steadily to a spur leading west a short distance to **Gorham Spring (10.6 mi.)** near the site of Gorham Lodge, which was removed in 2001. Camping and wood fires are not permitted here to allow the site to recover from fifty years of intensive use. Continue a gradual but rugged descent along Bamforth Ridge following the original Long Trail route developed by Prof. Will Monroe. The ridge is named in memory of dedicated trail maintainer and guidebook editor Eugene Bamforth.

North of the spring, drop to the first rocky opening along the ridge and reach the north end of the yellow-blazed **Alpine Trail (5) (11.0 mi.).** This side trail leads 1.7 mi. to the Long Trail south of the summit cone. Descend steeply over rocks and continue along the ridge, in and out of the woods with frequent views. Pass over several prominent knobs until reaching a **spur (13.4 mi.)** leading east 0.2 mi. to **Bamforth Ridge Shelter**. This cedar log lean-to was built by the Montpelier Section and other GMC volunteers in 2002, and has space for nine. The shelter is dedicated to the memory of section members David Morse and Harlan Farnsworth. There are tent platforms for group use and for campers who prefer to tent. There is a composting privy to protect water quality. Wood fires are prohibited at this site. The water source is the brook, which may fail during droughts, reached by a spur north from the shelter. **Montclair Glen Lodge to Bamforth Ridge Shelter, 5.6 mi., 9.0 km., 4 hr. (SB 4½ hr.)**

Follow the ridge north, passing an open ledge with a view south of Camel's Hump at the top of Spruce Knob (13.9 mi.). Drop steeply over "bannister ledge," passing under some prominent ledges, to Duxbury Window (14.5 mi.) with its tree-framed view of the Winooski Valley. From the window, steadily descend until reaching the former site of Buchanan Lodge (15.2 mi.), destroyed by fire in 1978, where it turns right to follow abandoned logging roads until descending to cross the **Gleason Brook bridge (15.5 mi.)**, built by the On Top School in 1994. Cross over a low ridge and descend to **Duxbury Road (16.1 mi.)** where there is a large parking lot. Turn left and follow the paved road along the Winooski River, then turn right (19.2 mi.) onto Cochran Road, and cross the **Winooski River bridge**, which was replaced in 2002. To the left, Cochran Road leads 4.0 mi. west to Richmond. Cross the New England Central Railway and U.S. 2, and enter Jonesville (19.3 mi.). **Bamforth Ridge Shelter to Jonesville, 6.1 mi., 9.8 km., 3¼ hr. (SB 4¾ hr.).**

Jonesville (326 ft.) is at the lowest elevation on the Long Trail. U.S. 2 leads west 0.3 mi. to the Jonesville Country Store. The Jonesville Post Office is located just west of the Long Trail on U.S. 2. Mail may be sent here in care of General Delivery, marked "Hold for Long Trail Hiker." See page 243 for more information.

From Jonesville, go north on the gravel-surfaced Stage Road. After passing beneath Interstate 89, climb toward a electric utility crossing. Just before the power lines, turn right off the road (19.8 mi.) and ascend the utility clearing. Bear north from the power lines (20.1 mi.), and climb to a lookout with fine local views of the Winooski Valley. Reenter the woods (20.5 mi.), following a rugged route uphill to a short spur leading south to **Duck Brook Shelter (21.0 mi.)**. This open-front frame shelter, with space for 12, was built by the Long Trail Patrol for the Burlington Section in 1966. Duck Brook, in a deep ravine below the shelter, is the water supply. **Bamforth Ridge Shelter to Duck Brook Shelter, 7.8 mi., 12.6 km., 4¼ hr. (SB 4¾ hr.).**

KNOW WHAT TIME THE SUN SETS! DON'T GET CAUGHT IN THE DARK.

From the shelter, follow an old woods road a short distance, cross a brook, and then turn sharp left, leaving the woods road. Hikers should follow the blazes carefully through this area. Proceed north and climb steadily, passing three lookouts and then descend first gradually, then steeply, before ascending to the top of a bedrock ridge. From the ridge, begin a gradual descent to a logging road (23.5 mi.), cross Duck Brook (24.0 mi.), and continue to the unpaved **Bolton Notch Road (24.3 mi.)**.

Cross the road and begin to ascend along a series of woods roads. Cross several unreliable small brooks, before reaching the top of Oxbow Ridge (25.2 mi.). Follow the ridge north, pass several lookouts to the east, then one to the west (25.5 mi.) that offers a view of Lake Champlain and the Adirondacks, and then yet another lookout (25.9 mi.) with views of Camel's Hump and the Adirondacks. From the lookout, reach the height-of-land along the ridge and, bearing east, arrive at a spur (26.0 mi.) that leads east 120 ft. to a lookout over Bolton Valley. Bear left, descend to cross a brook (26.5 mi.), and reach a **spur (26.6 mi.)**, sometimes easily missed due to recent logging activities, which descends east 0.3 mi. to Buchanan Shelter. This frame structure, built by the Burlington Section led by Basil Goodrich and Jack Lance in 1984, is named for Prof. Roy O. Buchanan, longtime leader of the Long Trail Patrol. It has an open-front porch and enclosed bunkroom with space for sixteen. Water is located 100 ft. to the north. **Duck Brook Shelter to Buchanan Shelter 5.9 mi., 9.5 km., 4 hr. (SB 3½ hr.).**

The steady ascent from Buchanan Shelter to Bolton Mtn. is characterized by numerous ups and downs. From the shelter spur, continue with minor changes in elevation to reach another **spur (27.6 mi.)** leading east 150 ft. to **Harrington's View**, named for its discoverer, Jack Harrington of the Burlington Section. It offers views of Mt. Mansfield, Bolton Mtn., Bolton Valley, and Ricker Mtn. After a short descent, continue east, cross a small brook (28.2 mi.), and make a zigzag ascent to a wooded, unnamed summit (3,236 ft.) (29.0 mi.) with a view south to Camel's Hump. Descend gradually to a saddle (29.7 mi.), then climb to the wooded summit of **Bolton Mtn. (30.3 mi.)**.

9

SIDE TRAILS

Refer to the Camel's Hump map (page 155) or the division map (page 148) for the location of numbered trails. All of Camel's Hump's side trails are marked with blue blazes, except for the yellow-blazed Alpine Trail.

1. HEDGEHOG BROOK TRAIL. This trail is located entirely on private land. Hikers are allowed to use the trail thanks to the generosity of the landowners. Please stay on the trail and respect all lands and buildings. Failure to do so could result in trail closure. The North Fayston Road leads west from Vt. 100, 4.5 mi. north of Vt. 17 in Waitsfield and 8.0 mi. south of U.S. 2 in Waterbury. Follow the North Fayston Road; at 2.5 mi. this road turns to dirt; at 4.0 mi. stay straight at a four-way offset intersection, continuing on Big Basin Road to the trailhead (5.0 mi.) at a heavy metal gate where a parking lot can accommodate ten cars.

The trail descends from the parking lot (0.0 mi.) to cross Hedgehog Brook over stepping stones. The trail then climbs the slope and contours north to a woods road (0.5 mi.). Turn left and follow the woods road uphill. Climb west steadily to the ridge and the Long Trail (2.0 mi.). **Big Basin Road to Long Trail, 2.0 mi., 3.2 km., 1¾ hr. (Rev. 1 hr.).**

2. ALLIS TRAIL. This loop trail by-passes Montclair Glen Lodge, following the ridgeline between Mt. Ethan Allen and Wind Gap, and its south end begins on the Long Trail 0.2 mi. south of the lodge. From the junction ascend east to a view south of Mt. Ethan Allen. At the top of the initial climb, reach Allis Lookout (0.1 mi.) with the David Morse Memorial Bench and a striking view of Camel's Hump. The bench was built by the Montpelier Section led by Bob Lindemann in 2000 and honors the memory of a long-time Montpelier Section volunteer and trail maintainer. Descend south and west to the Long Trail at Wind Gap, 0.2 mi. north of Montclair Glen Lodge. **Long Trail south of Montclair Glen to Long Trail at Wind Gap, 0.3 mi., 0.5 km., ¼ hr. (Rev ¼ hr.).**

3. FOREST CITY TRAIL. From Huntington Center follow the Huntington Road to the Camel's Hump Road, 6.1 mi. north of Vt. 17 and 2.5 mi. south of the Huntington Post Office. Follow Camel's Hump Road east 2.8 mi. to the trailhead, where there is limited parking. The road continues 0.7 mi. uphill to a larger parking lot and the beginning of the Burrows Trail. The Forest City–Burrows Connector (8) links these two trails.

From the road (0.0 mi.), follow an old logging road, cross Brush Brook, and reach Forest City (0.3 mi.), the site of a former 1930's CCC camp. Continue on the logging road, recross Brush Brook, reach the junction with the Forest City-Burrows Connector (8) (0.8 mi.), and then bear right, leaving the logging road. Climb gradually, with several brook crossings, to the Long Trail (2.2 mi.) 200 ft. north of Montclair Glen Lodge at the site of the original Montclair Glen Shelter, built in 1917. The Long Trail leads north 1.9 mi. to Camel's Hump and 1.0 mi. south to Mt. Ethan Allen. **Camel's Hump Road to Long Trail, 2.2 mi., 3.2 km., 1¾ hr. (Rev. 1¼ hr.); Camel's Hump Road to Camel's Hump, 4.1 mi., 6.3 km., 3½ hr. (Rev. 2¼ hr.).**

4. DEAN TRAIL. This trail diverges west from the Monroe Trail (7), 1.3 mi. from the Couching Lion parking lot, and makes a popular day hike loop over Camel's Hump with that trail and the Long Trail. From the Monroe Trail (0.0 mi.), descend west to cross the Hump Brook bridge (0.2 mi.), built by the Vermont Youth Conservation Corps, and reach a spur (0.3 mi.) leading south 0.1 mi. to Hump Brook Tenting Area, with tent

9

KEEP YOUR DRINKING WATER CLEAN

Proper disposal of human and pet waste prevents the spread of *Giardia* and other diseases. If an outhouse is not available, bury waste in a six-inch deep hole 200 feet from water and 50 feet from trails.

---

platforms and campsites. A GMC caretaker is in residence during the hiking season. A fee is charged for overnight use.

From the spur, climb steadily to a beaver pond (0.7 mi.) with views of Camel's Hump. Ascend more gently to Wind Gap (1.0 mi.), and the junction with both the Long Trail and the north end of the Allis Trail (2). The Long Trail leads south 0.2 mi. to the Forest City Trail and then Montclair Glen Lodge, and leads north 1.7 mi. to Camel's Hump. **Couching Lion parking lot to Montclair Glen Lodge, 2.5 mi., 4.0 km., 2 hr. (Rev. 1¼ hr.); Couching Lion parking lot to Camel's Hump via Monroe, Dean, and Long Trails, 4.0 mi., 6.4 km., 3½ hr. (Rev. 2 hr.).**

5. ALPINE TRAIL. Named by Will S. Monroe for one of his Saint Bernard dogs, the yellow-blazed Alpine Trail skirts the east side of the Camel's Hump summit cone and is rarely in deep woods. Although this trail can provide a safer route around Camels Hump in bad weather, its elevation and exposure makes it a poor choice in a thunderstorm, when you should seek shelter or descend immediately.

From the Long Trail (0.0 mi.) at treeline, 0.2 mi. south of Camel's Hump, descend east moderately, to the Monroe Trail (7) (0.5 mi.). Continue north and proceed, mostly along ledges featuring views toward the summit and with little change in elevation, before dropping to a brook crossing (1.0 mi.). Continue north over Basque Ledges, and then descend to the north junction with the Long Trail (1.7 mi.), 1.1 mi. north of the summit of Camel's Hump. **Long Trail south of Camel's Hump to Long Trail north of Camel's Hump, 1.7 mi., 2.7 km., 1 hr. (Rev. 1½ hr.).**

6. BURROWS TRAIL. Refer to directions to the Forest City Trail (3). From the Forest City trailhead continue up the Camel's Hump Road 0.7 mi. to the large gravel parking lot at the end of the road, 3.5 mi. east of Huntington Center. The Forest

LEARN BACKCOUNTRY TRAVEL SKILLS —— TAKE A GMC WORKSHOP!

City–Burrows Connecter (8) descends south from the trailhead to the Forest City Trail.

Enter the woods (0.0 mi.) in an internationally recognized site for research on acid deposition, soils, insects, and other forest health issues. Cross a brook, ascend moderately to a ridge between Camel's Hump and Bald Hill (1.7 mi.), and follow the ridge to the Long Trail and the Monroe Trail (7) at the Camel's Hump Hut Clearing (2.1 mi.). The Long Trail ascends south 0.3 mi. to the summit. **Camel's Hump Road to Long Trail, 2.1 mi., 3.4 km., 2¼ hr. (Rev. 1 hr.); Camel's Hump Road to Camel's Hump, 2.4 mi., 3.9 km., 2½ hr. (Rev. 1¼ hr.).**

7. Monroe Trail. This trail begins at the end of North Duxbury's Couching Lion parking lot. *Eastern approach via Waterbury's Winooski Street bridge:* From the junction of U.S. 2 and Vt. 100 (0.0 mi.) just off I-89's exit 10, drive south on Vt. 100 and pass under a railroad trestle. Turn right on Winooski Street (0.1 mi.) and cross the Winooski Street bridge (0.4 mi.). Turn right onto River Road and proceed west to Camel's Hump Road (5.0 mi.). Turn left (south.) and ascend, passing several side roads off the Hump Road; be sure to stay on the main road. At 6.4 mi. bear left at a fork and cross the bridge. Continue across another bridge and pass a sign that says "Welcome to Camel's Hump State Park." A side road to the left leads to the Camel's Hump View Trail and the winter parking area. Bear right and continue to climb to two large parking areas (8.7 mi.). The Monroe Trail begins at the far end of the upper parking lot.

Emergency vehicles and local residents require access to both the trailhead and the gated woods road near the parking area; please avoid blocking the gated road and do not park on the shoulder of this narrow road. *Note:* If the upper parking lots are full, please use the winter parking area.

Western approach via the Jonesville bridge: Camel's Hump Road is 6.0 mi. west of the Jonesville bridge on Duxbury Road (it becomes River Road in Duxbury). Turn right onto Camel's Hump Road and follow the previous directions to the trailhead.

The estate of Prof. Will S. Monroe left Couching Lion Farm to the State of Vermont. Prof. Monroe sponsored the planting of many of the trees surrounding the parking lot, including the Norway spruce from which the caretaker cabin was built in 1973 by the Department of Forests, Parks, and Recreation as well as the spruce and larch harvested in 1999 to rebuild Butler Lodge. Professor Monroe, his sister Katherine, and his beloved dogs are buried in a small cemetery 100 ft. north of the parking lot.

From the parking lot (0.0 mi.), enter the woods, pass a trailhead bulletin board and trail register, and begin a steady ascent. Shortly after leaving the registration box, cross the first of three footbridges. Cross the third footbridge at 0.8 mi. and ascend to the Dean Trail (4) (1.3 mi.). Resume climbing to a crossing of Hump Brook (2.1 mi.).

Recross the brook, turn north and ascend steadily, cross the Alpine Trail (5) (2.5 mi.), and continue uphill to the Long Trail (3.1 mi.) at the Camel's Hump Hut Clearing. The Long Trail ascends 0.3 mi. south to Camel's Hump. **Couching Lion parking lot to Long Trail, 3.1 mi., 5.0 km., 2¾ hr. (Rev. 1½ hr.); Couching Lion parking lot to Camel's Hump, 3.4 mi., 5.5 km., 3 hr. (Rev. 1¾ hr.).**

8. Forest City–Burrows Connector. This trail starts at the Burrows Trail (6) trailhead and connects with the Forest City Trail to eliminate a road walk in the Burrows–Forest City circuit over Camel's Hump. Bear right off the Burrows Trail just beyond the parking lot and proceed south, crossing a small brook on a wooden bridge. Cross a large bridge built by the On Top School over the impressive gorge of Brush Brook and descend to the Forest City Trail. **Burrows Trail to Forest City Trail, 0.1 mi.**

DIVISION 10

Bolton Mountain to
Lamoille River

DIVISION 10 PROFILE

Elevation (in feet)

Distance (in miles)

BOLTON MTN.
NEBRASKA NOTCH
FOREHEAD
MT. MANSFIELD, CHIN
SMUGGLERS' NOTCH
STERLING POND
MADONNA PEAK
WHITEFACE MTN.
BEAR HOLLOW SHELTER
LAMOILLE RIVER

Bolton Mountain to Lamoille River

miles north-bound	▲ NORTH	elevation at Long Trail (feet/meters)	miles south-bound
27.2	**Vt. 15; Lamoille River bridge**	500/152	0.0
26.6	**Vt. 15** at West Settlement Road	500/152	0.6
23.3	**Bear Hollow Shelter**, E via spur	1380/421	3.9
20.2	**Whiteface Mtn.**	3714/1132	7.0
19.7	**Whiteface Shelter; Whiteface Trail** (32) to **Beaver Meadow Lodge** (2214 ft/675 m), 1.0 mi S	3156/962	7.5
18.9	**Morse Mtn.**, east slope	3380/1030	8.3
18.6	**Hagerman Overlook**	3190/972	8.6
18.2	**Chilcoot Pass; Chilcoot Pass Trail** (31) to **Beaver Meadow Lodge** (2214 ft/675 m), 0.8 mi E	2950/899	9.0
17.4	**Madonna Peak**, chairlift	3668/1119	9.8
16.2	**Sterling Pond Shelter; Elephant's Head Trail** (28) to **Watson Camp**, 450 ft S	3030/924	11.0
16.0	**Sterling Pond** outlet	3000/915	11.2
15.9	**Sterling Pond Trail** (29) to Vt. 108, 1.1 mi W	3040/927	11.3
15.6	**Snuffy's Ski Trail; Elephant's Head Trail** (28) to **Sterling Pond Shelter**, 0.7 mi E	3080/939	11.6
14.9	**Elephant's Head Cliff** (2800 ft/853 m), 0.1 mi W via spur	3020/920	12.3
12.6	**Smugglers Notch Picnic Area; Vt. 108** at **Long Trail** north	1600/488	14.6
12.4	**Vt. 108** at **Long Trail** south	1600/488	14.8
10.7	**Profanity Trail** (24); **Taft Lodge**, 200 ft S via spur, **Hell Brook Cutoff** (27)	3650/1113	16.5
10.4	**Eagle Pass; Adam's Apple Trail** (25) to **Adam's Apple** (4060 ft/1250 m), 0.1 mi N; **Hell Brook Trail** (26) to Vt. 108, 1.5 mi E	3990/1217	16.8
10.1	**Chin**, Mt. Mansfield's highest peak	4393/1340	17.1
9.9	**Sunset Ridge Trail** (21) to **Laura Cowles Trail** (23), 250 ft W; to Underhill State Park, 3.1 mi W; **Profanity Trail** (24) to **Taft Lodge**, 0.5 mi E	4260/1299	17.3

Bolton Mountain to Lamoille River

9.7	**Cliff Trail** (15) to Cliff House (3600 ft/1098 m), 0.4 mi E	4020/1226	17.5
9.6	**Lower Lip**	4030/1229	17.6
9.4	**Upper Lip**	3964/1209	17.8
9.2	**Drift Rock; Amherst Trail** (14) to **TV Road**, 0.3 mi S	3940/1202	18.0
8.9	**Halfway House Trail** (20) to Underhill State Park, 2.3 mi W	3880/1183	18.3
8.7	**Mt. Mansfield Visitor Center: Toll Road** to **South Link** (11) and **Haselton Trail** (13), 0.5 mi E	3849/1173	18.5
8.4	**Forehead By-Pass**, north end; **TV Road**	3900/1190	18.8
8.1	**Forehead; Wampahoofus Trail** (10) to **Butler Lodge**, 0.8 mi S; to Underhill State Park via **Maple Ridge Trail** (9), 3.6 mi W	3940/1202	19.1
7.4	**Needle's Eye; Forehead By-Pass** (8) to **Long Trail** north of Forehead, 1.2 mi N	3080/939	19.8
7.2	**Wallace Cutoff** (4) to **Butler Lodge** (3030 ft/924 m), 0.1 mi W; to Stevensville parking lot via **Butler Lodge Trail** (5), 1.9 mi W	3100/945	20.0
6.0	**Twin Brooks Tenting Area**, 100 ft W via spur	2300/701	21.2
4.6	**Nebraska Notch Trail** (3) to Stevensville parking lot, 1.5 mi W	1780/543	22.6
4.3	**Clara Bow Trail** (2) to **Taylor Lodge**, 0.4 mi E	1860/567	22.9
3.9	**Lake Mansfield Trail** (1) to **Taylor Lodge** and **Clara Bow Trail** (2), 0.1 mi E; to Nebraska Valley Road, 1.6 mi W	1850/564	23.3
2.8	**Mt. Clark**, east slope	2800/853	24.4
1.4	**Mt. Mayo**	3160/964	25.8
0.5	**Puffer Shelter**	3200/975	26.7
0.0	**Bolton Mtn.**	3725/1136	27.2

SOUTH
▼

Division 10
Bolton Mountain to Lamoille River

Massachusetts: 195.5 miles   *Canada: 77.2 miles*

This division's Long Trail travels mostly above treeline on Mt. Mansfield for 2.3 mi. from the Forehead to the Adams's Apple and is exposed to strong winds and sudden storms. The portions of the LT south from the Forehead and north from the Chin can be treacherous in poor weather. Hikers should be familiar with the side trails that can be used to avoid or escape the exposed summit ridge; particularly the Forehead By-Pass (8) and the Profanity Trail (24).

Mt. Mansfield, Vermont's highest summit, is one of three sites along the Long Trail with alpine vegetation. Take care to walk only on the rocks, not the plants. For more information on Mt. Mansfield, see pages 178.

Backpacking groups camping on Mt. Mansfield should use Twin Brooks Tenting Area rather than the mountain's heavily used shelter sites.

Due to radio frequency radiation from broadcast facilities that exceeds federal exposure standards, the Nose remains temporarily closed to hikers. Reopening of the Triangle Trail is anticipated following a proposed realignment of tower facilities. Planning is underway for replacement of Watson Camp at Sterling Pond.

The Long Trail north of Vt. 108 has been relocated onto the former Elephant's Head Trail, eliminating the road walk along the highway through the notch.

GMC is also trying to relocate the Long Trail across the Lamoille River Valley to eliminate the road walk on Vt. 15 and Hogback Road.

Side trails in this division, blazed blue unless otherwise noted in the descriptions, are numbered to correspond with the division map on page 168 and Mt. Mansfield maps on pages 174 and 175.

SUGGESTED HIKES

STERLING POND. This popular destination features a subalpine pond with striking views of Mt. Mansfield across Smugglers Notch. Follow the Sterling Pond Trail, the former route of the Long Trail, north from the height-of-land on Vt. 108 at Smugglers Notch. Round trip from Vt. 108, 2.4 mi., 2 hr.

NEBRASKA NOTCH. This climb on the Lake Mansfield Trail to the rugged notch features a glacial cirque with views of the north wall of the notch, a large beaver meadow, and a fine view of the rugged ridges of Bolton Mtn. from Taylor Lodge. Continue on the Clara Bow trail through the boulders on the floor of the notch and return to Taylor via the Long Trail south. Return by reversing your direction on the Lake Mansfield Trail. Round trip, 4.0 mi., 2¾ hr.

BUTLER LODGE LOOP. This hike, with views of the Forehead from the Long Trail and of Lake Champlain and the Adirondacks from Butler Lodge, follows the Nebraska Notch, Long, Wallace Cutoff, and Butler Lodge Trails from the Stevensville Road parking lot. Round trip, 6.0 mi., 4 hr.

10

MANSFIELD TRAVERSE. Ascending through the picturesque forest of the Haselton Trail under Mt. Mansfield's Nose, this route features a 2.0 mi. alpine ridge walk along the Long Trail north to the Chin, Vermont's highest point (4,393 ft.). The descent on the Long Trail passes Taft Lodge and returns to Vt. 108, less than a mile north of the ski area. Round trip from the gondola parking lot, 6.5 mi. 4¾ hr.

Beaver Meadow. Featuring a subalpine ridge with views along the Sterling Range, this rugged trip utilizes the Beaver Meadow, Chilcoot, Long, and Whiteface Trails. This circuit passes Beaver Meadow Lodge and Whiteface Shelter and makes a fine backpack. Traveling uphill on the Chilcoot Trail is recommended. Round trip from Mud City, 8.7 mi., 6 hr. A climb of Whiteface Mtn. via the Long Trail north lengthens this trip to 9.7 mi., 7 hr.

Camping and Fires

This division's Long Trail south of Smugglers Notch crosses state, Stowe Mountain Resort, and University of Vermont land. North of the notch it crosses both state and private property. Camping above 2,500 ft. is allowed only at shelters (tenting is allowed only if a shelter is filled to capacity) and designated tenting areas. Primitive off-trail camping with small wood fires below 2,500 ft. is allowed.

Wood fires are prohibited in Division 10 at all shelters south of Whiteface Mtn. to protect the vulnerable vegetation at these sites. Small wood fires, although discouraged, are permitted in established fire rings at Twin Brooks Tenting Area, Bear Hollow Shelter, and Beaver Meadow Lodge.

Refer to Leave No Trace principles (pages 9 to 11) to minimize your impact.

Note: Camping and wood fires above timberline on Mount Mansfield are illegal and may be subject to a fine.

Group Use

Groups hiking this division's Long Trail may need a Commercial Use Permit from the Vermont Department of Forests, Parks, and Recreation. Group tenting space is available at Twin Brooks Tenting Area, Taylor and Beaver Meadow Lodges, and Sterling Pond and Bear Hollow Shelters. Groups can stay at Taft Lodge, where tenting is not permitted. Underhill State Park Campground, on the west side of Mt. Mansfield, and Smugglers Notch State Park Campground, on the east side, are available for base camp hiking. Elmore State Park, east of the Long Trail off Vt. 15 and Vt. 12 South, is also available for base camp hiking. Refer to pages 11 to 17 for additional group use guidelines.

WINTER USE

All suggested hikes listed for this division, except for the Beaver Meadow trip, make good snowshoe trips, although some may be longer than indicated owing to unplowed approach roads. Much of the terrain in this division is too difficult for beginner and intermediate cross-country skiers. Vt. 108 through Smugglers Notch (closed to vehicles in winter) and the Nebraska Notch Trail out of Stevensville make challenging trips for intermediate skiers. The approach trail to Beaver Meadow offers easier terrain for skiing.

ACCESS TO LONG TRAIL

VT. 108. There are two Long Trail trailheads on this road. The south trailhead, leading to the Chin of Mt. Mansfield, is 8.2 mi. north of Vt. 100 in Stowe and 9.6 mi. south of Vt. 15 in Jeffersonville. A pull-off on the west side of the road is just north of the trailhead. The north trailhead, leading to Elephant's Head, is the state picnic area 0.2 mi. north of the south trailhead. Vt. 108 through Smugglers Notch is designated a Scenic Highway by the State of Vermont.

During the winter a 3.5 mi. stretch of Vt. 108 through Smugglers Notch between the Mt. Mansfield Ski Area maintenance entrance (0.3 mi. south of the Long Trail) and the Smugglers Notch Ski Area upper parking lot (1.3 mi. north of the notch height-of-land) is not plowed.

VT. 15. There is parking at three locations at the north end of this division. To avoid a 0.6 mi. road walk along this busy highway, follow Vt. 15 west out of Johnson, cross the Lamoille River just beyond the Long Trail Tavern, and continue 0.6 mi. west of the river to West Settlement Road. Turn and follow this road south 0.4 mi., and bear left at a fork for another 0.3 mi. to an iron gate where limited parking is available. Be sure to park without blocking the road or the gate. West Settlement Road is also 6.7 mi. east of Vt. 108 in Jeffersonville.

There is also parking at both ends of the Lamoille River bridge along Vt. 15.

MT. MANSFIELD AREA

Vermont's highest mountain, Mt. Mansfield (4,393 ft.) is known for its distinctive ridgeline, which resembles the profile of a human face, especially when viewed from the east. The names of its more prominent south-to-north features reflect this: Forehead, Nose, Upper and Lower Lips, Chin, and Adam's Apple. The Abenaki called the mountain Mose-o-de-be-Wadso (mountain with the head of a moose), and it received its present name from the town of Mansfield, disestablished and divided among adjacent towns over a century ago.

The Mansfield summit ridge supports the largest community of alpine tundra found in Vermont. This unique and delicate plant life is a remnant of the era when ice sheets covered northern New England. Few species are able to survive the extreme conditions of the summit ridge; those that do grow very slowly and hang in a delicate balance. Although these plants are hardy to the weather, they are extremely fragile to foot traffic. Please take special care to walk only on the rocks, not the plants. Above treeline, walk only on marked trails. Camping is not permitted in any of Vermont's alpine zones.

Mt. Mansfield is the most frequently visited mountain in Vermont with over 40,000 visitors and hundreds of dogs annually. This use threatens its fragile alpine ecosystem. Please leash your dog on the busy summit out of consideration for other visitors and to reduce impact to the surrounding alpine vegetation. GMC summit caretakers are stationed on the summit ridge to assist hikers and other visitors and explain the fragile nature of the alpine ecosystem. The summit ridge of Mt. Mansfield, owned and managed by the University of Vermont as a Natural Area, has been declared a State Natural Area and National Natural Landmark. The university, the Stowe Mountain Resort, and the Vermont Department of Forests, Parks, and Recreation help fund the caretaker program.

Although most people hike the mountain via the well-known Long Trail from Vt. 108 and the Sunset Ridge Trail from Underhill State Park, the many other trails on the mountain are exciting and challenging. Hikers using these side trails should be in good physical condition and have sturdy boots. Backpackers may encounter difficulty on some of these trails due to their ladders and tight squeezes through crevices and ledges.

Base camping in the area can be found at Smugglers Notch and Underhill State Parks. Overnight facilities can also be found at hotels and other tourist lodgings in the surrounding area. GMC lodges are often overcrowded and should not be used by organized groups.

Groups are encouraged to use Twin Brooks Tenting Area or the group camping area at Underhill State Park. Information is available from the Department of Forests, Parks, and Recreation, Essex Junction Regional Office, 111 West Street, Essex Junction, Vermont 05452; (802) 879-6565.

Long Trail Description

Descend east from the summit of **Bolton Mtn. (0.0 mi.)**, then turn north and continue downhill on rugged trail to **Puffer Shelter (0.5 mi.)**. This shelter was built by the Burlington Section in 1975, with the help of over one hundred volunteers who carried the materials over Bolton Mtn. to the site. It replaced a log cabin that burned in 1974 and is named in honor of Louis B. Puffer, long active in many capacities with the GMC. There is space for six. A small brook to the west is an unreliable water source. Wood fires are prohibited at Puffer Shelter. **Buchanan Shelter to Puffer Shelter, 4.5 mi., 7.2 km., 3 hr. (SB 2½ hr.).**

Drop to a sag in the ridge, and then climb to the wooded summit of **Mt. Mayo (1.4 mi.)**. Descend to pass several views of Mt. Mansfield and, after reaching the Mayo-Clark col

10

(2.0 mi.), climb to the south ridge of **Mt. Clark**. Follow the contour around the ridge to pass east of the summit **(2.8 mi.)** and reach a lookout (3.0 mi.) with Lake Mansfield below and the Worcester Range beyond. Proceed east and drop steeply over rugged terrain, using a ladder at one point, to a beaver pond. Cross the dam and descend through challenging ledges to the **Lake Mansfield Trail (1) (3.9 mi.)**. This trail leads east 300 ft. to **Taylor Lodge** and descends 1.6 mi. east to Lake Mansfield and Stowe's Nebraska Valley Road. The east end of the **Clara Bow Trail (2)**, which passes through the boulders on the floor of Nebraska Notch, leaves the Lake Mansfield Trail behind Taylor Lodge.

Taylor Lodge, named for James P. Taylor, founder of the GMC, was built by the Burlington Section in 1978. The lodge, with an open front porch, has an enclosed bunkroom with space for fifteen and one tent platform for overflow camping. Water runs from a reliable spring 0.2 mi. down the Lake Mansfield Trail. Because two GMC lodges have already burned at this site, wood fires are prohibited at Taylor Lodge. **Puffer Shelter to Taylor Lodge, 3.4 mi., 5.5 km., 2 hr. (SB 2¾ hr.).**

Turn left at the Lake Mansfield Trail junction to climb over a low ridge, by-passing rugged Nebraska Notch. Descend to pass the west end of the **Clara Bow Trail (2) (4.3 mi.)**. Continue west to a large, shallow beaver pond, then climb north back to the ridge and the **Nebraska Notch Trail (3) (4.6 mi.)**, which descends west 1.5 mi. to Stevensville Road in Underhill Center.

Proceed north in a gentle ascent while circling around the west slope of Mt. Dewey, crossing two brooks. Beyond the second brook is a **spur (6.0 mi.)**, which descends west 100 ft. to the **Twin Brooks Tenting Area**, rebuilt in 1997 by Burlington Section volunteers in memory of Roland Boucher, a dedicated trail maintainer. Tent platforms are provided, and small wood fires are permitted in the established fire ring near the group site. The water supply is the brook 0.2 mi. south on the Long Trail.

Continue north from the junction, cross another brook (6.2 mi.), and then cross the Overland cross-country ski trail (6.3 mi.), which can be followed east to a rock feature called the Devil's Dishpan near the ridgeline. Climb through a glade to the ridge (6.8 mi.). Proceed along the ridge to the **Wallace Cutoff (4) (7.2 mi.)**, which descends west about 0.1 mi. to **Butler Lodge**. This trail is the shortest (and from this ridge, the only) route to the lodge from the Long Trail. In good weather, the Wallace Cutoff and Wampahoofus Trail is the best route for backpackers to follow to the Forehead.

Butler Lodge, of log construction, was originally built by the Long Trail Patrol in 1933 and reconstructed by Burlington Section volunteers led by Leo Leach in 2000. It is named for Mabel Taylor Butler, who was a member of the Burlington Section and loved the Green Mountains. The reconstructed lodge was dedicated in celebration of James C. Taylor, a Long Trail end-to-end hiker. There are bunks and loft space for fourteen. Water, though unreliable in late summer, is available at a small brook 75 ft. to the east of the lodge. A GMC caretaker is in residence during the hiking season to assist and educate hikers, help maintain the lodge and local trails, and compost sewage to protect water quality. A fee is charged for overnight use. Wood fires are prohibited at Butler Lodge. **Taylor Lodge to Butler Lodge, 3.4 mi., 5.5 km., 2½ hr. (SB 2 hr.).**

From the lodge there are views of the Champlain Valley and Adirondacks to the west, and the south escarpment of the Forehead of Mt. Mansfield to the north. The **Butler Lodge Trail (5)** descends west 1.8 mi. to the Stevensville Road parking lot. The Rock Garden Trail (7) follows along the foot of the Forehead cliffs north to the Maple Ridge Trail (9). The Wampahoofus Trail (10) climbs steeply north 0.8 mi. to the Long Trail at the Forehead.

From the Wallace Cutoff, continue north to pass through the **Needle's Eye**, an opening created by two large boulders, to the south end of the **Forehead By-Pass (8) (7.4 mi.)**. It is the less-exposed route to the summit in bad weather.

Bear left and begin a steep and rough climb over rocks and ledges, using ladders in some places. Emerge from the ledges and continue to ascend in the open to the highest point of the **Forehead (8.1 mi.)**, Mt. Mansfield's southmost peak, and the junction of the **Wampahoofus Trail (10)**. This trail descends west and south 0.2 mi. to the **Maple Ridge Trail (9)** and 0.8 mi. to Butler Lodge.

10

Proceed north from the Forehead, enter the woods and arrive at the north end of the **Forehead By-Pass (8)**, an alternate route in stormy weather. Just beyond is the **TV Road (8.4 mi.)**, which leads south to the north slope of the Nose, and its television station buildings.

Turn left to follow the TV Road north and in 150 ft. pass the south end of the Lakeview Trail (12) on the left. Turn right and reenter the woods (8.6 mi.), then reach the Summit Station and **Mt. Mansfield Visitor Center (8.7 mi.)**. The toll road parking lot is just below the Summit Station to the east. The Visitor Center occupies part of the Summit Station and contains displays on the mountain's natural history, research efforts, and the ridge's alpine ecosystem. It is open from Memorial Day to Columbus Day.

The Summit Station is built on the site of the old summit house. One of the last of the famous mountain hotels, the Mt. Mansfield Summit House was razed and burned in 1964 after more than one hundred years of operation. The **Mt. Mansfield Toll Road** is open during summer and foliage seasons and provides automobile access to the Long Trail from Vt. 108. From the Summit Station the Toll Road descends east 0.3 mi. to the Runny Nose spring and 0.5 mi. to a road leading left to the Octagon and the upper station of the Mt. Mansfield quad chairlift. At this road junction, the **Haselton Trail (13)** bears northeast down the Nose Dive ski trail. At the parking lot across from the junction, the **South Link (11)** leads west to the Forehead By-Pass (8). The toll road continues east downhill another 4.0 mi. to Vt. 108.

Continue north past the Summit Station where the coinciding Lakeview (12) and Canyon (16) Trails lead west to parallel the ridge. Cross the TV Road (8.8 mi.), which leads east 200 ft. to the Amherst Trail (14). Beyond the TV Road, emerge from the stunted spruce and fir trees on the rocky ridge of the mountain. From this point north over the Chin, hikers must take special care to protect the alpine tundra by walking only on the

VISIT WWW.GREENMOUNTAINCLUB.ORG!

marked trail. Pass the **Halfway House Trail (20) (8.9 mi.)**, which descends west 2.3 mi. to Underhill State Park, and then climb to Frenchman's Pile, a cairn marking the spot where a traveler was killed by lightning many years ago. Electrical storms on the exposed ridge of Mt. Mansfield are sudden and severe. Hikers are strongly urged to take shelter on any side trail leading off the ridge during thunderstorms (they are usually brief). To the east, use the Profanity, Cliff, or Amherst Trails; to the west, the Laura Cowles or Halfway House Trails. Fissures and overhanging rocks along the open ridge do not provide adequate shelter from lightning strikes.

Proceed north from Frenchman's Pile to **Drift Rock (9.2 mi.)**, a large glacial erratic, and the north end of the **Amherst Trail (14)** which provides a sheltered route south to the TV Road on the east side of the ridge. Ascend the **Upper Lip (9.4 mi.)**, then pass just west of the **Lower Lip (9.6 mi.)** with its Rock of Terror (a prominent boulder that appears ready to topple down the east side of the ridge), and reach a junction **(9.7 mi.)** where the **Cliff Trail (15)** descends very steeply east 0.4 mi. to the Cave of the Winds and the Cliff House. To the west at this junction are the Canyon North Extension (18) and the Subway (19).

Follow the ridge north, pass the north end of the Subway, and reach another junction (9.9 mi.) in a sedge meadow where the **Sunset Ridge Trail (21)** descends west 250 ft. to the more sheltered **Laura Cowles Trail (23)** and 3.1 mi. to Underhill State Park. The **Profanity Trail (24)** drops steeply east 0.5 mi. to Taft Lodge, and is the recommended bad weather route off the Chin. Straight ahead, ascend the **Chin (10.1 mi.)**, Mt. Mansfield's highest summit.

The view from the Chin is dramatic. East of north lie the Sterling Range and Jay Peak. Under very favorable conditions, Montreal's Mt. Royal in Canada is visible to the northwest. To the east is the Worcester Range. Mt. Washington in New Hampshire is south of east. Right of Mt. Washington lie the Franconia Range and Mt. Moosilauke. To the south the Green Mountains are visible to Killington Peak. To the west beyond Lake Champlain is lofty pointed Whiteface, which lies north of the dense cluster of Adirondack peaks surrounding Mt. Marcy.

10

From the Chin's highest point, continue north to an escarpment where there is a view of the Adam's Apple, the Lake of the Clouds, and the cliffs of Smugglers Notch. Drop steeply from the Chin on precipitous ledges to **Eagle Pass (10.4 mi.)**, where the **Hell Brook Trail (26)** bears north to the Lake of the Clouds before plunging 1.5 mi. to Vt. 108 in Smugglers Notch. Descending the Hell Brook Trail is not recommended. The **Adam's Apple Trail (25)** leads 0.2 mi. over the Adam's Apple to the Lake of the Clouds.

Bear right and descend through scrub to a junction with the lower end of the **Profanity Trail (24)**. Just beyond is a **spur (10.7)**, opposite a composting privy, leading south 200 feet to **Taft Lodge**, perched on a shelf below the Chin. This log structure, largest shelter on the Long Trail, sleeps twenty-four. Originally built by the Burlington Section in 1920, it was a gift of Judge Elihu B. Taft of Burlington. A large corps of volunteers, led by the Burlington Section and Dana Baron and Fred Gilbert, reconstructed the lodge in 1996. Daan Zwick, Taft caretaker from 1938 to 1940, generously funded the project. Water is found in a reliable brook 300 ft. south of the lodge. A GMC caretaker is in residence during the hiking season to assist and educate hikers, maintain the lodge and nearby trails, and compost sewage to protect water quality. A fee is charged for overnight use. Wood fires are prohibited at Taft Lodge. **Butler Lodge to Taft Lodge, 3.6 mi., 5.8 km., 2¾ hr. (SB 2¼ hr.).**

Just north of the spur is the **Hell Brook Cutoff (27)**, which follows the contours of the Adam's Apple north 0.7 mi. to the **Hell Brook Trail (26)**. Descend steadily on ledges, level out briefly, and bear left near the Chin Clip ski trail (11.3 mi.). Continue to drop to **Vt. 108** south of Smugglers Notch **(12.4 mi.)**. Vt. 108 leads south downhill 0.3 mi. to the Mt. Mansfield Ski Area, 0.5 mi. to the Spruce Peak Ski Area, 0.6 mi. to Smugglers Notch State Park Campground, and 8.2 mi. to Vt. 100 in Stowe.

Turn left and follow the highway north to the **Smugglers Notch Picnic Area (12.6 mi.)**. Turn right to leave the highway and bear right to follow the path at the south end of the picnic area. Here the Long Trail follows the former Elephant's Head Trail out of the notch. From the picnic area, descend to and cross Notch Brook, then start a steady ascent on switchbacks to the ridge south of Spruce Peak, crossing and recrossing a slide with views of Mt. Mansfield. Continue to ascend at a more moderate grade along the steep sidehill before descending to a **spur (14.9 mi.)** leading 0.1 mi. west to the top of **Elephant's Head Cliff**, which towers over the notch. When peregrine falcons nest on the east wall of the notch, the spur is closed during the nesting season (generally mid-March to mid-August, posted by the State of Vermont) to keep from disturbing these rare, majestic birds.

Beyond the spur, bear east and climb steadily to **Snuffy's ski trail (15.6 mi.)**, a service road that leads south 0.2 mi. to the top of Spruce Peak chairlift. The **Elephant's Head Trail (28)** continues across the ski trail and rejoins the Long Trail at the east end of Sterling Pond. Turn left and follow Snuffy's ski trail past the **Sterling Pond Trail (29) (15.9 mi.)**, which leads west downhill 1.1 mi. to Vt. 108 at the height-of-land in Smugglers Notch. Descend to the **Sterling Pond outlet (16.0 mi.)**. Cross the outlet and ascend to a chairlift (16.1 mi.) just above a ski area warming hut. Follow the ridge east to **Sterling Pond Shelter (16.2 mi.)** and the **Elephant's Head Trail (28)** leading south 450 ft. to **Watson Camp**.

Sterling Pond Shelter is a frame lean-to, built by the Montpelier Section in 1972, and has space for eight. There is a small, unreliable spring 300 ft. south of the shelter on the Elephant's Head Trail. A GMC caretaker is on duty during the hiking season to assist and educate hikers, help maintain the local trails and shelters, and compost sewage to protect water quality. A fee is charged for overnight use. Wood fires are prohibited at all Sterling Pond sites. **Taft Lodge to Sterling Pond Shelter, 5.5 mi., 8.9 km., 3½ hr. (SB 3¾ hr.).**

A second overnight facility, Watson Camp, is located at the east end of Sterling Pond. This frame camp was donated to the GMC in 1980 by Thomas J. Watson, Jr. of IBM. It has bunk space for eight. The GMC Sterling Pond caretaker is in seasonal residence, and a fee is charged for overnight use.

From Sterling Pond Shelter, climb over a knob, the Sawtooth, and ascend steadily to the ridge of the Sterling Range, which includes Spruce and Madonna Peaks and Morse and

10

Whiteface Mtns., and is named for the now-defunct town of Sterling. Cross the Drifter ski trail, climb to rejoin the ski trail, and follow it uphill to the summit of **Madonna Peak (17.4 mi.)**, where open areas at the chairlift upper station afford views in all directions. Descend east down the Chilcoot ski trail. Bear north into the woods near the Catwalk ski trail and drop steeply to **Chilcoot Pass** and, just north of the ski area, the **Chilcoot Trail (31) (18.2 mi.)**. This trail descends steeply south 0.8 mi. to **Beaver Meadow Lodge** and the Beaver Meadow Trail (30). Beaver Meadow Lodge, a log cabin built by the Sterling Section, was completed in 1947. It has space for fifteen. Water is found in several adjacent brooks. Beaver Meadow Lodge, while a convenient base camp for hiking the Sterling Range, is well below the ridgeline and isn't usually a destination for a long-distance backpacking trip. **Sterling Pond Shelter to Beaver Meadow Lodge, 2.8 mi., 4.5 km., 1¾ hr. (SB 2½ hr.).**

Follow the ridge north and climb gradually to **Hagerman Overlook (18.6 mi.)**, named in memory of Robert L. Hagerman, an active member of the Sterling Section, author of a detailed history of Mt. Mansfield, and former editor of the Long Trail News. The overlook affords a unique view of Mt. Mansfield. Ascend to pass just east of the summit of **Morse Mtn. (18.9 mi.)** and reach an eastern vista of Beaver Meadow below. Bear east and descend gradually to **Whiteface Shelter (19.7 mi.)** Here the **Whiteface Trail (32)** drops 1.0 mi. south to Beaver Meadow Lodge.

Whiteface Shelter, a log lean-to with space for five, was built by the Long Trail Patrol in 1958. The water source is a brook 150 ft. east on the Whiteface Trail. From the shelter, Madonna Peak is visible above the Beaver Meadow Basin. To its right, Mt. Mansfield can be seen above Chilcoot Pass. Wood fires are prohibited at Whiteface Shelter. **Sterling Pond Shelter to Whiteface Shelter, 3.5 mi., 5.6 km., 2¼ hr. (SB 2¾ hr.).**

From the shelter, climb steadily north to the wooded summit of **Whiteface Mtn. (20.2 mi.)**. A spur leads straight ahead to several openings, which permit views in almost every direction, including vistas of Mt. Mansfield and the west wall of Smugglers Notch. Descend moderately following the summit ridge, and reach a shelf with views of the Lamoille River Valley below. Descend steeply along an exposed ledge and then descend to cross Waterman Brook at an overhanging rock. Follow the brook downstream to a scenic cascade, then leave the brook to enter open hardwood forest and cross a major logging road. After several minor brook crossings, bear right onto an old woods road and descend to a **spur (23.3 mi.)** leading east to **Bear Hollow Shelter**, perched on a rocky knoll above the Trail. Built by Bob Lindemann and the Sterling Section in 1991, this open-faced frame shelter sleeps twelve. The water supply is a brook just south of the shelter along the Long Trail. **Whiteface Shelter to Bear Hollow Shelter, 3.6 mi., 5.8 km., 2¼ hr. (SB 3 hr.).**

Beyond the shelter, cross French Hill Brook (23.7 mi.), enter a logged area, and follow old logging roads north. After crossing Smith Brook, enter a clearing, turn right, and follow a gravel road. Pass an iron gate (25.9 mi.), where parking is available in dry seasons, and continue to an intersection with West Settlement Road (26.2 mi.) where there is limited parking. Follow this road north to the former railbed of the Lamoille Valley Railroad and, just beyond, **Vt. 15 (26.6 mi.).**

Turn right and follow Vt. 15 to the east end of the **Lamoille River bridge (27.2 mi.)**, 1.8 mi. west of the village of Johnson. Beware of fast-moving traffic on Vt. 15.

SIDE TRAILS

Refer to the division map on page 168 and the Mt. Mansfield maps on pages 174 and 175 for the location of numbered trails. Many of the side trails are steep and rough. Rugged footwear, allotting extra time is recommended.

1. LAKE MANSFIELD TRAIL. This trail begins on the private land of the Lake Mansfield Trout Club. Please be considerate of club guests, stay on the trail, and respect all lands and buildings while in this area. Take the Moscow Road west from Vt. 100, 2.5 mi. south of Stowe. Follow the paved road, which becomes the Nebraska Valley Road. Continue beyond the end of the pavement on the gravel-surfaced road, past an open gate to the Trout

Club, 6.7 mi. west from Vt. 100. Hiking season day-use parking is available at a large lot to the north of the main building. Winter parking is available next to the gate, just before the Trout Club. The land around the lake and for approximately ¼ mi. beyond is private property.

From the parking lot (0.0 mi.), follow the path into the woods and parallel the woods road that follows the north shore of the lake. Descend to join the road briefly, reenter the woods, and cross a bridge. Near the west end of the lake (0.5 mi.), descend to the road again and follow it away from the lake. Cross a small brook and steadily ascend on an old logging road. Bear right near the top of the rise and continue uphill to the alternate winter route (1.1 mi.), which bears left to cross the brook and ascend 0.4 mi. directly north to Taylor Lodge. The main trail continues at a steeper grade to the entrance of the gorge. This route may not be passable in icy weather. Pass a piped spring (1.4 mi.) which is the water source for Taylor Lodge, and gently climb to a beaver meadow with views of the north wall of Nebraska Notch. Cross the brook, climb to Taylor Lodge (1.6 mi.) and the junction with the east end of the Clara Bow Trail (2), and continue to the Long Trail. **Trout Club to Long Trail, 1.6 mi., 2.6 km., 1¼ hr. (Rev. 1 hr.).**

2. CLARA BOW TRAIL. This trail provides a challenging alternate route through the floor of Nebraska Notch just north of Taylor Lodge. Starting behind the lodge (0.0 mi.), travel north to the entrance of the notch, and climb over and under enormous boulders through the notch, using a ladder to negotiate a vertical drop. Rejoin the Long Trail 0.4 mi. north of Taylor Lodge. Taylor Lodge to Long Trail, 0.4 mi., 0.6 km., ⅓ hr. (Rev. ⅓ hr.).

3. NEBRASKA NOTCH TRAIL. From Underhill Center take the Pleasant Valley Road north 0.2 mi. and turn east onto the Stevensville Road. Pass Maple Leaf Farm at 1.1 mi. and reach the parking lot at the end of the road at 2.8 mi. This parking area is maintained by the state year-round, although the road can be challenging to negotiate in winter.

From the parking lot (0.0 mi.), bear right at the trailhead bulletin board, and pass the Overland cross-country ski trail (not suitable for hiking use due to wetlands). Climb at an easy grade to an area of beaver activity (1.4 mi.) and bear left to ascend to the Long Trail (1.5 mi.) at the west end of Nebraska Notch. The Long Trail leads south 0.7 mi. to Taylor Lodge. **Stevensville Road to Long Trail, 1.5 mi., 2.4 km., 1¾ hr. (Rev. 1 hr.).**

4. WALLACE CUTOFF. This trail is the shortest route from the Long Trail to Butler Lodge. From the Long Trail, 1.2 mi. north of Twin Brooks Tenting Area and 0.2 mi. south of the Needle's Eye, descend steeply west to the Butler Lodge Trail 100 ft. below Butler Lodge. The lodge is to the right. **Long Trail to Butler Lodge, 0.1 mi.**

5. BUTLER LODGE TRAIL. Refer to directions to the Nebraska Notch Trail (3). From the Stevensville parking lot, this trail follows a logging road east from the trailhead bulletin board. After passing a gate, the Butler Lodge Trail and Frost Trail (6) leave the road to the left at 0.2 mi.

From the logging road (0.2 mi.), bear right from the Frost Trail and begin a steady ascent, passing the Wallace Cutoff (4) (1.8 mi.) 100 ft. before Butler Lodge. Owing to unstable terrain and erosion, the former Butler Lodge Trail above the lodge to the Long Trail has been closed. Use Wallace Cutoff. **Stevensville Road to Butler Lodge, 1.8 mi., 2.9 km., 1¾ hr. (Rev. 1 hr.).**

6. FROST TRAIL. Refer to directions to the Nebraska Notch Trail (3). From the Stevensville parking lot, this trail follows a logging road east from the trailhead bulletin board. After passing a gate, the Butler Lodge Trail (5) and Frost Trail leave the road to the left at 0.2 mi.

From the logging road (0.2 mi.), bear left from the Butler Lodge Trail and cross Stevensville Brook. Climb steadily to the southmost knob of Maple Ridge (0.9 mi.), then ascend the ridge through spruce-balsam scrub to the Maple Ridge Trail (9) (1.4 mi.). The Maple Ridge Trail climbs very steeply 1.1 mi. to the Forehead via the Wampahoofus Trail (10). **Stevensville Road to Maple Ridge Trail, 1.4 mi., 2.3 km., 1½ hr. (Rev 1 hr.); Stevensville Road to Forehead, 2.5 mi., 4.0 km., 2½ hr. (Rev. 1½ hr.).**

10

7. ROCK GARDEN TRAIL. This trail connects the Maple Ridge Trail (9) with the Wampahoofus Trail (10) across the base of the Forehead's south face. Its north end starts at the Maple Ridge Trail 0.8 mi. from the old CCC Road and 2.9 mi. from Underhill State Park. From the junction on the ridge (0.0 mi.), follow the south side of the ridge, mostly in the woods among the boulders at the base of the cliff, to the Wampahoofus Trail (0.6 mi.), 0.1 mi. from Butler Lodge. **Underhill State Park to Butler Lodge, 3.6 mi., 5.8 km., 2¼ hr. (Rev. 1¾ hr.).**

8. FOREHEAD BY-PASS. This white-blazed trail offers a less exposed ascent of the Forehead; although recommended in severe weather conditions, it is rough and slippery when wet. From the Long Trail (0.0 mi.) just north of the Needle's Eye, bear right and steadily ascend the east slope of the Forehead. After the South Link (11) diverges right (0.9 mi.) to the Octagon, the By-Pass climbs to the ridge and joins the Long Trail (1.2 mi.) just south of the TV Road. **Needle's Eye to TV Road, 1.2 mi., 1.9 km., 1 hr. (Rev. ¾ hr.).**

9. MAPLE RIDGE TRAIL. From Underhill Center, take the Pleasant Valley Road 1.0 mi. north and turn east onto the Mountain Road (Town Highway 2). Follow the road 2.7 mi. to its end at Underhill State Park (nominal fee for parking). The Mountain Road is 3.8 mi. south of Vt. 15. The upper 1.5 mi. of the Mountain Road to the state park is not plowed in winter.

From the parking lot (0.0 mi.), follow the old gravel CCC Road uphill past the locked gate, passing the group camping area and continuing to a sharp right turn (1.0 mi.) where the Sunset Ridge Trail (21) leads north to the Laura Cowles Trail (23) and Sunset Ridge. Much of this road walk can be by-passed by the Eagle's Cut Trail which rejoins the road just below the Sunset Ridge Trail. A gentle ascent on the road leads to the Halfway House Trail (20) (1.2 mi.). Follow the narrowing road to the Maple Ridge Trail (2.1 mi.).

From the old CCC Road (0.0 mi.), climb steeply over a rough footpath and emerge on the open ridgeline (0.3 mi.) and climb to the Frost Trail (6) (0.4 mi.) which descends south to the Stevensville parking lot. Continue uphill to the Rock Garden Trail (7) (0.8 mi.), a sheltered route to Butler Lodge.

Climb very steeply over open ledges to the Wampahoofus Trail (10) (1.3 mi.), 0.2 mi. below the Forehead. *Use caution in wet weather, especially if descending.* **Underhill State Park to Forehead, 3.6 mi., 5.8 km., 3 hr. (Rev. 2 hr.).**

10. WAMPAHOOFUS TRAIL. This rugged trail provides another alternate route up the Forehead from the south and is the easiest route for backpackers in good weather. Proceed north from Butler Lodge (0.0 mi.) and pass the Rock Garden Trail (7) (0.1 mi.), which leads northwest to Maple Ridge. Climb steeply, squeezing through crevices and caves, to a large rock overhanging the trail (0.6 mi.). The Long Trail Patrol thought this rock resembled the open jaws of the mythical "Sidehill Wampahoofus." Just beyond the rock, the Maple Ridge Trail (9) descends west to the old CCC Road. Bear right and follow the open ridge uphill to the Long Trail (0.8 mi.) at the Forehead. **Butler Lodge to Forehead, 0.8 mi., 1.3 km., 1 hr. (Rev. ¾ hr.).**

11. SOUTH LINK. This trail connects the Toll Road near the Octagon with the Forehead By-Pass (8). From a parking area on the Toll Road opposite the spur to the Octagon, follow a rugged, rocky path through the woods to the Forehead By-Pass, 0.3 mi. south of the TV Road. **Toll Road to Forehead By-Pass, 0.6 mi., 1.0 km.**

12. LAKEVIEW TRAIL. Leave the TV Road just north of the Long Trail from the Forehead and emerge on an open shelf. Descend over and between large boulders using an underpass, several switchbacks, and a ladder. Follow a shoulder of the mountain, with views of the Champlain Valley and Adirondacks. Reenter the woods, join the Canyon Trail (16) and, crossing the TV Road, rejoin the Long Trail at the Summit Station. **TV Road to Summit Station, 0.8 mi., 1.3 km.**

13. HASELTON TRAIL. This trail, named after Judge Seneca Haselton of Burlington, the first vice president of the GMC, was part of the original route of the Long Trail between Mt. Mansfield and the Sterling Range. It begins at the far end of the Mt. Mansfield Ski Area Gondola Base Lodge parking lot (the upper lot), 0.6 mi. south of the Long Trail on Vt. 108. From the parking lot adjacent to the gondola station, pass under the

DOG ETIQUETTE

The American Dog Owners Association makes the following recommendations regarding hiking with your pet:

- Leashes protect dogs from becoming lost and from backountry hazards like porcupines and bears and sick, injured, or rabid animals.

- Unleashed dogs intimidate other hikers and their dogs, depriving them of the peace the backcountry provides.

- A leashed dog's keen senses can enhance your awareness of nearby wildlife and other backcountry visitors.

- Unleashed dogs harass, injure, and sometimes kill wildlife.

gondola, then follow a ski service road uphill to the left (south) of the Midway Lodge. The trail begins on the left about 150 ft. from where the road enters the woods.

Enter the woods (0.0 mi.) and climb steadily. After following a hogback separating two brooks (0.6 mi.), cross the south brook (0.7 mi.), then cross a ski trail, and ascend steeply through glades to join the Nose Dive Ski Trail (1.3 mi.). Climb steeply on the uppermost switchbacks of the ski trail to the Toll Road (1.6 mi.) near the Octagon. The Toll Road leads uphill 0.5 mi. to the Summit Station and the Long Trail. **Midway Lodge to Long Trail, 2.1 mi., 3.4 km., 2¼ hr. (Rev. 1¼ hr.).**

14. AMHERST TRAIL. This trail provides a sheltered route between Drift Rock and the Summit Station, by-passing Frenchman's Pile. From the Long Trail just north of the Summit Station, follow the TV Road east for 200 ft., and turn left into the woods. Pass the Cliff Trail (15) which bears off to the right. Continue north, passing between two ledges and following an open shelf before ducking back into the shelter of the trees and joining the Long Trail at Drift Rock. **TV Road to Drift Rock, 0.3 mi., 0.5 km.**

15. CLIFF TRAIL. This trail is not recommended for backpackers. From the Amherst Trail (14) (0.0 mi.) proceed north and begin a series of ascents and descents on the east side of the summit ridge, some involving ladders and cables. After passing through two "caves" and "Wall Street" (0.7 mi.) a spur (0.8 mi.) leads downhill 0.1 mi. to the Cliff House (i.e., the top of Stowe Mountain Resort's gondola). Continue straight, passing over and under rocks to another spur (1.0 mi.), leading left to the Cave of the Winds where there may be snow as late as July or August. Inside the "cave," there is a 60-foot descent that should only be attempted by experienced parties with ropes. Beyond the spur, climb steeply to join the Long Trail (1.1 mi.), just north of the Lower Lip. **Amherst Trail to Long Trail, 1.1 mi., 1¼ hr. (Rev. 1¼ hr.).**

16. CANYON TRAIL. This trail passes through the Canyon, a large joint in the mountain's west wall. From the Long Trail at the Summit Station (0.0 mi.), proceed west, cross the TV Road

10

to enter the woods, and coincide with the Lake View Trail (12) for a short way. Bear north and emerge from the woods to follow an open shelf with views to the west. After squeezing through narrow passages too tight for a backpack, enter the Canyon, a large chamber overhung by the mountain wall. After climbing ladders and passing through a second chamber, reach the Halfway House Trail (20) (0.6 mi.), 0.1 mi. west of the Long Trail. **Summit Station to Halfway House Trail, 0.6 mi., 1.0 km.**

17. CANYON NORTH TRAIL. This north extension of the Canyon Trail (16) begins on the Halfway House Trail (20) a few feet west (downhill) of the Canyon Trail junction. Cross an open shelf with views to the west before squeezing through a series of caves and crevices. Regain the shelf, reaching the Canyon North Extension (18), then bear right and climb to the Long Trail just south of the Upper Lip. **Halfway House Trail to Long Trail, 0.6 mi., 1.0 km.**

18. CANYON NORTH EXTENSION. This continuation of the Canyon North Trail (17) leaves that trail near the Long Trail just south of the Upper Lip. Climb steadily with fine views to the west, then pass through a crevice and emerge on a narrow ledge, with outstanding views of Sunset Ridge. After another crevice, bear right, passing the Subway (19), and end on the Long Trail opposite the north end of the Cliff Trail (15). **Long Trail south of Upper Lip to Cliff Trail, 0.6 mi., 1.0 km.**

19. THE SUBWAY. This trail is not recommended in unfavorable weather. From the Long Trail across from the Cliff Trail (15) junction, join the Canyon North Extension (18) for a short way, then bear right to a ladder and drop steeply into a maze of crevices, boulders, and caves which require agile maneuvering. After leaving the boulders, follow a steep, winding climb in the open and return to the Long Trail a few hundred feet north of the Cliff Trail. **Cliff Trail to ridge, 0.3 mi., 0.5 km.**

20. HALFWAY HOUSE TRAIL. This trail once served as a bridle path from the old Halfway House to the ridge. Refer to access directions for the Maple Ridge Trail (9) to get to Underhill State Park. Proceed east from the old CCC Road (0.0 mi.), 1.2 mi.

from the parking lot. Enter the woods and begin a winding course along switchbacks. Climb steeply over ledges to the Canyon North Trail (17) (0.9 mi.) to the left, then the Canyon Trail (16) to the right. Continue straight up on ledges to the Long Trail (1.1 mi.) at the ridge just south of Frenchman's Pile. The Long Trail leads south 0.2 mi. to the Summit Station, and north out in the open 1.2 mi. to the Chin. **Underhill State Park to Summit Station, 2.5 mi., 4.0 km., 2¼ hr. (Rev. 1½ hr.).**

21. SUNSET RIDGE TRAIL. Refer to access directions for the Maple Ridge Trail (9) to get to Underhill State Park. Proceed north from the old CCC Road (0.0 mi.), at the sharp right turn in the road 1.0 mi. from the parking lot. Pass the Laura Cowles Trail (23) (0.1 mi.), continue uphill past the Cantilever Rock Trail (22) (0.7 mi.), then bear east and climb to the open ridge. Follow cairns (rock pile trail markers) in addition to blue blazes above treeline. An active effort is underway to narrow the trail to protect the ridge's fragile alpine vegetation. Pass the upper end of the Laura Cowles Trail (2.1 mi.) and, 250 ft. beyond, reach the Long Trail on the ridge opposite the Profanity Trail (24), 0.2 mi. south of the Chin. **Underhill State Park to Chin, 3.3 mi., 5.3 km., 3 hr. (Rev. 1¾ hr.).**

22. CANTILEVER ROCK TRAIL. Cantilever Rock, discovered in 1960 by Clyde F. and Clyde H. Smith, is a horizontal blade of rock 60 ft. above the ground wedged into the vertical face of a 100 ft. cliff. It is 40 ft. long, with 31 ft. extending beyond the cliff. Proceed north from the Sunset Ridge Trail (21), 0.7 mi. above the CCC Road, for 0.2 mi. to this striking phenomenon.

23. LAURA COWLES TRAIL. This trail provides a steep but sheltered route on the west side of the mountain. It was named for the first woman president of the Burlington Section, and was built by her husband, Judge C.P. Cowles, a charter member of the GMC. Refer to directions to the Maple Ridge Trail (9). Proceed west from the Sunset Ridge Trail (21) (0.0 mi.), 1.1 mi. from the Underhill State Park, and follow a brook upstream. Cross a bridge built by Boy Scout Troop 627 and ascend steeply in the hollow to the south of Sunset Ridge. After passing a small ledge (0.9 mi.), continue uphill to the Sunset

10

Ridge Trail (1.4 mi.), 250 ft. west of the Long Trail. **Underhill State Park to Chin, 2.7 mi., 4.3 km., 2¾ hr. (Rev. 1½ hr.).**

24. Profanity Trail. This trail connects the ridge south of the Chin with Taft Lodge and provides a fairly sheltered route around the Chin in unfavorable conditions. It is not as exposed as the Long Trail north of the Chin. Summer thunderstorms blowing in from the west are not visible from this trail. Dogs should be leashed on the lower part of the trail to protect the Taft Lodge water supply. From the Long Trail, just above the Taft Lodge spur, bear left and climb steeply through the scrub under the west face of the Chin. Emerge into the open and gently ascend to the Long Trail opposite the Sunset Ridge Trail (21), 0.2 mi. south of the Chin. **Taft Lodge to Long Trail, 0.5 mi., 0.8 km., ½ hr. (Rev. ⅓ hr.).**

25. Adam's Apple Trail. From the junction of the Long Trail and Hell Brook Trail (26) in Eagle Pass ascend north 0.1 mi. to the open summit of the Adam's Apple, with views of the Chin, the east wall of the mountain, and the Lake of the Clouds. Descend north 0.1 mi. to rejoin the Hell Brook Trail near Lake of the Clouds. **Eagle Pass to Lake of the Clouds, 0.2 mi., 0.3 km.**

26. Hell Brook Trail. This trail starts on the west side of Vt. 108 in Smugglers Notch, 9.1 mi. north of Vt. 100 in Stowe and 8.7 mi. south of Vt. 15 in Jeffersonville. It leaves Vt. 108 just 150 ft. north of the Big Spring pullout, which provides limited parking for hikers. Descending this trail is not recommended.

From the highway (0.0 mi.), climb steeply to the ridge, frequently on precipitous ledges, through woods with several views of the cliffs on the east side of the notch. Pass the Hell Brook Cutoff (27) (0.9 mi.) leading 0.7 mi. south to Taft Lodge, and continue uphill to the Adam's Apple Trail (25) (1.3 mi.) near Lake of the Clouds. Follow the west side of the Adam's Apple to the Long Trail (1.5 mi.) in Eagle Pass. **Vt. 108 to Long Trail, 1.5 mi., 2.4 km., 2 hr. (Rev. 1 hr.).**

27. Hell Brook Cutoff. From the Hell Brook Trail (26), 0.9 mi. above Vt. 108, follow the contour of the steep east slope of the Adam's Apple south 0.7 mi. to the Long Trail near

Taft Lodge. **Hell Brook Trail to Taft Lodge, 0.7 mi., 1.1 km., ½ hr. (Rev ½ hr.).**

28. ELEPHANT'S HEAD TRAIL. This trail links the north end of Sterling Pond with the Long Trail at Snuffy's ski trail above Elephant's Head Cliff. From the Long Trail (0.0 mi.) at Sterling Pond Shelter, descend to the spring that feeds the pond, pass Watson Camp (0.1 mi.), and follow the rocky shoreline of Sterling Pond. Climb over a low knoll and descend to Snuffy's ski trail and the Long Trail (0.7 mi.). The Long Trail south crosses the ski trail and descends 0.7 mi. to the spur leading west to Elephant's Head Cliff; the Long Trail north turns right and follows the ski trail to Sterling Pond. **Sterling Pond Shelter to Long Trail at Snuffy's ski trail, 0.7 mi., 1.1 km., ½ hr. (Rev. ½ hr.); Sterling Pond Shelter to Elephant's Head Cliff, 1.5 mi., 2.4 km., 1 hr. (Rev. 1¼ hr.).**

29. STERLING POND TRAIL. This trail begins on Vt. 108 at the top of Smugglers Notch, 9.8 mi. north of Vt. 100 in Stowe and 8.0 mi. south of Vt. 15 in Jeffersonville. Formerly the Long Trail out of Smugglers Notch, this route was originally called Mould's Trail, in honor of Fred Mould of Morrisville, an active volunteer trail builder.

From the east side of the highway (0.0 mi.) opposite the parking area and information booth, climb a rock staircase built by the Long Trail Patrol. Continue the steady ascent on the rough path that was once a woods road. Reach the Long Trail (1.1 mi.) at Snuffy's ski trail, a service road linking Spruce Peak and Smugglers Notch ski areas. Turn left to descend on the Long Trail north along Snuffy's ski trail 0.1 mi. to Sterling Pond, or turn right to follow the Long Trail south 0.3 mi. to the Elephant's Head Trail leading around Sterling Pond, and 3.3 mi. to the Smugglers Notch Picnic Area on Vt. 108, 1.3 mi. south of the Sterling Pond trailhead. **Smugglers Notch to Sterling Pond, 1.2 mi., 1.9 km., 1¼ hr. (Rev. ¾ hr.).**

30. BEAVER MEADOW TRAIL. This trail provides access from the east to Beaver Meadow in a bowl 1,500 ft. below the Long Trail and the summits of the Sterling Range. From Vt. 100, 1.0 mi. south of Morrisville (0.0 mi.), follow Morristown Corners Road west, then immediately bear left to Morristown Corners. At the four-way stop sign (0.7 mi.), continue straight on Walton Road. Pass Cote Hill Road by bearing left on Walton Road, and then pass Cole Hill Road on the left before taking the next left on Mud City Loop Road (1.7 mi.). Turn left at the junction with Bryan Road (3.5 mi.) to continue on Mud City Loop Road, and follow it to a fork (4.4 mi.). At a farm, bear right onto Beaver Meadow Road and follow it to a large winter parking lot (5.4 mi.) to the right, or continue on an unimproved road to a small clearing on the right opposite an iron gate where the trail begins (6.0 mi.).

Pass the iron gate (0.0 mi.), and ascend gradually on old logging roads to an intersection with the Beaver Meadow Cut-off Trail (1.8 mi.). Turn left, leaving the logging road, and cross Beaver Meadow Brook (1.9 mi.). Pass near a beaver pond and, after crossing a stream, reach Beaver Meadow Lodge (2.3 mi.) and the Chilcoot Trail (31). The Beaver Meadow Cut-off Trail bears right to circle the meadow. From the Beaver Meadow Trail, continue straight ahead on the woods road, passing the Whiteface Trail (32) (0.3 mi.), and reach Beaver Meadow Lodge (0.5 mi.). **Iron gate to Beaver Meadow Lodge, 2.3 mi., 3.7 km., 1½ hr. (Rev. 1¼ hr.).**

31. CHILCOOT TRAIL. This trail links Beaver Meadow Lodge with the Long Trail north of Madonna Peak. Follow the path behind the lodge (0.0 mi.) and initially ascend gently, then steeply to the Long Trail (0.8 mi.) at Chilcoot Pass. **Beaver Meadow Lodge to Long Trail, 0.8 mi., 1.3 km., 1 hr. (Rev. ¾ hr.).**

32. WHITEFACE TRAIL. From Beaver Meadow Cutoff Trail (0.0 mi.), 0.2 mi. east of Beaver Meadow Lodge, steadily climb to the Long Trail (1.0 mi.) at Whiteface Shelter. **Beaver Meadow Lodge to Whiteface Shelter, 1.0 mi., 1.6 km., 1 hr. (Rev. ½ hr.).**

DIVISION 11

Lamoille River to
Tillotson Camp

DIVISION 11 PROFILE

Lamoille River to Tillotson Camp

miles north-bound	▲ NORTH	elevation at Long Trail (feet/meters)	miles south-bound
26.7	**Frank Post Trail** to **Tillotson Camp**, 50 ft E; to Tillotson Road, 2.0 mi E	2560/780	0.0
23.9	**Belvidere Saddle; Forester's Trail** to **Belvidere Mtn.** (3360 ft/1024 m), 0.2 mi SE; to Tillotson Road via **Frank Post Trail**, 2.7 mi NE	3200/975	2.8
21.3	**Vt. 118** at **Eden Crossing; Babcock Extension** to **Long Trail** via **Babcock Trail**, 1.8 mi W	1320/402	5.4
19.6	**Ritterbush Lookout**	1300/396	7.1
19.3	**Babcock Trail** to **Vt. 118**, 1.4 mi N; to **Long Trail** via **Babcock Extension**, 1.8 mi NE	1100/335	7.4
18.7	**Devil's Gulch**, south entrance	1260/384	8.0
18.3	**Spruce Ledge Camp** (1565 ft/477 m), 830 ft E via spur	1515/469	8.4
17.4	**Bowen Mtn.**, north summit	2200/671	9.3
15.9	**Bowen Mtn.**, south summit	2290/698	10.8
14.7	**Basin Brook**	1890/576	12.0
12.9	**Butternut Mtn.**	2715/828	13.8
11.7	**Corliss Camp; Davis Neighborhood Trail** to Cross Road, 1.5 mi S	1900/579	15.0
9.0	**Laraway Mtn.**	2790/850	17.7
8.7	**Laraway Lookout**	2620/799	18.0
6.9	**Codding Hollow Road**	1230/375	19.8
4.5	**Plot Road**	1254/382	22.2
3.6	**Roundtop Shelter**	1650/503	23.1
2.0	**Prospect Rock Road**	960/293	24.7
1.7	**Prospect Rock**	1040/317	25.0
0.9	**Ithiel Falls Camp Meeting Ground**	510/155	25.8
0.0	**Vt. 15**; Lamoille River bridge	500/152	26.7

SOUTH
▼

Division 11
Lamoille River to Tillotson Camp

Massachusetts 222.7 miles   *Canada 50.0 miles*

From the Lamoille River to Belvidere Mtn., the Long Trail is named for Marjorie Hulburd whose father, the Honorable R. W. Hulburd, funded the original trail construction.

GMC is trying to relocate the Long Trail across the Lamoille River Valley to eliminate the road walk on Vt. 15 and Hogback Road.

Suggested Hikes

Laraway Lookout. This hike north on the Long Trail from Codding Hollow passes impressive cliffs and features a splendid view. Round trip, 3.6 mi., 2½ hr.

Ritterbush/Big Muddy Pond Loop. This trip passes Ritterbush and Big Muddy Ponds, two backcountry ponds. The loop includes the Long Trail south from Vt. 108, the Babcock Trail, and Babcock Trail Extension to return to the trailhead. Round trip, 3.9 mi., 2½ hr.

Belvidere Mtn. This challenging hike offers sweeping views from the summit fire tower. One route takes the LT north from Vt. 118 and follows the Forester's Trail to the summit. Round trip, 5.6 mi., 3¾ hr. A second option is a loop hike from Tillotson Road that follows the Frank Post, Long, and Forester's Trails past Tillotson Camp and the summit of Belvidere Mtn. This trip is suitable for backpacking. Total loop, 7.9 mi., 5 hr.

Camping and Fires

This division's Long Trail crosses private and state land. Camping is allowed only at shelters. Small wood fires, although discouraged, are permitted at the shelters' established fire rings. Refer to Leave No Trace principles (pages 9 to 11) to minimize your impact.

Note: Wood fires are not permitted at Spruce Ledge Camp to protect surrounding vegetation.

Group Use

Groups hiking this division's Long Trail may need a Commercial Use Permit from the Vermont Department of Forests, Parks, and Recreation. Group tenting space is available at Corliss, Spruce Ledge, and Tillotson Camps. Elmore State Park, east of the Long Trail off Vt. 15 and Vt. 12 South, is available for base camp hiking. Refer to pages 11 to 17 for additional group use guidelines.

Winter Use

This division's suggested hikes make good snowshoe trips. The Davis Neighborhood Trail is suitable for intermediate cross-country skiers.

Access to Long Trail

Vt. 15 and Hogback Road. The Long Trail leaves Vt. 15 just east of the Lamoille River bridge, 1.8 mi. west of Johnson and 7.3 mi. east of Vt. 108 in Jeffersonville. The trail is a road walk along the Hogback Road for 0.9 mi. north (toward Waterville) to Ithiel Falls Camp. There is parking on both sides of the Lamoille River bridge, and limited parking at the Hogback Road trailhead, which is shared with visitors to the camp. *Use caution; vehicles travel fast on Hogback Road.*

PLOT ROAD. The Long Trail crosses this road west of Johnson and north of Vt. 15. From Johnson at the junction of Vt. 15 and Vt. 100C (0.0 mi.), take Vt. 15 west to Foote Brook Road (1.2 mi.). Turn right and follow Foote Brook Road north to an offset intersection (2.7 mi.). Turn left onto Plot Road and continue west to the Long Trail (4.6 mi.). From Waterville, Plot Road leaves Vt. 109 0.3 mi. south of town and leads 3.1 mi. east to the trailhead. There is limited parking along the road. A parking lot is planned for the south side of the road near the trail crossing.

CODDING HOLLOW ROAD. From Waterville (0.0 mi.) follow Vt. 109 north to Codding Hollow Road (1.8 mi.). Turn right and proceed east on this road, crossing a covered bridge over the North Branch of the Lamoille River, and continue, bearing left at the only fork, to the last farm where the road becomes a narrow, unimproved country lane. Pass a winter parking lot on the right at 2.2 mi. The road continues and at 2.5 mi. the Long Trail enters the road from the south to follow it briefly east before turning left into a former log landing where there is parking. Please make sure to park beyond the last house in the designated parking lot; do not block private access. To the east it is 1.9 mi. by unimproved road, impassable to vehicles, to Davis Neighborhood.

VT. 118 AT EDEN CROSSING. The Long Trail crosses this road 4.8 mi. west of Vt. 100 in Eden, and 2.0 mi. east of Vt. 109 at

---

TREAT YOUR WATER!

Any water supply can become contaminated. The purity of water supplies cannot be guaranteed. Filter, boil, or chemically treat water before drinking. Keep water clean — wash self and dishes away from the source.

11

Belvidere Corners. There is an off-road parking lot on the north side of the highway, accessed by a short road 300 ft. west of the Long Trail crossing.

LONG TRAIL DESCRIPTION

Turn left off **Vt. 15** at the east end of the **Lamoille River bridge (0.0 mi.)** and follow the paved Hogback Road west along the Lamoille River to the **Ithiel Falls Camp Meeting Ground (0.9 mi.).** Turn right and climb up a gravel driveway, and then bear left into the woods on an old logging road. Follow the road past the base of a cliff, and climb steeply up its west side to **Prospect Rock (1.7 mi.),** with a commanding view of the pastoral Lamoille River Valley below the Sterling Range.

Continue north on an old road and descend to the **Prospect Rock Road (2.0 mi.).** Turn left and follow it a short distance before turning right (2.1 mi.) to reenter the woods. Ascend gradually to the broad summit of Roundtop before dropping down to **Roundtop Shelter (3.6 mi.).** This unique log shelter, with space for ten, was built by Todd and Wendy Jenner with the Laraway Section and other GMC volunteers in 1994. It is dedicated to Todd's brother Jeff. The logs were cut on Roundtop and skidded to the site by hand the previous winter. The water source is a hand pump found at the end of a 450-ft. spur trail, which leaves the Long Trail a short distance north of the shelter. Pump water, like all water along the Long Trail System, should be treated. This source can run dry in drought conditions. In case of pump failure, water might be found in a seep just beyond the pump. **Bear Hollow Shelter to Roundtop Shelter, 7.5 mi., 12.1 km., 4½ hr. (SB 4¼ hr.).**

From the shelter follow the ridge north before descending to Plot Road (4.5 mi.). Cross the road and ascend to a shallow saddle (5.5 mi.), before descending into Codding Hollow. Turn right, cross over a stone wall, and continue to the unpaved Codding Hollow Road (6.9 mi.). To the left, this road leads 0.3 mi. west to the winter parking lot.

Turn right and follow the road east about 200 ft., then turn left over a brook into an old log landing where there is additional parking. Enter the woods at the north end of the landing, and ascend on old logging roads, crossing several small brooks and then a large stream (7.1 mi.). Leave the logging road, bear left and reach some impressive cliffs. Follow along the base of the cliffs before climbing to **Laraway Lookout (8.7 mi.)**. This vista affords a sweeping view from southeast to northwest, featuring Mt. Mansfield from a unique angle. Continue north, then east, along the boggy ridge to the summit of **Laraway Mtn. (9.0 mi.)** with a limited view.

Follow the ridge east and descend at a moderate grade, before making a steeper descent (11.3 mi.) to an old woods road. Follow it downhill to **Corliss Camp and the Davis Neighborhood Trail (11.7 mi.)**, which leads 1.5 mi. south to Cross Road. Corliss Camp, a frame cabin, was built by Peter Hayden and the Laraway Section in 1989 and is named for Robert Corliss of St. Albans, who was an active section volunteer. It has sleeping space for fourteen. Water is found at a small brook about 350 ft. from the camp at the end of a spur to the left off the Davis Neighborhood Trail. **Roundtop Shelter to Corliss Camp, 8.1 mi., 13.1 km., 5½ hr. (SB 5¼ hr.).**

From Corliss Camp proceed east and climb steadily to the highest peak of **Butternut Mtn. (12.9 mi.)** where there is a limited view. Descend moderately to cross the main branch of **Basin Brook (14.7 mi.)**. Cross the brook, follow several woods roads, and then join a gravel road. Follow this road for 0.2 mi. before turning right to reenter the woods and climb to the lower of two south summits of **Bowen Mtn. (15.9 mi.)**. Illegal access by all-terrain vehicles is a chronic problem in this area.

Continue along a ridge with easy grades to a north summit of **Bowen Mtn. (17.4 mi.)**. Descend to a stream crossing and

11

MANY THANKS!

The Green Mountain Club thanks the private landowners who allow portions of the Long Trail and side trails to cross their properties.

a **spur (18.3 mi.)** leading 830 ft. east uphill to **Spruce Ledge Camp**. This frame camp with space for 8 was built by Gil Patnoe and Cheryl Vreeland, the Laraway Section, and other GMC volunteers in 1998. The camp is dedicated to Don Hill, long an inspiring trail maintainer in northern Vermont. Water sources are the small steam crossed at the beginning of the spur and a spring 250 ft. behind the camp. Devil's Perch Outlook, just beyond the camp, affords a view of Ritterbush Pond and Belvidere Mtn. **Corliss Camp to Spruce Ledge Camp, 6.7 mi., 10.8 km., 4 hr. (SB 4 hr.)**.

From the spur, descend to enter **Devil's Gulch (18.7 mi.)**. Follow the challenging route along the floor of the gulch among jumbled boulders and then descend to a junction with the **Babcock Trail (19.3 mi.)** just west of Ritterbush Pond. This trail leads 1.4 mi. north to Vt. 118. Cross a brook, and then climb steeply on a series of stone stairs to **Ritterbush Lookout (19.6 mi.)** on a cliff overlooking Ritterbush Pond. Continue to the top of a low ridge (20.2 mi.), descend, and then pass under a power line. Reenter the woods and follow the east side of the ridge downhill to **Vt. 118 at Eden Crossing (21.3 mi.)**.

Cross the highway and descend to a parking lot. From the parking area, the **Babcock Trail Extension** bears west 0.4 mi. to the Babcock Trail at Vt. 118. Continue north around a gate to cross Frying Pan Brook (21.5 mi.) and then climb steadily with some steep grades over ledges to **Belvidere Saddle (23.9 mi.)** and a trail junction between the two summits of Belvidere Mtn. To the right, the **Forester's Trail** leads 0.2 mi. uphill to the main summit of Belvidere Mtn. and its fire tower, and straight ahead it descends east 2.7 mi. to Tillotson Road.

Turn left at Belvidere Saddle and proceed north to follow the ridge through spruce-fir forest devastated by Hurricane Floyd in 1999, leading to a sag at Lockwood Pond. Bear right to skirt the south shore of the pond past some beaver activity and reach the **Frank Post Trail (26.7 mi.)** leading 50 ft. east to **Tillotson Camp** and then 2.0 mi. downhill to Tillotson Road. This classic "Buchanan era" frame camp, with bunks for eight, was built in 1939, replacing the original shelter built by Red Tillotson in 1930. Brook water, draining beaver ponds, is

100 ft. to the north on the Long Trail. From the front of the camp there is a limited view to the east. **Spruce Ledge Camp to Tillotson Camp, 8.5 mi., 13.7 km., 6 hr. (SB 5 hr.).**

SIDE TRAILS

DAVIS NEIGHBORHOOD TRAIL. This trail utilizes a Class 4 town road and an old logging road in the so-called Davis Neighborhood, north of Johnson. Take Foote Brook Road north from Vt. 15, 1.2 mi. west of Johnson and 0.4 mi. east of the Lamoille River. Drive straight through two offset intersections, then turn right on Cross Road to Davis Neighborhood Road, the trailhead, with limited roadside parking at 4.0 mi. Summer parking is also located 0.2 mi. down Davis Neighborhood Road. From Cross Road (0.0 mi.), follow Davis Neighborhood Road north and ascend moderately past a camp to the Long Trail State Forest boundary. Continue on the now-abandoned road uphill past the site of the former Parker Camp (1.2 mi.) to the Long Trail (1.5 mi.) just east of Corliss Camp. **Cross Road to Long Trail, 1.5 mi., 2.4 km., 1 hr. (Rev. ¾ hr.).**

BABCOCK TRAIL EXTENSION. This trail starts at the Long Trail parking lot at Eden Crossing. From the Long Trail, bear left and travel west, downhill, to cross a small brook, and then reach a dirt road. Turn left and follow the road 0.1 mi. before re-entering the woods to the left and climbing to Vt. 118 directly across from the north end of the Babcock Trail. **Long Trail to Babcock Trail on Vt. 118, 0.4 mi., 0.6 km., ¼ hr. (Rev. ¼ hr.).**

BABCOCK TRAIL. This trail provides an alternate route to Ritterbush Pond and Devil's Gulch from Vt. 118. Leave Vt. 118 across the highway from the Babcock Trail Extension, and ascend gently on old woods roads south to Big Muddy Pond (0.5 mi.). Climb over a low knoll at the north end of the pond and then continue south above the west shore of the pond. Cross the height-of-land (1.1 mi.) at the south end of the pond, then descend steadily on old woods roads to the Long Trail (1.4 mi.) just above Ritterbush Pond. **Vt. 118 to Long Trail, 1.4 mi., 2.3 km., 1 hr. (Rev. 1 hr.).**

11

FRANK POST TRAIL. This trail is named for a former Boy Scout leader and Burlington Section member. From Vt. 100 in Eden Mills, follow North Road (which becomes Mines Road at the county line) 5.2 mi. north and turn left on Tillotson Road, a gravel public road. Follow Tillotson Road to the trailhead (5.8 mi.). Tillotson Road is also 3.1 mi. south of Vt. 58 in Lowell via Mines Road. Enter the woods at the parking area (0.0 mi.) and follow a logging road to the Forester's Trail (0.6 mi.), which leads 2.1 mi. to the Long Trail near the summit of Belvidere Mtn. Continue west, cross a brook and follow old woods roads steadily uphill. At a right turn (1.6 mi.), begin a steep ascent to Tillotson Camp (2.0 mi.), and 50 ft. beyond, the Long Trail. **Tillotson Road to Long Trail, 2.0 mi., 3.2 km., 1¾ hr. (Rev. 1 hr.).**

FORESTER'S TRAIL. This trail begins at the Frank Post Trail, 0.6 mi. west of the trailhead on Tillotson Road. From the Frank Post Trail (0.0 mi.), ascend gradually at first, crossing a small brook and then the larger Lockwood Brook. Cross several more small brooks and old woods roads, and then climb, following some switchbacks, to Belvidere Saddle (2.1 mi.) and the Long Trail. Turn left and continue uphill to the summit of Belvidere Mtn. (2.3 mi.).

The summit of Belvidere Mtn. features a fire tower maintained by the GMC. From the tower, the Green Mountains are visible south to Camel's Hump; Big Jay and Jay Peak are prominent to the north; to their right stands Owl's Head and other Canadian mountains in Quebec near Lake Memphremagog. On a clear day the White Mountains are visible to the east. An inactive asbestos mine, once a mainstay of northern Vermont's economy, lies at the eastern base of the mountain, with another inactive mine on the south slope. **Tillotson Road to Belvidere Mtn., 2.9 mi., 4.7 km., 2½ hr. (Rev. 1½ hr.).**

DIVISION 12

Tillotson Camp to
Canadian Border

DIVISION 12 PROFILE

Elevation (in feet)

4000
3000
2000
1000

TILLOTSON CAMP
HAYSTACK MTN.
HAZEN'S NOTCH
BUCHANAN MTN.
JAY PASS, VT. 242
JAY PEAK
DOLL PEAK
NO. JAY PASS, VT. 105
NO. TERMINUS OF LONG TRAIL

0   5   10   15   20   25

Distance (in miles)

Tillotson Camp to the Canadian Border

miles north-bound	▲ NORTH	elevation at Trail (feet/meters)	miles south-bound
	JOURNEY'S END TRAIL		
1.3	**Northern terminus** of **Long Trail**	2100/640	0.0
0.5	**Journey's End Camp**	1550/472	0.8
0.0	**Journey's End Trail** parking	1350/411	1.3
	LONG TRAIL		
23.3	**U.S.–Canadian Border, Line Post 592,** northern terminus of **Long Trail**	2100/640	0.0
21.9	**Carleton Mtn.**, lookout	2670/814	1.4
20.7	**Vt. 105** at **North Jay Pass**	2150/655	2.6
19.5	**Burnt Mtn.**	2608/795	3.8
18.9	**Shooting Star Shelter**	2260/689	4.4
16.0	**Unnamed peak** of **North Jay Massif**	3320/1012	7.3
15.5	**Doll Peak**	3409/1039	7.8
14.6	**Laura Woodward Shelter**	2800/853	8.7
13.1	**Jay Peak**	3858/1176	10.2
11.7	**Jay Loop**, north end to **Jay Camp**, 0.2 mi W	2460/756	11.6
11.5	**Jay Loop**, south end to **Jay Camp**, 0.2 mi W	2238/682	11.8
11.4	**Vt. 242** at **Jay Pass; Atlas Valley Shelter** (no camping)	2220/677	11.9
10.6	**Gilpin Mtn.**, south summit	2920/890	12.7
9.6	**Domey's Dome**	2880/878	13.7
8.6	**Chet's Lookout**	2900/884	14.7
8.4	**Buchanan Mtn.**	2940/896	14.9
7.5	**Bruce Peak**	2900/884	15.8
6.1	**Hazen's Notch Camp**, 0.1 mi W via spur	2040/622	17.2
4.6	**Vt. 58** at **Hazen's Notch**	1780/543	18.7
2.7	**Haystack Mtn.**, east slope; summit (3223 ft/982 m), 0.2 mi W via spur	3180/969	20.6
0.6	**Tillotson Peak**, east slope	2980/908	22.7
0.0	**Frank Post Trail** to **Tillotson Camp**, 50 ft E; to Tillotson Road, 2.0 mi E	2560/780	23.3

SOUTH
▼

Division 12

Tillotson Camp to Canadian Border

Massachusetts 249.4 miles   *Canada 23.3 miles*

Much of the Long Trail runs on or near the ridgeline in this division. Water is scarce and hikers should take advantage of sources noted in the text.

The north terminus of the Long Trail is in the woods at the Canadian border west of North Troy. The Journey's End Trail, which leads to the border from the east, is the only approach trail to the north terminus. It is described on page 222 and included in the division summary on page 214.

Suggested Hikes

Carleton Mtn. This hike follows the Long Trail north from Vt. 105, ascending to a lookout. Round trip, 2.4 mi., 1¼ hr. Continuing north to the Canadian border along the ridge offers views into Québec from the boundary clearing at Post. 592. Total round trip, 5.2 mi., 3¼ hr.

Jay Peak. This steady climb on the Long Trail north from Vt. 242 features views from the open summit. Round trip, 3.4 mi., 2½ hr.

HAYSTACK MTN. The Long Trail south from Vt. 58 in Hazen's Notch climbs a steep, rugged route to the spur leading to the summit lookouts. Round trip, 4.0 mi., 2¾ hr.

CAMPING AND FIRES

This division's Long Trail crosses private and state land. Camping is allowed only at shelters. Small wood fires, although discouraged, are permitted at the shelters' established fire rings. Refer to Leave No Trace principles (pages 9 to 11) to minimize your impact.

Note: Atlas Valley Shelter is not intended for overnight use, and wood fires are prohibited.

GROUP USE

Groups hiking this division's Long Trail may need a Commercial Use Permit from the Vermont Department of Forests, Parks, and Recreation. Group tenting space is available at Hazen's Notch and Jay Camps and Laura Woodward Shelter. Refer to pages 11 to 17 for additional group use guidelines.

WINTER USE

The suggested hikes from Jay and North Jay Passes make good snowshoe trips. This division's terrain is not suitable for beginner and intermediate cross-country skiers. Deep snow often makes the white-blazed route very difficult to discern.

ACCESS TO LONG TRAIL

VT. 58 AT HAZEN'S NOTCH. The Long Trail crosses unpaved Vt. 58 just west of the height-of-land 5.3 mi. east of Montgomery Center and 5.2 mi. west of Vt. 100 in Lowell. Limited parking is available on the south side of the road just east of the trail. The road through the notch is not plowed in winter and is part of the Catamount Trail. Refer to Catamount Trail information on page 26.

VT. 242 AT JAY PASS. The Long Trail crosses this highway at Jay Pass, 5.1 mi. west of Jay Village and 6.4 mi. east of Montgomery Center. There is a large parking lot on the south side of the highway.

VT. 105 AT NORTH JAY PASS. This road intersects the Long Trail at North Jay Pass, 5.2 mi. west of Vt. 101 near North Troy and 7.4 mi. east of Vt. 105A near Richford. Parking is on the north side of the road. Overnight parking here is not recommended.

LONG TRAIL DESCRIPTION

From the **Frank Post Trail (0.0 mi.)**, 50 ft. west of **Tillotson Camp**, proceed north and ascend wooded **Tillotson Peak (0.6 mi.)**, passing just east of the summit. Descend into a deep col and climb gradually to **Haystack Mtn. (2.7 mi.)**. A spur leads west 0.2 mi. to the summit knob where there are lookouts. Continue downhill at a moderate, though uneven, grade along the ridge, then drop very steeply to a brook (4.4 mi.) and then to unpaved **Vt. 58 at Hazen's Notch (4.6 mi.)**.

The Notch is named for General Moses Hazen who, with General Jacob Bayley in 1778 to 1779 built a military road, originally intended to reach Canada, from Peacham to this point. A granite marker just east of the Long Trail commemorates this effort. The south face of Sugarloaf Mtn. rises 700 ft. vertically above the road.

Cross the highway and follow a nearly level grade under the cliffs, then turn right to climb steeply over the west shoulder of Sugarloaf Mtn. Cross the west slope of Sugarloaf and descend moderately to a **spur (6.1 mi.)** leading west 0.1 mi. to **Hazen's**

WEATHER CHANGE

The weather can change quickly. Always be prepared for rain, cold, and wind.

12

Notch Camp. Built by the Long Trail Patrol in 1948 at a site just below the highway, the camp was dismantled, hand-carried, and reassembled by the VYCC with GMC volunteer support in 1997. There are bunks for eight. The water source is a small brook crossed by the spur leading to the camp; it may go dry during droughts. The camp features a view north to Bruce Peak, Buchanan Mtn., Big Jay, and Jay Peak. **Tillotson Camp to Hazen's Notch Camp, 6.2 mi., 10.0 km., 4 hr. (SB 4½ hr.).**

Proceed north from the spur, and cross several ravines where there may be water. Ascend to the skyline at **Bruce Peak (7.5 mi.)**. Continue along the ridge to the summit of **Buchanan Mtn. (8.4 mi.)**, named in honor of Prof. Roy Buchanan of Burlington, longtime GMC Trails and Shelters chairman and leader of the Long Trail Patrol. Formerly called Old Splatterfoot, this mountain has a view of Jay Peak and Big Jay. It is Bruce Peak is named for Bruce Buchanan who helped his brother Roy scout the final miles of the Long Trail from Jay Peak to Canada in 1930.

Continue north from Buchanan Mtn. to **Chet's Lookout (8.6 mi.)** on a boulder to the right reached by a ladder, with views north of the ridge. The lookout is named for one of Roy Buchanan's sons who worked with the Long Trail Patrol in the 1930s and continued to help with trail projects into the 1980s. Drop into a saddle and then climb to the summit of **Domey's Dome (9.6 mi.)**, named for Capt. R. H. Domey of St. Albans, long-time local trail maintainer. Just south of this summit, pass an opening with views to the east and south. Descend to a sag (10.2 mi), then climb to the south summit of **Gilpin Mtn. (10.6 mi.)**. Formerly called Double Top, it is named for the Gilpin brothers, northern Vermont newspaper editors. Follow the ridge, then descend steadily to the west, and after passing a spring on the right, arrive at **Vt. 242 at Jay Pass (11.4 mi.)**.

Cross the highway and pass **Atlas Valley Shelter** on its north embankment. This small structure, not intended for overnight use, was built in 1967 by a plywood company that owned the adjacent timberlands. There is no outhouse and wood fires are prohibited. Proceed north to the south end of **Jay Loop (11.5 mi.)**, leading 0.2 mi. west to **Jay Camp**. The Catamount Trail shares the south part of Jay Loop. Jay Camp, built in 1958, is a frame cabin with bunk space for ten. The site includes a tent platform and a moldering privy. The water source is a spring 50 ft. in front of the camp. Jay Loop continues north uphill 0.2 mi. to rejoin the Long Trail. **Hazen's Notch Camp to Jay Camp, 5.7 mi., 9.2 km., 4¼ hr. (SB 4¼ hr.).**

Ascend to the north end of **Jay Loop (11.7 mi.)** and then climb steadily on the southeast shoulder of Jay Peak. Bear left at the ridge's saddle, and continue uphill, steeply at times, to a ski trail (12.9 mi.). Cross a snowmaking pipeline and pass through a snow fence. Proceed directly across the Vermonter ski trail, reenter the stunted woods, then emerge into the open and climb to the rocky summit of **Jay Peak (3,858 ft.) (13.1 mi.).** In bad weather the open summit may be by-passed by turning left onto the Vermonter ski trail, bearing right at the next ski trail junction and ascending to the Jay Peak Tramway Station, which is located just below the summit.

The summit features views in all directions. In the immediate foreground to the west are Big Jay (3,786 ft.) and Little Jay and to the northwest, the Black Falls Basin and the Stanhope Ridge. These features are all on the 5,337 acres acquired by the Green Mountain Club and added to the Jay State Forest in 1993 and 2001. To the south the Green Mountains are visible to Camel's Hump, with the White Mountains to the southeast and the Adirondacks to the southwest. To the north is the Green Mountain ridge to the border, as well as Canada's Sutton Mountains, culminating in Round Top. To the northwest, the foreground ridge is Stanhope Ridge, which forms the northern rim of the Black Falls Basin, acquired by GMC and added to Jay State Forest in 2001. Beyond, Mt. Pinnacle stands alone. To the northeast are Sugarloaf, Owl's Head, and Bear Mtn., over which the border passes. The international waters of Lake Memphremagog lie beyond Bear Mtn.

From the tramway station, drop northeast on a ski trail, then turn left and cross another ski trail at right angles (13.3 mi.). Pass through a snow fence and cross a water pipeline, then enter the woods and turn right to descend steeply to Ullrs Dream ski trail. This ski trail drops 1.0 mi. east to the Jay Peak Ski Area base lodge and Vt. 242. Bear left to follow the north edge of this trail and then reenter the woods (13.8 mi.). Descend near

12

If you've hiked this far, here are three more steps to consider.

1 Buy the *Day Hiker's Guide to Vermont*, volume 2 of the Vermont Hiking Trail Series.

2 Check out our Web site: www.greenmountainclub.org

3 Join the Green Mountain Club today! *Your membership or gift supports hiking trails and land conservation in Vermont.*

**Green Mountain Club
4711 Waterbury-Stowe Rd
Waterbury Ctr, VT 05677
(802) 244-7037**

Maintaining and Protecting Vermont's Hiking Trails Since 1910 the top of the ridge to **Laura Woodward Shelter (14.6 mi.)**. Originally built in 1956, this three-sided post-and-beam shelter, which sleeps six, has been replaced twice, most recently by Tom Abbott and son with GMC volunteers in 2001. It is named for an early supporter of the Long Trail. Water is located at a spring west of the trail. **Jay Camp to Laura Woodward Shelter, 3.1 mi., 5.0 km., 2½ hr. (SB 2¼ hr.)**.

Continue north along the ridge and climb **Doll Peak (15.5 mi.)**, named for Charles G. Doll who, with Phillips D. Carleton, both University of Vermont professors, cut the route from Jay Peak to Canada. Descend from Doll Peak and follow the ridge uphill to an unnamed peak of the **North Jay massif (16.0 mi.)**. Begin a steady and sometimes steep descent east before crossing a small stream (17.9 mi.), the most reliable water source for Shooting Star Shelter. Follow the ridge north over several low summits to **Shooting Star Shelter (18.9 mi.)**. This post-and-beam shelter was built by Ferdinand Lauffer and Northern Frontier volunteers in 2001 and sleeps six. A display of shooting stars observed by the Long Trail Patrol during the construction of the original shelter in 1934 provided its name. The primary water source is a shallow well with a hand pump, located on a short spur leading west off the Long Trail, 190 ft. south of the shelter. Pump water, like all water along the Long Trail System, should be treated. The quality and quantity of water cannot be guaranteed. In case of pump failure, water might be found 450 ft. east and downhill of the shelter. This source is unreliable. **Laura Woodward Shelter to Shooting Star Shelter, 4.3 mi., 6.9 km., 2¾ hr. (SB 3 hr.)**.

From the shelter ascend **Burnt Mtn. (19.5 mi.)**, where a spur leads west to a lookout. Follow the ridge and descend gradually to cross **Vt. 105 at North Jay Pass (20.7 mi.)**.

North of the highway, turn right past a gated logging road, follow the edge above the top of the road cut, pass under a power line, then turn left. Cross the power line and ascend to the ridge, then climb to the summit of **Carleton Mtn. (21.9 mi.)**, named for Phillips D. Carleton, who helped Charles G. Doll cut the Long Trail from Jay Peak to Canada. A spur leads south to a view of the Jay Mountains. Turn north to descend and then pass over several minor summits to the Journey's End Trail, which leads east 0.8 mi. to Journey's End

Camp and 1.3 mi. to Journey's End Road. Continue a few feet beyond the junction to the **United States–Canadian Border at Line Post 592 (23.3 mi.), the north terminus of the Long Trail.**

The present line post was set in 1907 in accordance with the Webster-Ashburton Treaty, which in 1842 finally settled the U.S.–Canada boundary. The boundary swath provides views of the Missisquoi River Valley to the west and Québec's Sutton Mountains to the north.

APPROACH TRAIL

JOURNEY'S END TRAIL. This is the only approach trail to the north terminus of the Long Trail. From North Troy, follow the gravel North Jay Road west and then south 2.6 mi. to a junction with narrow, unpaved Journey's End Road opposite a dairy barn. Turn right and follow this road west. Or, from Vt. 105, follow the North Jay Road 2.0 mi. north to the same road and turn left.

This rough road leads 1.2 mi. west, mostly uphill, to a log landing where there is plenty of space to park. Bear right and descend 0.1 mi. more on a narrower road to a small trailhead parking area where the road is blocked by boulders. *Use caution on this road which is sometimes used for local logging operations.* Springtime (through June) road conditions may be poor.

From the trailhead at **Journey's End Road (0.0 mi.),** continue on the now-abandoned woods road west. Ascend gently to **Journey's End Camp (0.5 mi.).** This frame cabin, another classic "Buchanan era" camp, was built by the Long Trail Patrol in 1933 and has space for eight. The water source is the brook 300 ft. north on the trail. **Shooting Star Shelter to Journey's End Camp 5.2 mi., 8.4 km., 3¼ hr. (SB 3½ hr.).**

Continue west from the camp, then bear right to cross a sizable brook, before rejoining the old road again to an old farm settlement evidenced by stone foundations and rock piles. Turn left here and ascend gradually northwest, crossing several old woods roads, to the border swath. Parallel the border to the **north terminus of the Long Trail (1.3 mi.) at Line Post 592. Journey's End Road to Long Trail, 1.3 mi., 2.1 km., 1 hr. (Rev. ¾ hr.).**

About 1"

SEED POD

APPALACHIAN TRAIL 1

Long Trail at Maine
Junction to Vt. 12

THE APPALACHIAN TRAIL 1

SCALE IN MILES

1   0   1   2

N

Silver Lake

Barnard

Delectable Mountain

LES NEWELL WILDLIFE MAN. AREA

GREEN MTN. NAT. FOREST

GIFFORD WOODS S.P.

LONG TRAIL

Deer Leap Mtn.

Long Trail

Inn at Long Trail

Sherburne Pass

Pico-Peak Ski Area

Pico Peak 3957

Sherburne Pass Trail

PICO CAMP

Little Pico 3134

CHURCHILL SCOTT SHELTER

Bucklin Tr.

COOPER LODGE

Killington Pk. 4235

Killington Ski Area

COOLIDGE STATE FOR

APPALACHIAN TRAIL

Notown 2500

STONY BROOK SHELTER

Bull Hill Trail

2690

2570

The Lookout 2460

Pinnacle 2558

Chataraguay

Killington

Ottaquechee River

Gulf Stream

Barnard

Gulf Road

To Woodstock

CORRIDOR

Prosper

WINTTURI SHELTER

Montague Hill 2500

Bridgewater Center

To Bridgewater Corners and U.S. 4

AT 1 Profile

Elevation (in feet)

Distance (in miles)

MAINE /CT.

RIVER ROAD

QUIMBY MTN.

STONY BROOK

CHATEAUCUAY RD.

SAWYER HILL

VT. 12

Long Trail at Maine Junction to Vt. 12

miles north- bound	▲ NORTH	elevation at Trail (feet/meters)	miles south- bound
22.7	**Vt. 12; Gulf Stream bridge**	882/269	0.0
18.9	**Wintturi Shelter**, 0.2 mi N via spur	1900/579	3.8
16.5	**The Lookout**, 300 ft N via woods road	2320/707	6.2
14.8	**Lakota Lake Lookout**	2640/805	7.9
13.7	**Chateauguay Road**	2000/610	9.0
11.6	**Height-of-land**	2260/689	11.1
9.8	**Stony Brook bridge**	1360/415	12.9
9.0	**Stony Brook Shelter**, 250 ft S via spur	1760/536	13.7
7.9	**Height-of-land** on **Quimby Mtn.**	2550/777	14.8
4.7	**River Road**	1214/370	18.0
2.4	**Kent Brook bridge**	1580/482	20.3
2.3	**Vt. 100**	1580/482	20.4
2.0	**Gifford Woods State Park**, upper camping area	1660/506	20.7
1.2	**Ben's Balcony**, 50 ft S via spur	2220/677	21.5
0.9	**Deer Leap Trail** south end to **Deer Leap Overlook** via **Overlook Spur**, 0.6 mi; **Sherburne Pass Trail** north end: to **Sherburne Pass** and **Inn at Long Trail**, 0.5 mi S; to **Long Trail/Appalachian Trail** at **Jungle Junction**, 3.4 mi S	2440/744	21.8
0.1	**Deer Leap Trail** north end to **Deer Leap Overlook** via **Overlook Spur**, 1.1 mi S	2290/698	22.6
0.0	**Maine Junction** at **Willard Gap**; **Long Trail** to U.S. 4, 1.0 mi S; to **Tucker-Johnson Shelter**, 0.4 mi N	2250/686	22.7

SOUTH
▼

APPALACHIAN TRAIL 1
Long Trail at Maine Junction to Vt. 12

Vermont's Appalachian Trail (AT) leaves the Long Trail at Maine Junction, 1.0 mi. north of U.S. 4 and 104.9 miles north of the Massachusetts state line, and bears east 44.6 miles to the Connecticut River at Norwich and from there continues north over the White Mountains and ultimately to Maine's Mt. Katahdin.

The Appalachian Trail from Maine Junction south to the Vermont-Massachusetts state line is covered in Divisions 1 through 6. The AT between Vt. 12 and the Connecticut River is covered in Appalachian Trail 2.

GMC is working with Green Mountain National Forest, Appalachian Trail Conference, and the town of Killington to relocate the AT off Thundering Brook Road.

CAMPING AND FIRES

Much of the trail is on state land and a narrow strip of federal land surrounded by private property. Camping is allowed only at shelters. Small wood fires, although discouraged, are permitted at the shelters' established fire rings. Refer to Leave No Trace principles (pages 9 to 11) to minimize your impact.

GROUP USE

Groups hiking this division's Long Trail may need an Outfitter-Guide Permit from the Green Mountain National Forest. Gifford Woods State Park Campground, where the Appalachian Trail crosses Vt. 100, and Silver Lake State Park Campground, north of the Appalachian Trail off Vt. 12 in Barnard, are available for base camp hiking. Refer to pages 11 to 17 for additional group guidelines.

ACCESS TO APPALACHIAN TRAIL

VT. 100. The Appalachian Trail crosses this highway at the Gifford Woods State Park maintenance driveway, 0.5 mi. north of the west junction of Vt. 100 and U.S. 4. Parking is available at the boat landing on the east side of the highway.

RIVER ROAD. To access the south end of River Road from U.S. 4, turn north at 2.0 mi. east from the junction of Vt. 100 and U.S. 4. Continue on this road 1.5 mi. to the trail crossing at its junction with Thundering Brook Road. To access the north end of River Road from Vt. 100, turn east onto River Road approximately 2 mi. north of Gifford Woods State Park, or 6 mi. south of Pittsfield. The AT crossing is 2.4 mi. from Vt. 100.

VT. 12. The AT intersects this highway 4.2 mi. north of Woodstock and 12.2 mi. south of Vt. 107 in Beth Parking is available on the west side of the highway.

APPALACHIAN TRAIL DESCRIPTION

From **Maine Junction at Willard Gap (0.0 mi.)**, turn right and leave the Long Trail. Proceed south, passing the north end of the **Deer Leap Trail (0.1 mi.)**. Continue southeast, slabbing the east side of Deer Leap Mtn. and pass the south end of the **Deer Leap Trail** 200 ft. before reaching the north end of the **Sherburne Pass Trail (0.9 mi.)**. This side trail descends 0.5 mi. to U.S. 4 and the Inn at the Long Trail.

Bear left from the trail junction, climb a low ridge, then descend to a **spur (1.2 mi.)** leading south 50 ft. to **Ben's Balcony**, a vista with views of Pico and Killington Peaks. Descend steadily to the upper camping area of **Gifford Woods State Park (2.0 mi.)**, and pass through the camping and picnic areas to reach **Vt. 100 (2.3 mi.)** south of the park entrance and 0.5 mi. north of U.S. 4.

Gifford Woods State Park provides open shelters, tent sites, and picnic tables. Make reservations for the use of overnight facilities through the park office (Killington, VT 05751; 802 775-5354). Gifford Woods itself, located elsewhere within the park, is one of the few remaining stands of virgin hardwood forest in Vermont.

Cross Vt. 100 and parallel it south a short distance to Kent Pond Fishing Access, 0.4 mi. north of U.S. 4. Traverse the entry drive for the parking lot and reenter the woods. Cross a footbridge over **Kent Brook (2.4 mi.)**, bear left along the brook, and descend to the shore of Kent Pond (2.5 mi.). Follow the shore through the woods, then pass through a field to the gravel Thundering Brook Road (3.0 mi.). Cross the road and ascend to a height-of-land. Descend to the road again (4.2 mi.), and turn right to follow it downhill to the headwaters of the Ottauquechee River. Continue to the unpaved **River Road (4.7 mi.)**, 1.5 mi. north of U.S. 4.

Cross River Road and ascend through mixed hardwood forest to an old logging road. Turn left to continue climbing on the road, then bear right to leave it. Continue to climb, in part on old woods roads, to a vista (5.5 mi.) with late fall and early spring views of the Ottauquechee River Valley and the Coolidge Range.

From the vista, follow a logging road, level out, then begin to ascend via switchbacks to the summit of an unnamed hill (6.0 mi.). From the summit, descend to a ridge, and follow it to a power line clearing (6.5 mi.). Continue along the ridge, cross a woods road (6.8 mi.), and begin an ascent to an unnamed summit (7.1 mi.). Drop again before ascending to the north shoulder of **Quimby Mtn.** Descend to a shallow saddle, and then climb to a height-of-land (7.9 mi.), the watershed divide between the Ottauquechee River and Stony Brook.

Beyond the height-of-land, descend to a **spur (9.0 mi.)** leading south 250 ft. to **Stony Brook Shelter**. This shelter, a

AT 1

frame lean-to with space for six, was built by Erik and Laurel Tobiason and friends and Ottauquechee Section volunteers in 1997. It is dedicated to honor the section volunteers who relocated the AT between Vt. 100 and Vt. 12 from 1980 to 1990. Water is from a brook that crosses the AT 300 ft. north of the spur. **Tucker-Johnson Shelter to Stony Brook Shelter, 9.4 mi., 15.1 km., 5¾ hr. (SB 5¾ hr.).**

Descend steadily to the valley below, using a ladder to negotiate one ledge (9.2 mi.). Cross **Stony Brook** on a narrowed logging bridge (**9.8 mi.**), and turn left to reenter the woods before Notown Clearing, which is used for logging operations. Rock hop across Mink Brook and climb, via switchbacks at first, to a ridge. Follow the ridge across several knolls to a height-of-land (11.6 mi.). Pass a small pond and continue to a sag. Descend from the sag, crossing an intermittent brook and several logging roads. Climb over several small hills, winding just north of Bull Hill. There are occasional views to the west. Drop via switchbacks to the gravel **Chateauguay Road (13. 7 mi.).**

Cross the road and, just beyond, Locust Creek. After climbing over a low hill, cross another brook (14.1 mi.). Switchback up a steep evergreen-covered hillside. Reenter a mixed hardwood forest as the grade moderates, and cross an intermittent brook (14.6 mi.). Continue to ascend through a stand of paper birches, passing a southwestern view, before reaching **Lakota Lake Lookout (14.8 mi.).** Lakota Lake is below with the White Mountains in the distance.

DRESS IN LAYERS, LIKE AN ONION

Wear wicking underwear, an insulating layer, and a wind- and waterproof shell. Rather than cotton, wear wool or synthetics like pile or polypropylene. Regulate body temperature by adding and removing layers. Strip layers *before* you overheat; add layers *before* you chill.

From the lookout, follow the ridge with gradual elevation changes, cross an old woods road, and reach a woods road (16.5 mi.) leading north uphill 300 ft. to **The Lookout**, located on private property outside the AT corridor. Please respect this property.

At the junction, turn right to follow the old woods road, which continues to the Lookout Farm Road (17.3 mi.). Cross this road and continue to the King Cabin Road (17.4 mi.). Turn right and follow this road for a short distance, then turn left (17.6 mi.) off the road, and gradually ascend the south slope of the Pinnacle, to a southwestern view (18.2 mi.) of Killington and Pico Peaks. Continue to ascend to the height-of-land on Sawyer Hill (18.3 mi.). Begin a gradual descent, cross a woods road, and reach a **spur (18.9 mi.)** leading north 0.2 mi. to **Wintturi Shelter**. Wintturi Shelter, a frame lean-to with room for six, replaced an older shelter of the same name, and was built by Erik and Laurel Tobiason and friends in 1994. It is named in honor of longtime trail maintainer Mauri Wintturi. A spring 300 ft. north of the shelter provides water. **Stony Brook Shelter to Wintturi Shelter, 10.1 mi., 16.3 km., 6 hr. (SB 6 hr.).**

From the Wintturi Shelter spur, follow the contour of a wooded slope, then descend to an old road (19.7 mi.). Beyond the road, climb to the crest of a low ridge (19.9 mi.), where a spur leads right to a view of North Bridgewater. Descend to a woods road (20.5 mi.),where an old cellar hole and stone chimney to the north are all that remains of a past dwelling. Continue along the contour, then climb to an open ridge (21.3 mi.), with views of Mt. Ascutney. A second bald hilltop with panoramic views (21.5 mi.) is a short distance beyond.

Reenter the woods, make an abrupt left turn and descend through an open area. Continue through the woods with minor changes in elevation, and reach the edge of a hillside clearing where a wooden stile crosses an electric fence. Descend through two more fields with stiles, which provide pastoral views of the valley and hills beyond. Cross **Gulf Stream** on a footbridge constructed by Ottauquechee section volunteers, and enter the parking lot at **Vt. 12 (22.7 mi.).**

AT
1

SIDE TRAILS

DEEP LEAP TRAIL. This trail leads to the ledge looming over the highway to the north of Sherburne Pass. The Deer Leap Trail begins on the AT 1.9 mi. north of its crossing of U.S. 4 and 220 ft. from the north end of the Sherburne Pass Trail, 0.5 mi. north of U.S. 4 of Sherburne Pass.

From the AT (0.0 mi.), bear west and climb through an attractive birch forest to the Overlook Spur (0.4 mi.). The spur leads 0.2 mi. south to the dramatic rock outcropping visible from the pass below. The outcrop features views of the nearby Coolidge Range and to the west, New York's Adirondacks. Continue north from the spur, drop to a brook (0.5 mi.), climb again to the height-of-land on Deer Leap Mtn. (0.7 mi.), and then descend gradually to the north junction with the AT (1.3 mi.), 0.1 mi. south of Willard Gap and 0.8 mi. north of the Sherburne Pass Trail. **Deer Leap Trail from the AT near the Sherburne Pass Trail to the AT near Willard Gap, 1.3 mi., 2.1 km., 1¼ hr. (Rev. 1¼ hr.).**

SHERBURNE PASS TRAIL, NORTH OF SHERBURNE PASS. This trail extends north and south from U.S. 4, and is the former, historic route of the Long Trail. It connects with the Appalachian Trail on both sides of the pass, providing an alternate hiking route across U.S. 4. Trailhead directions and a trail description for the Sherburne Pass Trail south of Sherburne Pass is described on page 109.

From U.S. 4 at Sherburne Pass (0.0 mi.) enter the woods at the east end of Inn at Long Trail's parking lot and wind uphill to the Appalachian Trail (0.5 mi.). The south end of the Deer Leap Trail is 220 ft. beyond on the AT. The Long Trail is another 0.9 mi. north at Willard Gap. **Sherburne Pass north to Appalachian Trail, 0.5 mi., 0.8 km., ½ hr. (Rev. ¼ hr.). Sherburne Pass north to Long Trail, 1.4 mi., 2.3 km., 1 hr. (Rev. ¾ hr.).**

APPALACHIAN TRAIL 2

Vt. 12 to the
Connecticut River

AT 2 Profile

Vt. 12 to the Connecticut River

miles north-bound	▲ NORTH	elevation at Trail (feet/meters)	miles south-bound
21.9	Enter **New Hampshire**; **Ledyard bridge** over **Connecticut River**	380/116	0.0
20.9	**U.S. 5**; **Norwich Village Green**	537/164	1.0
20.1	**Elm Street trailhead**	750/229	1.8
18.2	**Newton Lane**	1120/341	3.7
16.8	**William Tucker Trail** to Happy Hill Road, 0.8 mi E	1320/402	5.1
16.6	**Happy Hill Shelter**, 0.1 mi S via spur	1420/433	5.3
14.0	**Podunk Brook**	860/262	7.9
12.6	**Iron bridge** over **White River**; **Vt. 14**	390/119	9.3
9.3	**Joe Ranger Road**	1280/390	12.6
7.8	**Thistle Hill Shelter**, 0.1 mi S via spur	1480/451	14.1
5.5	**Cloudland Road**	1370/418	16.4
3.7	**Pomfret–South Pomfret (County) Road**	980/299	18.2
3.0	**Bartlett Brook Road**	980/299	18.9
1.5	**Woodstock Stage Road**	820/250	20.4
0.0	**Vt. 12**; **Gulf Stream bridge**	882/269	21.9

SOUTH
▼

APPALACHIAN TRAIL 2
Vt. 12 to the Connecticut River

The Appalachian Trail (AT) between Vt. 12 and the Connecticut River is maintained by the Dartmouth Outing Club. See address information on page 244. The Appalachian Trail from Vt. 12 south to the Vermont-Massachusetts state line is covered in Appalachian Trail 1 and Divisions 1 through 6.

CAMPING AND FIRES

Much of the trail is on state land and a narrow strip of federal land surrounded by private property. Camping is allowed only at shelters. Small wood fires, although discouraged, are permitted at the shelters' established fire rings. Refer to Leave No Trace principles (pages 9 to 11) to minimize your impact.

GROUP USE

Groups hiking this division's Long Trail may need an Outfitter-Guide Permit from the Green Mountain National Forest. Group tenting space is available at Happy Hill Shelter. Silver Lake State Park Campground, north of the Appalachian Trail off Vt. 12, is available for base camp hiking. Refer to pages 11 to 17 for additional group use guidelines.

ACCESS TO APPALACHIAN TRAIL

VT. 12. Refer to directions on page 228 in Appalachian Trail 1.

WOODSTOCK STAGE ROAD. The Appalachian Trail crosses this road 0.9 mi. north of South Pomfret and 4.1 mi. north of Woodstock.

POMFRET–SOUTH POMFRET (COUNTY) ROAD. The AT crosses this road 1.3 mi. north of South Pomfret and 4.5 mi. north of Woodstock. There is parking available at a small pull-off on the west side of the road.

VT. 14. The Appalachian Trail joins this road at the bridge over White River in West Hartford, 6.9 mi. north of U.S. 4 and U.S. 5 in White River Junction.

U.S. 5. The AT joins this highway in Norwich Village across from the village green, 4.6 mi. north of Vt. 14 in White River Junction.

APPALACHIAN TRAIL DESCRIPTION

Cross **Vt. 12 (0.0 mi.)**, then a small field and reenter the woods. Ascend steadily, reaching a hilltop field on Dana Hill, with views of the surrounding countryside. Descend from Dana Hill, easily at first and then more steadily, to the paved **Woodstock Stage Road (1.5 mi.)**. Cross the road and then a footbridge over Barnard Creek and gradually climb through a field. Enter the woods, continue uphill to a sag between Totman and Breakneck Hills, and then descend, bear right at an obvious fork, and cross a narrow road.

Ascend through a field past some foundations to a height-of-land, then take a right-hand fork downhill. Follow woods roads downhill to a field and meet the gravel **Bartlett Brook Road (3.0 mi.)**. Cross the road and then a small creek, and follow an old fencerow through woods and fields before descending to cross Pomfret Brook and the paved **Pomfret–South Pomfret (County) Road (3.7 mi.)**.

From the road, climb steeply through mixed woods to a field with views. At the edge of the field, turn left and follow an old woods road. This is a remnant of the old Kings Highway, which used to be a major thoroughfare through Pomfret (the trail crosses another section of this old road near Bunker Hill). Continuing on the woods road, pass an old four-way junction and climb a small hill before descending to the east. Leave the former highway at a spur (4.6 mi.), which leads south uphill 50 ft. to an unreliable spring. Ascend to the top of DuPuis Hill, a bald summit with panoramic views, and then descend gradually through the woods to the gravel **Cloudland Road (5.5 mi.)**.

Turn right onto the road for 200 ft., then left into a field north of a house. Follow the south side of the field, then cross it to a gap in the stone wall. Pass through this gap and enter the woods. Ascend through woods, passing under a power line. After crossing over the top of **Thistle Hill (7.5 mi.)**, reach a spur (7.8 mi.), which leads 0.1 mi. south to Thistle Hill Shelter. Thistle Hill Shelter, with space for 8, was built by the DOC in 1995. Ample water is available in nearby streams. **Wintturi Shelter to Thistle Hill Shelter, 11.9 mi., 19.2 km., 6¾ hr. (SB 6¾ hr.).**

AT 2

From the spur, descend to cross a small brook, and then climb to an open field atop Arms Hill, with views. Follow a woods road to a second field, with views to the north and northeast. Continue to drop via switchbacks to the unpaved **Joe Ranger Road (9.3 mi.)**. Cross Joe Ranger Road by a small pond with a stone dam, and then climb via switchbacks to the wooded summit of Bunker Hill. Descend Bunker Hill, and cross an old town road (10.0 mi.) by a cemetery and several hilltop pastures with views to the southeast. Traverse an old farm road before descending through a stand of pines and bearing left through a sag, then climb to another hilltop pasture with views of the White River Valley. From the field (11.6 mi.), descend steadily through open hardwoods. Cross a small swampy area and puncheon, and turn left onto the paved Quechee–West Hartford Road. Follow this road to cross an iron bridge over the **White River to Vt. 14 (12.6 mi.)** in the village of West Hartford.

Turn left (north) on Vt. 14, passing a store, and follow it to Tigertown Road (13.0 mi.). Follow Tigertown Road to the right, cross railroad tracks, and bear left at a fork. After passing under Interstate 89, reach a road junction with Podunk Road. Turn right onto Podunk Road (13.2 mi.) and then left into the woods.

Climb through overgrown pasture and woods before descending back to Podunk Road. Cross the road, then **Podunk Brook (14.0)**, before ascending and crossing a woods road. Make a sharp left turn across a brook and several old town roads, and then traverse the south shoulder of Griggs Mt. (16.1 mi.) to reach a spur (16.6 mi.) that leads 0.1 mi. south to **Happy Hill Shelter**. This shelter, a stone structure with double-deck accommodations for eight, was built by the DOC in 1997 to 1998. **Thistle Hill Shelter to Happy Hill Shelter, 9.0 mi., 14.4 km., 5 hr. (SB 5 hr.).**

From the shelter, descend on an old road to a junction with the **William Tucker Trail (16.8 mi.)**, where the old road leads 0.8 mi. to a gate at Happy Hill Road. From the junction, bear to the right and follow the south side of the ridge and cross **Newton Lane (18.2 mi.)**. Wind through hardwood forest and pass under a power line (19.5 mi.) on the north flank of Mosley Hill. From the utility clearing, descend, cross a small stream, and follow the hill's contour to a two-car **trailhead on Elm Street (20.1 mi.)**. Bear right on Elm Street and descend, passing Hickory Ridge Road on the right, and follow the street to **U.S. 5 (20.9 mi.)** on the Norwich Village Green. A grocery store and the Norwich post office are to the left. Turn right and proceed south on U.S. 5 and then east on Vt. 10A under Interstate 91, enter **New Hampshire**, and cross the **Ledyard bridge over the Connecticut River (21.9 mi.)**.

SIDE TRAIL

WILLIAM TUCKER TRAIL. This trail provides an alternative route to the AT and the highlands around Griggs Mtn. from Norwich. From its junction with Dutton Hill and Meadow Brook Roads, 0.5 mi. west of the Norwich Village Green, Bragg Hill Road leads 1.3 mi. to a crossroads. The trailhead is another 0.5 mi straight ahead on the gravel Happy Hill Road beyond this junction. There is a turn-around with very limited parking. Follow an old woods road uphill for 0.8 mi. to the Appalachian Trail. **Happy Hill Road to AT, 0.8 mi., 1.3 km., ⅔ hr. (Rev. ½ hr.).**

Public Campgrounds Near the Long Trail

Divisions 1 and 2

Woodford State Park, Woodford
- (802) 447-7169 or Jan. to May 800-658-1622
- From Bennington: 10 mi. east on Vt. 9

Red Mill, Woodford (U.S. Forest Service)
- (802) 362-2307
- From Bennington: 10 mi. east on Vt. 9, then 1 mi. north on USFS Rd. 274

Divisions 2 and 3

Grout Pond, Stratton (U.S. Forest Service)
- (802) 362-2307
- From Stratton: 2.5 mi. west on Arlington–West Wardsboro Rd., then south on USFS Rd. 262

Divisions 3 and 4

Emerald Lake State Park, North Dorset
- (802) 362-1655 or Jan. to May 800-658-1622
- On U.S. 7 in North Dorset

Hapgood Pond, Peru (U.S. Forest Service)
- (802) 362-2307
- From Vt. 11 in Peru: 2.0 mi. north on Hapgood Pond Rd.

Division 5

Coolidge State Park, Plymouth
- (802) 672-3612 or Jan. to May 800-299-3071
- From junction of Vt. 100 and Vt. 100A in Plymouth Union: 3.0 mi. north on Vt. 100A

Divisions 5 and 6

Gifford Woods State Park, Killington
- (802) 775-5354 or Jan. to May 800-299-3071
- From junction of U.S. 4 and Vt. 100: 0.5 mi. north on Vt. 100

Divisions 6 and 7

Branbury State Park, Brandon
- (802) 247-5925 or Jan. to May 800-658-1622
- From junction of Vt. 73 and Vt. 53: 6.0 mi. north on Vt. 53

Moosalamoo, Ripton (U.S. Forest Service)
- (802) 388-4362
- From junction of Vt. 73 and Vt. 53 in Forest Dale: 1.6 mi. east on Vt. 73, then left on USFS Rd. 32 for 5.3 mi., and left again on USFS Rd. 24

Chittenden Brook, Chittenden (U.S. Forest Service)
- (802) 767-4261
- From the junction of Vt. 100 and Vt. 73: 5.2 mi. west on Vt. 73, then 2.5 mi. south on USFS Rd. 45

Divisions 8, 9, and 10

Little River State Park, Waterbury
- (802) 244-7103 or Jan. to May (802) 479-4280
- From the northern junction of U.S. 2 and Vt. 100 in Waterbury: 1.5 mi. west on U.S. 2 to Little River Rd., then right (north) for 3.5 mi.

Division 10

Underhill State Park, Underhill
- (802) 899-3022 or Jan. to May (802) 879-5674
- From Underhill Center: 1.0 mi. north on Pleasant Valley Rd., then east 2.7 mi. on the Mountain Rd. (Town Highway 2)

Divisions 9, 10, and 11

Smugglers Notch State Park, Stowe
- (802) 253-4014 or Jan. to May (802) 479-4280
- From Stowe: 8 mi. north on Vt. 108

Divisions 10 and 11

Elmore State Park, Lake Elmore
- (802) 888-2982 or Jan. to May (802) 479-4280
- From Morrisville: south 5 mi. on Vt. 12

Post Offices and Stores

The communities listed below are those nearest the Long Trail and its side trails. Each has at least one grocery or general store. Those in boldface are larger communities offering more goods, services, and accommodations. Communities without a postal zip code following the name do not have a post office. Address hiker's mail sent to post offices: "General Delivery, hold for Long Trail hiker, arriving [date]."

Division 1
North Adams, MA 01247; Greylock, MA; Williamstown Station, MA; Williamstown, MA 012676; Stamford, VT; **Bennington** 05201

Division 2
East Arlington 05252; Arlington 05250; West Wardsboro 05360

Division 3
Peru 05152; **Manchester Center** 05255; Manchester 05254

Division 4
Danby 05739; South Wallingford; East Wallingford 05742; Wallingford 05773

Division 5
Cuttingsville 05738; North Clarendon 05759;Killington 05751; **Rutland** 05701

Division 6
Chittenden 05737; Rochester 05767; Forest Dale 05745; **Brandon** 05733

Division 7
Hancock 05748; Ripton 05766; East Middlebury 05740; **Middlebury** 05753; Granville 05747

Division 8
Warren 05674; Lincoln; Bristol 05443; **Waitsfield** 05673

Division 9
Huntington 05462; Jonesville 05466; Richmond 05477; **Waterbury** 05676

Division 10
Moscow 05662; Underhill Center 05490; **Stowe** 05672; Morristown Corners; Morrisville 05661

Division 11
Johnson 05656; Waterville 05492; Belvidere Center 05442; Eden 05652

Division 12
Lowell 05847; Montgomery Center 05471; Westfield 05874; Jay; North Troy 05859; Richford 05476

Useful Addresses

Green Mountain Club
4711 Waterbury-Stowe Rd., Waterbury Center, VT 05677
(802) 244-7037; www.greenmountainclub.org

Appalachian Trail Conference
New England Regional Office
P.O. Box 312, Lyme, NH 03768-0312
(603) 795-4935; e-mail: atc-nero@appalachiantrail.org

Appalachian Trail Conference
799 Washington St., P.O. Box 807, Harpers Ferry, WV 25425
(304) 535-6331; www.appalachiantrail.org

Catamount Trail Association
1 Main St., Rm 308A, Burlington, VT 05401
(802) 864-5794; www.catamounttrail.org

Dartmouth Outing Club
Outdoor Programs Office
119 Robinson Hall, Hanover, NH 03755
(603) 646-2834; dartmouth.outing.club@dartmouth.edu
www.dartmouth.edu/student/doc

Green Mountain National Forest
Forest Supervisor's Office
231 N. Main St., Rutland, VT 05701
(802) 747-6700; www.fs.fed.us/r9/gmfl

U.S. Forest Service
Manchester Ranger District
2538 Depot St., Manchester Center, VT 05255
(802) 362-2307

U.S. Forest Service
Middlebury Ranger District
1007 Route 7 South, Middlebury, VT 05753
(802) 388-4362

U.S. Forest Service
Rochester Ranger District
99 Ranger Road, Rochester, VT 05767
(802) 767-4261

Vermont Department of Forests, Parks, and Recreation
Barre Regional Office
324 N. Main St., Barre, VT 05641-4109
(802) 476-0170

Vermont Department of Forests, Parks, and Recreation
Essex Junction Regional Office
111 West St., Essex Junction, VT 05452
(802) 879-6565

Vermont Department of Forests, Parks, and Recreation
Pittsford Regional Office
317 Sanitorium Rd., West Wing, Pittsford, VT 05763-9358
(802) 483-2314

Vermont Department of Forests, Parks, and Recreation
Vermont Agency of Natural Resources
103 S. Main St., Waterbury, VT 05671-0601
(802) 241-3655; www.state.vt.us/anr/fpr

Vermont Department of Travel and Tourism
6 Baldwin St., Drawer 33
Montpelier, VT 05633-1301
(800) VERMONT; (802) 828-3237
www.travel-vermont.com

Vermont State Police Headquarters
Waterbury State Complex
103 S. Main St., Waterbury, VT 05676
(802) 244-8727

GMC Publications

The Green Mountain Club welcomes inquiries about hiking and backpacking in Vermont. For more information, or to order GMC publications, write or call:

The Green Mountain Club, Inc.
4711 Waterbury-Stowe Road
Waterbury Center, Vermont 05677
Phone: (802) 244-7037
E-mail: gmc@greenmountainclub.org
www.greenmountainclub.org

Guidebooks

Day Hiker's Guide to Vermont (4th edition, 2002). Companion volume to *Long Trail Guide*; describes most of the hiking trails in Vermont outside of the Long Trail System. Comprehensive coverage of more than two hundred trails throughout the state, dozens of topographical maps, hiking tips and suggestions.

The Long Trail End-to-Ender's Guide (new edition annually). Handy supplement to *Long Trail Guide* for long-distance hikers. Up-to-date information on trail conditions, overnight accommodations, equipment sales and repairs, mail drops, and transportation.

A Trip Leader's Handbook (1997).

Periodicals

The Long Trail News. GMC's quarterly membership newsletter provides trail and shelter updates, hiking statewide trail information, Club history, and a Club activities calendar.

MOUNT MANSFIELD FROM LAKE OF CLOUDS

Pamphlets

"A Group Hiking Guide for Vermont's Long Trail and Appalachian Trail." Information about group permits, Leave No Trace, group size, and more.

"The Tundra Walk: An Interpretive Guide to the Mount Mansfield Alpine Region" (2002). This illustrated brochure describes a half-mile natural history hike along the Long Trail on the summit ridgeline of Mount Mansfield.

"The Long Trail: A Footpath in the Wilderness." Information and suggestions on hiking the Long Trail.

Additional Reading

The Green Mountain Club suggests the following books as you make your way through the natural world. They may make your trip safer and more enjoyable and help you identify the plants and animals you may encounter as you hike in the Northeast. All books are available from the Green Mountain Club headquarters.

Natural History and Field Guides

Birdwatching in Vermont (2002). Ted Murin and Bryan Pfeiffer, University Press of New England.

Field Guide to the New England Alpine Summits (1995). Nancy G. Slack and Allison W. Bell, Appalachian Mountain Club Books.

Mammal Tracks (2001). Lynn Levine and Martha Mitchell, Heartwood Press.

National Geographic Field Guide to the Birds of North America (4th ed., 2002). National Geographic Society.

The Nature of Vermont (2d ed., 1998). Charles W. Johnson, University Press of New England.

Newcomb's Wildflower Guide (1989). Lawrence Newcomb, Little, Brown & Co.

Owls Aren't Wise and Bats Aren't Blind (2001). Warner Shedd, Crown Publishing.

The Peterson Field Guides Series, Houghton Mifflin Co., or *Stokes Nature Guides,* Little, Brown & Co., include guides to flora, fauna, and ecology.

Reading the Forested Landscape (1999). Tom Wessels, Countryman Press.

Tracking and the Art of Seeing: How to Read Animal Tracks and Signs (2d ed., 1999). Paul Rezendes, HarperCollins.

Wetland, Woodland, Wildland (2000). Elizabeth H. Thompson and Eric R. Sorenson, Vermont Department of Fish and Wildlife and The Nature Conservancy.

Wildflowers of Vermont (2001). Kate Carter, Cotton Brook Publications.

Hiking "How to" Books

Be Expert with Map and Compass (1994). Bjorn Kjellstrom and Newt Heisley, John Wiley & Sons.

Beyond Backpacking (1999). Ray Jardine, AdventureLore Press.

The Complete Walker IV (2002). Colin Fletcher and Chip Rawlins, Alfred A. Knopf.

Medicine for the Backcountry (3d ed., 1999). Buck Tilton and Frank Hubbell, ICS Books.

The NOLS Cookery (1997). Claudia Pearson, Stackpole Books.

Winter Outings

AMC Guide to Winter Camping: Wilderness Travel and Adventure in the Cold-Weather Months (2d ed., 1999). Stephen Gorman, AMC Books.

Winterwise, A Backpacker's Guide (1997). John M. Dunn, Adirondack Mountain Club Books.

Ethics, Perspectives, and History of Outdoor Recreation

Backwoods Ethics: A Guide to Low-Impact Camping and Hiking (2d revised ed., 2002). Laura and Guy Waterman, Countryman Press.

Don't Die on the Mountain (1998). Dan Allen, Diapensia Press.

Forest and Crag: A History of Hiking, Trail Blazing, and Adventure in the Northeast Mountains (1989). Laura and Guy Waterman, AMC Books.

Forest under My Fingernails (1999). Walt McLaughlin, Wood Thrush Books.

Hands on the Land: A History of the Vermont Landscape (2000). Jan Albers, MIT Press.

Leave No Trace (1998). Annette McGivney, The Mountaineers.

Northeast Mountains Leave No Trace Skills and Ethics (2001). Glenn Goodrich and Tami Pokorny, Leave No Trace Inc.

A Walk in the Woods (1998). Bill Bryson, Broadway Books.

Wilderness Ethics: Preserving the Spirit of Wildness (1993). Laura and Guy Waterman, Countryman Press.

Green Mountain Trail Guides and Maps

Adventure Guide to Vermont (2d ed., 2000). Elizabeth Dugger, Hunter Publishing.

Appalachian Trail Guide to New Hampshire-Vermont (10th ed., 2001). Appalachian Trail Conference.

Paine Mountain Guidebook (1997). William E. Osgood, Northfield News & Printery. Available through GMC.

Fifty Hikes in Vermont (6th ed., 2003). Green Mountain Club, Backcountry Publications, Countryman Press.

Guide to the Taconic Crest Trail (1992). Taconic Hiking Club.

Hiker's Guide to the Mountains of Vermont (3d ed., 2001). Jared Gange, Huntington Graphics.

Hiking Green Mountain National Forest, Southern Section (2000). Bruce Scofield, New England Cartographics.

Mt. Ascutney Guide (6th ed., 1997). Ascutney Trails Association.

North Berkshire Outdoor Guide (1999). Williams Outing Club.

Hiking Vermont (1996). Larry Pletcher, Falcon Publishing.

Index